BUILD ME AN ARK

The author and Mauyak

BUILD
ME
AN
ARK

A LIFE WITH ANIMALS

BRENDA PETERSON

W. W. NORTON & COMPANY

NEW YORK LONDON

Sections of this book appeared in the following publications,
in very different forms:
"Who Will Speak for Wolf?" appeared in *New Age Journal*, fall 1994
Series of Alaska wolf control and wolf reintroduction articles appeared in the *Seattle Times*, 1993–97
"Silkie" appeared in *Orion* magazine, October 1997
"Beluga Baby: An Afterlife of Animals" appeared in *New Age Journal*, March/April 1993
"My Father Combing My Hair" appeared in *Washington* magazine, 1986
"Mermaid's Hideaway" appeared in *Underwire*, April 1999
"Apprenticeship to Animal Play" appeared in the anthology *Intimate Nature: The Bond Between Women and Animals* (Ballantine, 1998)
"The Whales of April" and "War Games in a Whale Nursery" appeared in different form in the *Seattle Times*, April 23, 1995, and February 15, 1998.

For information about permission to reproduce selections from this book, write to Permissions, W. W. Norton & Company, Inc., 500 Fifth Avenue, New York, NY 10110

The text of this book is composed in Electra
with the display set in Michelangelo
Composition by Tom Ernst
Manufacturing by Quebecor Fairfield
Book design by JAM design

Library of Congress Cataloging-in-Publication Data

Peterson, Brenda, 1950–
Build me an ark : a life with animals / Brenda Peterson.
p.   cm.
ISBN 0-393-05014-9
1. Peterson, Brenda, 1950– 2. Naturalists—United States—Biography. 3. Human-animal relationships. I. Title.

QH31.P46 A3 2001
599–dc21   00-060078

W. W. Norton & Company, Inc., 500 Fifth Avenue, New York, N.Y. 10110
www.wwnorton.com

W. W. Norton & Company Ltd., 10 Coptic Street, London WC1A 1PU

1 2 3 4 5 6 7 8 9 0

For Susan Biskeborn
Astute friend and first reader for two decades

~⌒

For Linda Hogan,
Whose own work with wildlife inspires my own

~⌒

In memory of Ivan Louis III; in playful celebration of Isabel

~⌒

For all the animals

And God told Noah, "Build me an ark!"
—From the old spiritual "Well, Well, Well"

Until one has loved an animal, a part of one's
soul remains unawakened.
—Anatole France

CONTENTS

ACKNOWLEDGMENTS

A MEMOIR IS one of the most challenging and mysterious of all writing projects. I could not have finished this book without help from true allies, readers, and friends. Thanks to Christine Lamb for her artistic alliance, for close and insightful readings by my agent Elizabeth Wales, and for her assistant Nancy Shawn's remarkably competent advice. Weekly dialogues on the natural world with my wonderful students, many of whom are fine nature writers, continue to enhance my own work. Vanessa Adams, Bill McHallfey, Tara Kolden, and Rebekka Stahl lent me invaluable editorial assistance in bringing this book to press. Many thanks to James Vesely, my editor at the *Seattle Times*, for believing in my work and to Louise Bode, my old-growth elder, for listening to my life. And my discerning editor, Jill Bialosky, has helped shape and focus this book during the long years of its gestation.

Of the many conservation and animal advocates well met in this book, I'd like to especially thank marine mammal biologists Dr. Toni Frohoff of Terra-Mar, Dr. Naomi Rose of HSUS, Cathy Kinsman of the Canadian Whale Sterwardship Project, naturalist Leigh Calvez, Dr. Marsha Green of Ocean Mammal Institute, and Howard Garrett and Susan Berta of Orca Conservancy. I'd also like to acknowledge the fine advocacy of Natural Resources Defense Council International Fund for Animal Welfare, and Ellen Beard and Sue Bennett at B&B Media.

The pack of wolf researchers and advocates who have helped me immensely in this book are Rick McIntyre of the Yellowstone Park Service; wolf specialist Diane Boyd of Glacier and now Yellowstone Park; the wolf champions at Defenders of Wildlife, Ken Goldman, Nina Facione, and Gerry Hamilton; and Joan Moody at Department of Interior. Also Bobbie Haliday of PAW (Protect Arizona's Wolves) and

Kent Weber of Colorado's Mission Wolf are models of citizen activists and animal advocates.

I am grateful to my parents for always keeping our family close to the wild and to my siblings, my first small pack and pod. Most of all, thanks to all the animal people who are building a bridge between species.

PART ONE

ANIMAL

APPRENTICE

*Not to hurt our humble brethren is our first duty
to them, but to stop there is not enough.
We have a higher mission—to be of service
to them wherever they require it.*

—Saint Francis of Assisi

O N E

SLIPSTREAM

O N THIS FAMILIAR, floating wooden dock, my feet are strong and secure in sleek black flippers, my snorkel mask adjusted like a transparent Cyclops eye, my wet suit tight against my body like a second skin. In my stomach, that familiar fluttering, my heart beating excitedly as I prepare to plunge into the chilly saltwater lagoon. It is my winter pilgrimage to a research center in Key Largo, Florida. I visit here, traveling cross-continent from my home in Seattle to meet both my human family and the dolphins we have come to call our "other relatives."

I can name all these dolphins, adolescent females who swim by, dorsal fins rising and falling in an arc that my eyes take in gratefully. Dinghy, Jessica, Samantha of the crooked jaw, and Dreamer glide by and then execute acrobatic leaps and spins in perfect sync. Dreamer is my favorite, with her half-lidded sleepy brown eyes and intimate scrutiny. She cruises up and with a graceful, glossy snout, or rostrum, gently lifts my flippers and legs so I fall backwards on the dock, laughing.

"Now they're ready to play with you, land-lubbers!" the researcher calls down from his perch above the lagoon. He is studying dolphin-human interaction for his doctoral thesis in marine mammal biology and has spent the summer here at Dolphins Plus Marine Mammal Research and Education Center gathering material on the dolphins' altruistic behavior toward children with life-threatening diseases.

In the next lagoon over a little girl with leukemia, so terribly thin her wet suit hangs on her like a sagging blue slicker, floats in the lagoon with a bouncy yellow life preserver. She is all elbows and arms, but no fear. Even through her mask, her astonishingly pale face reveals the wasting disease that will kill her. This time next month she will be dead, but for now all she knows is that this is her heart's desire—to be in the water with a dolphin. And though very weak, she is thrilled, giggling shyly as a dolphin circles, taking her in with a calm, contemplative eye. This twelve-year-old girl is participating in the Make a Wish Foundation, one of several therapeutic programs at this research center. I gaze at her surrounded by dorsal fins, dolphins tenderly lifting her above the water to carry her slowly around the lagoon, as if she were drowning and they her funeral bearers. In ancient Greece it was believed that dolphins carried human souls between our world and the watery realm of the dead. Dolphins were recognized as creatures who go between the worlds, as guides not only of the shipwrecked and drowning but of the living as well.

As I at last slip into the next cold winter lagoon, catching my breath, my chest heaving until the wet suit warms the saltwater against my skin, I feel as if I am also going between two worlds: between the exuberance of the past seven years, in which I've made this Key Largo trip to swim with these dolphins, and my present, conflicted emotions over continuing this bond when it means captivity for the dolphins I have come to love. This swim I must make a decision that weighs on my heart like the pressure of a fathoms-deep dive. But for now I can't bear to think that this might be my last swim with these sister creatures.

Once in this lagoon, which borders a bay into the Atlantic Ocean, I forget everything, even myself, for a moment as I listen: yes, the underwater ricochet of dolphin vocalizations. Bleeps, signature whistles, cetacean songs that sound like creaking doors and Geiger counters come closer and closer until suddenly out of the murky green of the lagoon a graceful glide of silver streaks past, one pectoral fin lightly touching my legs. It always amazes me to remember that inside each dolphin's pectoral is a perfect, five-fingered skeletal hand, remnant of their ancestors who returned to the sea as our mammal cousins. To be touched by this hand-fin is to feel chosen. For just as dolphins are conscious breathers and would suffocate if knocked unconscious, these creatures are so agile and synchronize each movement so thoughtfully that even the slightest touch is a conscious choice.

I long ago stopped wondering if a dolphin's memory or intelligence is equal to our own. I have ample evidence and experience that their capacity for flexible thinking, their myriad strategies for learning new behaviors are survival tools my species could find instructive. Dolphin societies have evolved highly sophisticated social structures and communication skills. Their altruism toward their own as well as other species and their astonishing capacity to outwit researchers are what makes them so beloved and yet so mysterious.

As a dolphin again streaks by with just the lightest touch to my arm, I wonder which of "the girls"—as my sister and her children call this group of dolphins—has chosen to reach out to me, remembering me from many other swims here. I lift my head above the surface and propel myself above the water with the borrowed power of my flippers. Calling out to the watchful researcher, I ask, "Was that Dreamer who touched me?"

"No," he laughs. "That's the new one. Alphonse."

"But he's so big!" I sputter in surprise and have to take off my face mask and snorkel to clear the fog of my breathing. "He was just a baby . . ."

"Yes, last time you were here. But he's a big boy now."

As Alphonse cruises by, turning his head to catch my eye, my heart is again captured and I am overjoyed to see he has survived so well, grown up in this lagoon with many doting aunts.

Only a year ago I had arrived with my sister Paula and her three daughters in tow for another swim only to find the lagoon closed because of a birth—Alphonse's long-awaited arrival. Paula has also been devoted to these dolphins ever since they first "midwifed" her third child, Lissy, in 1986. On Paula's first swim with "the girls" she'd been nine months pregnant and the dolphins had forced all the other swimmers out of the lagoon to focus their full attention on my sister. Practiced in echolocation, the dolphins listened to the fetal heartbeat and, as always, found it fascinating. But that day back in 1986, there had been something different, an agitation in the dolphins that prompted the researcher to ask my sister hesitantly, "Is everything all right with your baby?"

As a surgical nurse and the mother of two healthy girls, my sister had satisfied herself that this third birth would go without a hitch. The doctor had warned her however, after her last delivery that another pregnancy and cesarean section might be life-threatening. Paula listened to the warning of the dolphins' insistent concern and made sure to have blood donors and a specialist on hand for Lissy's birth. As it turned out, Lissy was born jaundiced and with a rare blood incompatibility that required an immediate transfusion of her body's entire supply of blood. In our family, we credit the dolphins and my sister's intuitive skills with saving Lissy's life. And Lissy considers herself half-sister to "the girls."

In 1993, when Lissy was seven years old, I arrived with my sister's family to find that a dolphin had just been born. This newborn dolphin was for us like coming full circle in the cycle that included human and animal birthing. The research director let us inside because we were old friends. As we tiptoed in, honored to be allowed to see a newborn dolphin, he whispered, "The little one's chances for survival are 50-50.

We have hope because this is Dinghy's second calf. The first one died, you know—as so many dolphin newborns do in the wild."

He went on to to remind us that in the wild, the many toxins, heavy metals, and PCBs in the oceans are absorbed by cetaceans and stored in their blubber. When a mother gives birth for the first time, her body purges these toxins through her milk and she literally poisons her own calf. "In some places where Eskimos still hunt and eat whales," he said sadly, "the Inuit women are now like cetaceans—when they nurse their young, they risk killing them with all the toxins in their milk. So you see, the way the oceans and the dolphins and whales go will be the way we humans go. It's just a matter of time."

The hope was that Dinghy's lactating purge released most of the toxins from her body into her firstborn calf; without as many pollutants and poisons, this one might survive. "We haven't named him yet," the research director said. "It's bad luck. And we don't want to get too attached, if he also dies."

Even as he spoke, the silver-haired director already showed how deeply attached he was to this newborn. "Look, see that long, deep wrinkle on his little side. That's from being so recently folded in the womb."

Such a tiny creature and so awkward for a dolphin! This newborn, who would one day be named Alphonse, swam right up against his mother, but his breathing had not the practiced glide and arc of a mature cetacean. Instead, as Dinghy surfaced to exhale that "twoosh, twoosh" of misting air at 100 mph, her son belly-flopped and let out a squeak that was more noise than breath. As Dinghy inhaled, then patiently dived, encouraging her calf to do the same with a guiding pectoral fin to his flanks, Alphonse instead sputtered and flailed sideways near the dock.

We all gasped, expecting him to crash into the floating wooden rectangle, but at the last minute one of his aunts glided between the newborn and the dock, gently guiding him back to his mother.

"This is the most important thing the newborn has to learn," the researcher told us. "To plan and synchronize each breath, not only for his own body, but in rhythm with his pod. Can you imagine humans trying to breathe together while moving so swiftly through the water?" he laughed. "I can't even do it for three minutes with one of my own children, much less my wife."

Nor could I imagine the intimacy and awareness it would take to time my own breathing and fluid movements with those of another human being. As I watched Alphonse and his mother pair-bonding and practicing breathing together, his mother twirling and pirouetting protectively near her newborn, I wondered what kind of life this new dolphin would have, if he survived the crucial first six months. Though he was born in captivity, I knew from my countless trips to Dolphins Plus that these dolphins were cared for and even loved, unlike in some aquariums or zoos where they are forced into tedious performances to "earn" their food. The researchers had assured me that these dolphins were let out every week or so into the open ocean and that they willingly returned to the shelter and safety of this lagoon. In this research facility, they were not expected to interact with humans and had "free zones" for retreat from human encounters. They were never fed as a reward for performance or interaction. The dolphins initiated contact, not us. So to be touched or swum alongside, to be eyed or played with was a dolphin's choice.

I also knew that here the dolphins were safe from many perils—from sharks to drift nets to boat parasites and heavy pollutants in the open ocean. They had excellent veterinary care and reliable, healthy food. Nevertheless, captive dolphins often die of sudden, unknown diseases. And the annual infant mortality rate among captive dolphins is no lower than in the wild. Why not?

During my last several swims in Key Largo, I had found myself troubled by the increasing demands that human visitors were placing on these dolphins. Were they stressed? I had seen the research center grow from a shack on the lagoon to a popular, well-run organization offering dolphin swims twice a day. What toll was this taking on the dolphins? A question haunted me: Is it fair to ask the dolphins to give up their freedom so that we can receive the pleasure of their company? What do the dolphins receive from us in return? Is it worth their lifelong captivity?

A TAP ON the flipper again from a pectoral fin brings me back to the lovely, dark-green depths of the lagoon. Four dolphins, upside down, reveal their pale white and pink bellies as they cruise in a blur below me. Swimming near me is my friend Laura, who has suffered chronic pain for many years. In her stiff wet suit and snorkel she is shy and awkward in the water, swimming at the edges of the lagoon just as she so often stays outside human circles, held back by what she has called "that other territory of physical pain that seems to separate me so from everyone else." Laura is here to swim with the dolphins, not seeking some miracle cure or healing, but simply to float without the pressure and pain of gravity, to rest in another element that is easy on her body, the benevolent buoyancy of this saltwater. Her hopes of an encounter with a dolphin are muted by her desire not to intrude on them—for more than any of my friends, Laura is loathe to invade or demand anything of anybody.

So she floats hesitantly away from the delighted splash and play of those of us in the middle of the lagoon, surrounded by curious dolphins. Samantha with her crooked dolphin smile is pushing my feet now as if I were a favorite float toy, and we skim through the water barely touching the surface. I am propelled through the lagoon so fast that the palm trees and other people all blur into green fronds, black-suited figures in bright life preservers, and turquoise water. Right before we run into the dock, Samantha swerves to miss the wooden rectangle and deposits me at the fence. I am at once exhilarated from the encounter but suddenly aware that here I am again facing my dilemma: Samantha and I cannot race into the open ocean together or explore the fifty-plus miles a day that she is capable of traveling. Nor can we leap together over the fence, because although it is low, she is "psychologically imprisoned," as the animal behaviorists call it. Samantha and all the other dolphins here could easily leap the barricade, but will not leave their pod—or their people. Samantha is held captive here as much by her sense of community and belonging as by the underwater fences.

Troubled by these thoughts, I propel myself off the fencing with a strong thrust of my fins and streak through the lagoon, undulating my hips and legs, my hands straight at my sides in imitation of the dolphin's movements. But whereas they are graceful, my back is sore from such heavy work after only a few laps around the lagoon. I do not have the flexible, long spine that stretches from neck to tail fluke to slide through the waters. Without tail flukes, with separate legs that can paddle but not propel, with ungainly arms that can pull water but not aerodynamically slip through the waves using currents and my body weight to speed up to 30 mph, I can only crawl as best I can. Added to this indignity is the fact that as a human I splash at both ends, unlike the dolphin, who can enter and exit water almost without a ripple.

Back-paddling now to rest my weary spine, I glance over at Laura, who is clinging to the fencing, as if out of breath. Is she in trouble? A cramp or some muscular seizure from deep within her pain-wracked body as her mysterious illnesses, her "physical poltergeists," clench? I turn on my belly and begin to swim over to her, but I am not the first to arrive. By the time I can see Laura through the murky depths and the one eye of my snorkel mask, she is surrounded by six carefully circling dolphins. All of a sudden, their sonar echolocation is very loud as they bounce their sonar off her body and listen to what vibrations come back. This is how dolphins "see" the world, with ultrasound—most of it at a higher frequency than human hearing can detect—in much the same way we have so recently figured out how to use radar in submarines to "see" acoustically canyons and valleys and other ships without our eyes.

Dolphin sonar is so sophisticated that for years the Navy has been studying captive dolphins to learn how better to adapt to an underwater world of sound. Ultrasound, which humans have used to image a fetus or to shatter and dissolve a kidney stone or break up a heart clot, is being studied as "vibrational medicine." Human ultrasound is also being used to open narrow blood vessels to help some heart patients avoid bypass surgery by relaxing artery walls and softening fatty deposits. Medical science is discovering that ultrasound is a less-invasive alternative for treating cataracts and even certain kinds of tumors. And some recent evidence indicates that ultrasound frequencies in the region of 2,000 Hz, high above human hearing, nevertheless have a calming and pleasurable effect on human brain waves, possibly by triggering the release of endorphins. Perhaps this accounts for many people's sensations of ecstasy upon encountering dolphins, particularly in the wild.

Over the years I've come to believe from firsthand experience that it is not so much that the dolphins use ultrasound to heal themselves or us; it is simply a vibrational resonance so sophisticated and strong that it works like a tuning fork. Another tuning fork held near a tuning fork that is struck will begin to vibrate at the exact same pitch as the struck one. Our proximity to dolphins or their echolocation and vocalization might simply encourage our own bodies to resonate with a higher frequency, thus bringing our brain waves into the same Delta or Theta brain waves as the dolphins'. These waves are akin to what we humans experience as meditation or dreaming—but Delta and Theta waves are the dolphins' natural state.

Our immune systems may be triggered by the dolphin sonar, which supports our natural healing. But do we actually have to be next to real live dolphins to experience the same resonance? Or could it happen by listening to audio tapes of dolphin vocalizations, which hospitals have found help women in labor get through birthing with less stress. Or in the future, could we develop three-dimensional, IMAX-like sensory-surrounding movies that recreate the same experience as actually swimming with a dolphin in the wild? A kind of virtual healing?

Dr. Horace Dobbs, author of *The Magic of Dolphins*, has researched human depression and dolphins for years; he has combined visualization techniques and audio tapes of dolphin vocalizations to pioneer a therapy he calls the "audio pill." His audio tape *Dolphin Dreamtime* is a combination of dolphin vocalizations, sounds of the sea, the human heartbeat, and a background choir. It seems to placate people suffering from mental illness, depression, and other neurological ills, as well as offering relaxation and meditative support. Dobbs believes that much healing can come about through hydrotherapy, visual hologrammatic images, and audio vocalizations—the combination of which approximates the experience of a dolphin encounter without requiring the capture of live animals. Using such techniques, we can borrow skills from the dolphins without enslaving them or mistaking them for some living form of Prozac.

⁓

I KEEP A respectful distance from Laura and the dolphins swimming in ever closer circles around her so that she is held in the exact eye of their whirlpool. Even underwater I can hear her small murmurs of surprise as suddenly all the dolphins leap above her head—all except one. I struggle to see which dolphin is now performing a pirouette to come belly to belly with Laura in a behavior I have never before witnessed. Vertical alongside Laura, this dolphin opens pectoral fins and tenderly takes my friend in an interspecies embrace. Laura gasps, tiny bubbles leaving her lips. Dreamer clasps Laura to her long, silver body. In slow motion, dolphin and woman twirl together through the water, Dreamer always careful to keep Laura's snorkel above the water so she can breathe—which she does now steadily and calmly, as if Dreamer is sharing oxygen with her human body, which had for too long been suffocating. What Dreamer shares in that embrace I will never know. I can only theorize.

Laura swears it was not healing as much as it was animal kindness. "My pain did not disappear," she says afterwards as Dreamer swims her to the dock, lifts her bodily up onto the flat wooden platform, and dives deep. "When that dolphin held me and carried me through the water, I felt whole and a sense of well-being." She pauses and pulls off her snorkel mask, tears streaming from her eyes. "That's it!" she says. "I felt what it was like to be well again, because I was with such a well being."

As Laura steps from the dock onto the shore, her legs collapse under her; one of the researchers helps her walk. Her entire body is trembling, as if still vibrating to another frequency not her own, one borrowed from the dolphins and their buoyant world where the effects of gravity cannot curse a body. She trembles like this for more than two hours and then falls into a deep sleep from which she awakes refreshed.

"The dolphins didn't heal me," she still says to this day, whenever we talk about that rare underwater, interspecies embrace. "I have to do that myself. But they left me with the feeling that anything is possible—even that one day I might be without pain."

I ponder this gift of possibilities that the dolphins bestowed so kindly on my friend Laura the next day when I visit another dolphin research center farther down in the Keys called the Dolphin Research Center.

Here at the research and educational center in Grassy Key, the dolphins are unfamiliar to me, since I've come here only three or four times before. Though the facility is concerned and very committed to its dolphins' care, I have never felt comfortable with its program of rewarding dolphins for interaction with humans—too much like "singing for their supper." But today I am here to observe the work of Dr. David Nathanson, a neuropsychologist who has worked for years with stroke victims, Down's syndrome children, and other children at risk. Using flash cards and interaction with dolphins as a reward for learning, Dr. Nathanson's work shows impressive results in terms of increased learning skills for these disabled children.

"But could this learning increase come about just as well from inter-action with domestic animals?" A respected marine mammal biologist and dear friend, Dr. Toni Frohoff, has posed an important question. "Say, like cats or dogs—those therapy animals used by the blind or the disabled in programs such as the Delta Society, which trains domestic animals to help people who are blind or disabled or in the hospital?"

With these questions in mind, I again observe Dr. Nathanson at work with a little Down's syndrome boy who has made his animal-assisted therapy internationally famous. This little boy, Dean Paul Anderson, was never expected to talk, let alone learn. But after five years of working with the dolphins at the Dolphin Research Center, Dean Paul has proven himself somewhat of a prodigy, his symptoms less intense than medical authorities predicted. Is it the dolphins who have made a difference?

According to his mother, Cathy Anderson, the dolphins have made a huge difference in her son's development. "Dean Paul thinks of him-self as more dolphin than human," she laughs, watching her son pro-pelled around the lagoon by his favorite dolphin, Santini. "When he draws a picture of his family, some of us have dorsal fins. And there are always several dolphins in the drawing, like brothers and sisters. If you watch my son closely you'll see him exhibit definite dolphin-like behaviors—like he'll turn his head sideways to give you his full atten-tion, the way dolphins, with their 180-degree vision, will do. Sometimes when he doesn't make words, Dean Paul makes dolphin bleeps and vocalizations. He even seems to have his own signature whistle."

There is another disabled child in the lagoon with Dean Paul, a little girl who has delayed motor skills and at the age of five still has not said her first word. After working with the dolphins for several days, she amazes her parents by saying quite distinctly and with perfect diction, "Coca-Cola!"

The exuberant parents are so happy to hear their child's first speech that they immediately insist that Dr. Nathanson let their other, nondisabled child swim in the lagoon. But other people's sessions are scheduled and Dr. Nathanson patiently explains that these sessions are therapeutic only.

"Listen, you," says the suddenly hostile parent. "I've paid a lot of money to come here and get my kid some help. As far as I'm concerned, as long as I'm paying for the time, I *own* these dolphins and I can get anything from them I want!"

Dr. Nathanson sighs and walks calmly back to the lagoon to continue his work with the other disabled children, leaving the girl's parents to fume and mutter. Their furor has blown over, but I am still reeling from the woman's words as if caught up in an inner emotional storm.

I own these dolphins and I can get anything from them I want! Her words spin around me and I feel a wave of nausea deep in my belly. Here is the naked human greed that for years I have tried not to face whenever I have watched dolphins at work and play with humans, even in semicaptivity. The woman had revealed the selfish and dominating demands of humankind. Our species has for too long seen other animals as existing only to serve our needs, believing that animals have no distinct life beyond what they can give to us.

Though the palm trees reveal little breeze and the lagoon is calm, my own body trembles with an inner tumult as if a great wind surges through me, changing my own landscape. This is a turning point in my life. Where there had been uneasiness there is now a decision, where there was ambivalence there is now a new awareness. I realize that I can no longer participate in any encounter with wild animals that keeps them captive. A childhood in the forest has taught me this, but I had forgotten those long-ago lessons in my joy to find connection with this, my other family. I remember that in Hawaii a native friend once told me, "Dolphins are obviously your *aumakua*, the animal you belong to, whether you know it or not. Fortunately, you found out who you are and the animal you're meant to be with. Whom you must protect as a relative and who protects you." I had received the graceful lessons and protection of the dolphins as my interspecies siblings, but what had I done to protect them?

Standing in Grassy Key now, outside the Dolphin Research Center where people pay to have their children "healed" by dolphin encounters, where some parents believe they own another animal whose altruism is simply natural, I make my stand. I can no longer support such entrapment, even if it means I will have to give up my own deep connection to the dolphins in Key Largo. It is my responsibility now to give back to the dolphins, they who have given me so much. It is simple reciprocity—resonance. The tuning fork is struck, and I must respond.

Because dolphins have helped shape my character and my life's work with other animals, now I must try to help shape the future for the dolphins, whether in captivity or in the wild. That night I rent a small motel room next to the Dolphin Research Center. It is a place I've stayed before, right on the water. It offers small kayaks, which I have often paddled out to the lagoon, to float there just outside the fence and watch the dolphins inside. The night sky features a new moon and Venus is sitting inside the luminous crescent like an intimate visitor. As I paddle the still waters I can already hear the Geiger counter bleeps and ricochets of dolphin vocalizations. Keeping a respectful distance so as not to disturb the dolphins, who have already worked all day long with other humans, I bob in the moonlight, humming low, sometimes randomly singing a nonsense tune.

Suddenly two dolphins swerve from their synchronized leaps and streak toward the fence, skidding to a stop at the last moment. It is this stutter and stop of the dolphins' natural speed at the underwater fencing that finally breaks my heart. The fencing symbolizes the invisible, psychological restraint put on these creatures whose natural exuberance should know no limits—certainly not our own.

As I watch the two dolphins leap around their small saltwater lagoon, I cannot bear to think of giving up my long relationship with the dolphins at Dolphins Plus. I know full well that dolphins will continue to be captured worldwide for human use. I argue with myself: Won't they feel abandoned if people who truly care for them don't keep visiting, keep restoring the bond? Don't I have a responsibility toward them and our interspecies friendship?

At that moment one of the Dolphin Research Center trainers comes out into the night to check on the dolphins. Whistling softly, calling out to several of the dolphins in a fond, singsong voice, the researcher sits on his haunches on the dock and carries on a whimsical conversation with one of the dolphins. I can't hear what he is saying, but the dolphins' pleasure in their bond is evident. These dolphins, like those up at Dolphins Plus in Key Largo, are loved and nurtured. During their long captivity, the dolphins are cared for and given everything they need. All but their real lives, their families, their freedom.

"I'm so sorry," I hear myself whisper now to the two dolphins breathing near me behind their underwater fence. "I'm so sorry you've given up so much. I hope knowing us humans has made up for some of what you lost."

Soon the two dolphins are "talking" to me, opening their mouths to vocalize in return, nodding their long, graceful rostrums as if to say, "Can you stay out late and play?" I do, but my heart is subdued. I stay with these two for almost an hour before the wind whips up from the ocean and my kayak is too unsteady to stay afloat. Besides, it is almost midnight and I need to rest. I know, of course, that these dolphins will not sleep; they will simply shut one eye and, in an adaptation that is so simple, yet so sophisticated, rest one hemisphere of their brains, while remaining conscious. Perhaps, I reflect as I paddle back to the motel room, dolphins don't need to sleep because they spend their entire lives in a lucid dream.

The next morning I make my way back up the single-lane road to Dolphins Plus. Though it is a slow and sometimes endless road along these reefs connected like a bright coral necklace for a hundred miles between Miami and Key West, I want the trip to take more time than it does. Before I can even grasp what I am about to do, I arrive at Dolphins Plus in the late afternoon, just in time for another swim with "the girls."

"Welcome back," the director grins, "always room for you."

I have not called ahead as I should have. The programs are always full to overflowing, but I am welcome here. Can I really go through with this—my last swim with these beloved dolphins? Giving up my encounters with the girls feels at once like losing relatives or like abandoning those whose lives and well being seem intricately connected to my own.

Sure enough, here are Dreamer and Samantha welcoming me back "home." They are eager to engage and Dreamer leaps over my legs before I can even get my flippers pulled on. As I enter the lagoon I try to tell them by body language or telepathy that this is my last time with them, that it is not a rejection but a commitment not just to their group but to all dolphins. Somehow this philosophic rationale seems silly or hollow when greeted with such fondness and familiarity. It feels like telling siblings that I can't ever see them again because I'm off to save the world.

Silly, I tell myself, self-righteous, and above all humorless—quite a sin in the cetacean world. In spite of myself I laugh as Samantha prods at my knees teasingly, as if to ask, "Want to race?"—certain she will win.

As I swim leisurely on the surface, my snorkel mask down to watch when dolphins swim below me, upside down, or right by my side, eye to eye, I try to get some sense of how well these dolphins are doing. Are they are depressed or overworked, like my sisters who have each endured grueling years as intensive-care nurses? As I watch the dolphins leap over other swimmers and meet my eye with grace and familiarity, I believe that these dolphins are probably in the best shape of any dolphins I've ever witnessed in captivity. Yet they are still not free to come and go as they please. Like ambassadors from another realm, they are perhaps resigned to teach and translate, ever going between two worlds. Like those who must always speak a second language because they are in exile from their homeland, perhaps these dolphins have somehow even volunteered for the job of helping humans recognize other species' intelligence.

A pang of sorrow strikes as I realize that soon I, too, will be in exile from these dolphins. I swim with a heightened awareness of the lagoon and creatures around me—the way one would memorize a beloved face, landscape, or home for the last time. It is like leaving a second home: I take in the lush lagoon, each dolphin eye holding mine, even the raucous cry of the brown pelican who also makes his home here, as I swim. My eyes blur behind my fogged snorkel mask. I can't see a thing now, but before I can rise to the surface and clean my mask, I sense that I am suddenly surrounded by all six dolphins in the lagoon.

Three ahead of me and three behind me: this is an unusual formation. Usually the dolphins flank me at each side like protective scouts, but now they have placed me within their center in the position of a calf learning to swim. As the three lead dolphins streak forward, their powerful tail flukes pull me in their fast wake. The three dolphins behind me propel me forward with their pectorals, so I need make no movement with my own arms and legs—yet I speed along with them, aerodynamically held in their glide.

Slipstream! My mind recognizes what my body has already enjoyed. The dolphins are swimming for me, carrying me aloft in their waves, just as a dolphin will ride a boat's wake, easily pulled along in another's path. This is how I am honored, as if I am a newborn and can be carried along by the pod.

Never before have the dolphins allowed me this privilege, one usually reserved for their own kind. And in this moment of following, being flung forward without any effort, I feel as if the dolphins understand that they are like rockets, fondly flinging me out into some unknown orbit, some other space that we will no longer share. So fast is this propulsion, it's as if we are no longer in the heavy element of water, but above it. And as I speed along, held in their gravity, an image suddenly comes to my mind. Hundreds of dolphins in the open ocean, porpoising across whitecaps, leaping out of the water together so quickly that their bodies never seem to touch down. Only the tips of their tail flukes splash to show they are swimming, not flying.

"Crossover" is the word scientists use to describe dolphins' soaring over seas, their traveling so free and fast, so high-spirited and almost effervescent that their sleek bodies barely skim the waves. The suggestion of splashes from tail and pectoral leaves a luminous wake across the water. For these crossover miles, the dolphins, like their human terrestrial mammal kin, belong more to the element of air than to sea. Crossover behavior is a wonder to see, and I had not yet witnessed it myself. So where was the vivid image in my mind coming from? The dolphins or me?

As I swam in the dolphins' slipstream, I closed my eyes and watched the bright crossover images expand. Now I saw a superpod of wild dolphins flying over the waves, jubilant and exuberantly free. Had the dolphins carried me not only with their bodies but also with their minds? Was this the hologrammatic intelligence that some dolphin researchers believe exists, what we might experience as a kind of photographic telepathy?

Held in their fluid embrace, I pulled my arms close against my sides and our communal speed increased. The dolphins swam so fast now, swerving at the fences in an expert curve of wake and small waves. Racing around the lagoon, I opened my eyes again to see nothing but an emerald, underwater blur. And then I remembered what I had either forgotten long ago or never quite fully realized. This feeling of being carried along by other animals was familiar.

Animals had carried me all my life. I was a crossover — carried along in the generous and instructive slipstream of other species. And I had always navigated my life with them in mind, going between the human and animal worlds — a crossover myself. By including animals in my life I was always engaging with the Other, imagining the animal mind and life. For almost half a century, my bond with animals had shaped my character and revealed the world to me. At every turning point in my life an animal had mirrored or influenced my fate. Mine was not simply a life with other animals, but a life *because of animals*. It had been this way since my beginning, born on a forest lookout station in the High Sierras, surrounded by millions of acres of wilderness and many more animals than humans. Since infancy, the first faces I imprinted, the first faces I ever really loved, were animal.

AND NOW AS these beloved dolphins held me in their moving wake, I followed them one last time. As I glanced over at Alphonse, his brown, benevolent eyes held mine and I tried to send him a mental picture of his own beautiful, wrinkled body at birth. My eyes blurred in my mask as I apologized that I would not be there to see him through his new life. It was a life that broke my heart. Captive-born, he would serve humans and their healing; he would never know a watery world without fences or exult in the company of a wild pod crossing over air and sea.

Straight ahead three dolphins ululated the strong currents that carried me still and as I raced with them, I felt more dolphin than human. In that moment, I knew the crossover images in my mind were not mine alone, but shared. For all the other dolphins carrying me were once free, born in open sea, given a birthright that was now denied.

But still they had the memory of speed and slipstream, of spacious ocean and traveling thirty miles a day, their powerful pectorals and tail flukes never flung against fences.

In that lagoon on my last swim with the dolphins whom I will always hold as dear as my own brother and sisters, I promise myself that I will begin the real work of helping to release and restore captive dolphins to the wild. And that perhaps one day before I die, I will hope to be blessed with seeing what these generous ambassador dolphins can only remember: a crossover of thousand-strong dolphins slipping wildly through wide open seas.

The dolphins still remember their wild birthright. And so do I.

TWO

THE WILD

THE HIGH SIERRAS, 1950

ONE OF MY earliest memories is of lying in my cabin crib, my eyes wide open to seek the solace of deer and elk heads above me while I listened to every slither and broken branch, every soft padding of possum and fox, all the animals moving through the woods at midnight. In our Forest Service lookout cabin high in the Sierra Nevada, I was raised under the steady, clear gaze of animals I believed were my guardians. The doe's dark eyes fondly followed me as I crawled, bare belly, against the itchy rag rug; an elderly elk witnessed my first steps. When I slept, a young buck right above my crib kept a watchful eye, his black, protective nose lifted to catch the scent of any stranger.

It never occurred to me that these animals who stood such patient guard over me were not alive. I did not know that I was different from the animal heads mounted on our cabin walls, their eyes so intent, dark, and luminous—no blanker than the window glass that revealed another world. Inside each of these animals lingered spirit, an aliveness that always stayed with its skin and bone and muscle.

My father tells a story of checking on me in my crib one midnight. I was several months old, barely able to keep my head from wobbling on my frail neck; he was astonished to see that I had hoisted myself up by the crib railings and was reaching to touch the black lips of his deer trophy. Sometimes my father would lift me up to run my hands over the tanned fur of these deer, the first faces I ever loved; I touched the long slope of jawbones and sensitive snouts, the pricked ears and tufts at the top of their heads. Most amazing were the antlers—I expected I would grow my own someday.

As I swooped around the cabin on my father's shoulders, often eye level with the deer faces, I believed it was I who carried this man on my own tiny back, like a turtle its shell. At night, because my mother had no milk to nurse me, it was my father who would get up to feed his colicky baby. Making animal noises—clicking crow calls and chipmunk chitters—he'd carry me into the cabin kitchen where the wood stove was soon bright and murmuring. Boiling water for my glass bottle, Father sang me a lullaby while the bottle clanked and bobbed in the syncopated saucepan.

> Baby sails the silver sea,
> Searching for the moon . . .

Then he lay me on his belly—taut and muscular, a human plateau—and I would at last sleep, rocked by his steady, slow breathing.

One night when I was a toddler and sleeping in my own, real bed, my father woke me up. "Listen," he whispered. "Do you hear that?" There were thin, wavering howls coming through the tall trees, almost like wind crying. "No wolves around here for years. . . ." Again, those haunting, high-pitched calls. Not the "yip-yip" of coyotes but the full-throated singing of a wolf pack. "No, can't be." My father shook his head and tucked me back in bed. "Maybe wild dogs have got some wolf left in them."

Then my father told me the story of the wild wolf who once inhab-
ited these forests where we now lived, who hunted game to survive, just
as we did. "They have families, like us," he told me. "But they're all
gone now." Then, with a soft laugh, he said, "I can tell you: If there
were wolves still round these parts, even our mounted deer heads here
might just up and skeedaddle."

I looked up at my animal guardians and felt a sudden, sharp sorrow,
a loss. What would I do without their company? If the wolf drove them
away, would I go hungry? Would I be all alone? My father reassured me
that it was the other way around. The wolves couldn't take our game,
because we'd driven the wolves away, so far away that few had been
seen lately in all the Lower Forty-Eight states—or in any other part of
the world, for that matter. "Go to sleep, honey," he cooed in his soft,
bass voice. "There's no more Big Bad Wolf. You'll never go hungry. I'll
see to that."

Long before I attended school or church, I was told that these animals who gazed down on me had sacrificed their lives so that I might
live. These devoted deer and old elk had made the first communion
that my parents later taught me belonged to a saviour who lived in the
sky. Before every meal, they said grace to this god, not the animals. In
the tiny mountain church I heard the minister declare, "This is the
body and blood of Christ. Take ye and eat—eat all of me," but I knew
we were not subsisting on these communion wafers and grape juice
every day. On that forest station, we few human families surrounded by
millions of acres of lodgepole and ponderosa pine, of bugling elk and
tender deer, of succulent, sweet rattlesnake and mysterious moose—we
were eating wild game given us by the animals. A meal-time grace that
seemed less confusing to a small child would have been "Give us this
day, our daily animals."

Then there was my hunter father, himself part dark Swede,
Seminole, and French-Canadian Indian. Perhaps he was confused, too,
or maybe his mixed blood and shame about his backwoods roots led

him to share the Southern Baptist prayers with my mother. But when
we were alone, my father taught me a more pragmatic faith. He said,
"These animals in the forest are your brothers and sisters, if you can
just look under the skin of things and truly see them." My father would
always honor any deer or elk he shot with small offerings before he carried it back to our cabin. We used all the animal, including its innards,
and from the soft, tanned skins we made moccasins on Christmas Eve.
As a child, I'd watch my father flense a doe in our back shed with the
same loving hand he used to stroke fine horses and redwood trees. He'd
call me animal names like "Gopher" and "Raccoon," then he'd remind
me of a secret: "Some people say there was a time when animals and
humans remembered how to talk together."

This was no secret to me. Hadn't I listened in on the daily dialogues
of hawks and hoot owls, the calls of wild coyotes and cats, hadn't diamondback rattlesnakes warned me away as I crawled across the forest
floor, and mountain lions screamed me awake in the night? There
were more animal conversations in that forest lookout station than
human talk.

In the forest there were posters everywhere of my father's stalwart
boss and my first, reassuring divinity—Smokey Bear. My father was
fond of telling me that Smokey Bear had been dreamed up by the U. S.
Forest Service during World War II, before I was born. Smokey's
friendly but firm bear face first showed up on official posters for the fire
season of 1945—the year we bombed Hiroshima and Nagasaki. When
I was born in the tiny community clinic in the forest in August 1950,
the fire season was at its summer peak. The threat of fire was everywhere; red-zone forest postings screamed out "Fire Danger: High!" But
alongside these warnings of fire Smokey Bear's reassuring furry face
gazed out from every signpost and bulletin board. Smokey was as
omnipresent as God and certainly as concerned with our daily survival.

The real, rescued Smokey Bear soon gave flesh and fur to the official
cartoon Smokey. "Think of it, honey," my father would tell me in my first

Smokey Bear stories as I toddled behind him through the forest. "Firefighting soldiers found that little bear cub the same year you were born, down in a forest in New Mexico. This sturdy little bear cub had climbed up a tree that was charred down to almost nothing but hollowed-out bark. Why, it was a wonder the tree still stood after such a horrible forest fire. But it did. It stood tall enough to hold Smokey just above the flames. Even so, the little guy's baby fur was burned up pretty bad . . . all black and singed." My father's voice would fall. "No one knows what happened to Smokey's mother. Most likely she was lost in the fire."

My father told me how the firefighters heard his tiny bear-cub bleat—a half-hoarse whimper and snuffling sob. One soldier climbed up and carried him down as he clung to the man's strong back, snapping whenever any other human came near. How often did I cling to my own stuffed Smokey Bear with his sensible, broad-brimmed hat, blue dungarees, and kind but firm brown eyes. Sometimes I even prayed to Smokey Bear.

In my worst nightmares up there on the forest station, I'd heard the call and screech and cry of wild animals running before hungry flames. I'd seen men run out of the forests with tears and sweat streaking their sooty faces as they dug trenches to distract the fury of a wildfire. My own father sometimes came home in filthy overalls, black ash falling as he tore off his Forest Service helmet, his upper arm swollen from shoveling. Once, years later in another California forest, my father would find a wood tick bloated as big as a baseball on his skin. While his forest burned, so did my father's near-fatal Rocky Mountain Spotted Fever.

As a toddler, when people talked about forest fires, I knew what that little bear cub and my father had survived. I knew what devastation little Smokey must have seen from the lookout atop his burning tree: his forest was a fiery wasteland. In a world where the Biblical "fire next time" singed my earliest bedtime stories, a decade in which images of a fiery nuclear waste would one day haunt my nightmares, I believed Smokey Bear would somehow save me as he had been saved. Smokey would save my family, and all human beings — just as he protected the forest creatures from terrible flames.

When I was a child, it didn't seem odd to worship a bear, especially so brave and wise an animal who took care of his forest the way my father did and reminded people not to start the terrifying fires that had killed bears and humans alike.

Often I'd follow my quiet father into the forest, which smelled like him — tart, fragrant timber. On that forest floor were moss and lichen to slide into, pine needles to prick my palms, and against my cheeks the moist sweetness of leaf rot. Everything vegetable in me loved this smell, rooted in it on all fours — knees, hands, face pressed into the bottom of the forest that was never still, but talking with wet clouds walking low through blue spruce and Douglas fir.

Once while trailing after my father as he entered his woods, I found myself suddenly eye to eye with a rattlesnake. She hissed her name in greeting, rattled, and I, a child-cobra, raised my head, my tongue sticking out, too, feeling the warm air. I listened with my tongue as the snake did and I met those tiny agate eyes that resembled black stones. Slowly the rattlesnake, gold and coral, coiled around my wrist like those bracelets my mother sometimes wore. Then the serpent encircled my arm, her cool scales a comfort in this summer's heat. No rattle now, just the tongue touching me here and there on the breastbone, the throat, the forehead — a light tickle like a blade of grass. I stretched out flat on my back and let the snake nestle on my belly, her soothing weight like an end to hunger.

My father found me asleep in the dazzling sun, the thin, high-altitude air so clear and nourishing I nursed on it. Looking down, he saw the rich, coiled folds of a mountain rattler in a black-and-tan diamond circle on my chest. The old rattlesnake rose and fell with my dreaming breath.

Someone was whispering. It was not the trees nor the mist, it was my father. His voice was just a quiet echo in my ear so I could hardly hear him. "Be very still . . . ," he breathed.

Sleepily I opened my eyes and was about to stretch when I saw my father raising up a large stick. Hissing, he thwacked the air and lifted the mountain rattler off my chest. Whip-like, he wrapped her around a solitary silver fir. Terrible snapping sounds cracked like dead branches as her long spine shattered. My bare chest was still radiant from the warmth of the rattlesnake, but now her long diamondback body hung limp in my father's hands. I screamed. Then silence.

Squirrels discussed it, but I couldn't understand them now because my father was crying out. His heart clanged as I'd never heard before. It made the hacking steel sound of an ax ringing down on iron wedges. I'd heard this sound before fires blazed in our kitchen, but now the clanging of my father's heart filled the forest and for the first time in my life I felt the clear, resonant pitch of his fear. I wept as I watched my father hack off the snake's rattler—a present for me.

I refused ever to play with that rattler and for a long while after my father tried to protect me by killing that snake, I shied away from him, but every day he still combed my hair.

"How did you get so many tangles?" my father would ask, exasperated at the curls and gnarls of ashen hair that reached out like tentacles to encircle his fingers even as he tried to straighten and twist and braid. My hair did not behave itself, although I was a quiet, watchful child.

Ever since I could remember, my father had been in charge of combing my hair. My own mother was too impatient and high-strung to take over that chore, so to my more maternal father fell the management of my unruly hair. I put up with all my father's fussing and disciplining my hair because when he finally unloosed all the tangles, there was a time of complete rest for both of us. It reminded me of something I could hardly remember, only feel—a time when I had rested on my father's belly as deeply as I now did on those flat summit rocks in the sun.

As I grew into an independent and shy child, my father rarely took time with me because he had grown busier and more important, plus there was my new sister to hold. I was long and gangly like my father and his trees. When I sat on his lap as he combed my hair, my legs dangled, scraping the cabin floor.

As my father eased the bristle-brush through my hair, the curls relented and flowed into bright waves, like a waterfall down my back. Everything in my father that was tall and tight as timber fell away when he combed my hair. Soon, I knew, when I started school, my father would start correcting my mind, the way he did my hair. He would groom me then as he once had his horse; maybe he might even put a bit between my teeth when my imaginings were too wild. Even though we lived in this wilderness, his job was to manage it, just like he did his daughters' hair.

"Do you know," my father asked me one morning as he combed what he called my "rat's nest" of hair, "that I only went to school every *other* day?"

"But you still won the state spelling bee," I answered proudly, having heard this story many times. I felt him grab a long curl between forefinger and thumb, cinch it there like a horse's harness to hold my head still as he yanked the comb through a particularly stubborn knot.

"Why, it's pine gum in your hair," he laughed. "Where did you sleep last night—the woodpile?" His voice was teasing and fond, yet somehow reprimanding, the way he would speak to a high-spirited horse. It was the way I'd heard him talk to the pack horse he rode through the forest; it was the way he'd talk to elk and deer before he shot them. Once I'd heard him talking easily this way to a doe he'd hunted down and was skinning in the back shed. The doe swung back and forth gently from the rafters, swaying like a gleaming white-barked birch, but upside down.

"Sorry, little girl," he'd said as he flensed away the pale, shining skin. He sliced a length from the doe's flank to its shoulder; it shimmied and hung from his hand like a luminous snake. "This time," he said, "I was just a tad faster."

Last time, I knew, the deer had heard him coming. She'd stood with magnificent eyes tuned, dark and listening to the dawn light as my father crept on his belly over the ridge. Father said she smelled him first and I was surprised that she noticed he was any different from the smell of trees. Father met the doe's eyes; he was that close to her. And as he raised his gun, squinting for the shot, he could already see this exquisite deer head mounted on the wall to watch over his daughters. It was a perfect shot, my father said, right through the heart he saw throbbing in her tawny breast. On the hillside, the doe was poised as if she had all the time left in the world. But she did not drop to the forest floor. She just stood gazing steadily down at him. And then, he said, like some sort of guardian spirit, the doe disappeared.

WHEN MY OWN family disappeared from the forest, leaving behind all the other wild animals, I endured my first near-death experience. I was almost four years old and the descent from high above the Sierra Nevada timberline to San Diego sea level was dizzying, disorienting. The dive left me breathless, and as my blood thickened, I moved slowly, uneasy with my new heaviness. It was like learning to walk all over again, but this time as if underwater. Gravity weighed on my thin body and often I envied my two baby sisters, who still crawled across the well-cut grass. I longed to be eye level again with the garter snakes patrolling my father's vegetable garden looking for those green, bulbous tomato slugs we kids were supposed to spy out and crush in two with a hoe.

I remember standing among pungent tomato vines as high as my chest and hesitating over a chartreuse slug as it inched and nibbled the precious leaves. When we squashed the slugs, their fuzzy bodies popped with a juicy burst. This sound hurt my ears and made me want to cry—not at all the behavior expected of an oldest child familiar with life and death in the wilderness. But this fatal sound was not made by red-tailed hawk sinking talons into fleeing, brown rabbit; it was not even the ricochet and ringing of rifle shot felling a deer for our supper. No, this plop and burst of a lowly tomato slug beneath our farmer's hoe was a new sound—a domesticated and somehow unnatural sound. It belonged to the new realm of our domestic life, like automobiles louder than the small stands of trees and a multitude of other children claiming only a vacant lot as their wilderness.

Very little remains with me of that year in San Diego and another year in San Bernadino, except the garden, the Arrowhead Mountains like a pink, jagged mirage shimmering up from our backyard. But to this day I cannot bear to hear the sound of someone stomping an insect. It reminds me of the first animals I ever killed, their green blood haunting me more than the sight of their severed bodies. Sometimes I would lie awake at night in my bunk bed, remembering the forest sounds of deer hooves and animal crossings in the dark. And then I would weep for the tomato slugs I had harmed, the vast forests, and all the other wildlife I had lost.

It was during one of these garden patrols that my father called to us one summer afternoon. "We're going to the ocean!" he said happily. "Forget the garden for now."

I had rarely seen the ocean, just Crater Lake, the world's deepest mountain body of water. Some old foresters had teased me, telling me it had no bottom. My father had told stories about the sea from his U.S. Navy days and it seemed to me that my older cousin Nelda must have practically lived in the ocean because she had so many swimsuits. Her father, Uncle George, was part Choctaw Indian who both thrilled and terrified us kids because he was so contemplative, and his wry sense of humor was way beyond us.

But that day, not even Uncle George's keen eyes could anticipate that at the sight of the Pacific Ocean's rolling, luminous waves, I would run straight from my family picnic into the surf. To this day at family reunions, when my father's family tells stories of wild animals—from grizzlies to coyotes to runaway horses—my father includes the story of my near death by drowning, as if I were also a wild animal.

"It was high tide," my father often recalls, "and we look up from eating to see this blur of a toddler dash right down to the surf and dive in. No stop, no testing the water with her foot, but plunging deep into this huge wave like it was just an open door. Except this wave swamped her and she disappeared so long we knew an undertow had taken her down." My father's face always falls at this minute and then he looks very young again, as if he has shed the heaviness of his seventy years and is again a slim, agile athlete—a forester and farmer boy reckoning with an ocean that has stolen his small daughter.

"I dove in and searched blindly for her, but nothing," Dad tells the story. "I remember thinking, 'She's just too little to lose. Please, God, don't take her away so soon!' "

What I remember is spinning in a kaleidoscopic underworld of blue-green, grabbing onto kelp, which encircled my belly like another slippery umbilical cord. The undertow was as strong as my father's arms and held me down so long that soon I simply breathed in saltwater, so familiar, so like that other womb that I'd recently swum out of to find a few people and many guardian trees. This other water world was not the forest with its sheltering tall people, but it was populated just the same with starfish and bright tropical beings who flickered past my face like butterflies.

And nearby there was a rapid ricochet of clicks and bleeps from a passing dolphin pod. It was my first encounter with these quixotic sea creatures and their echolocation felt like a delightful inner tickling that made me laugh and gulp more seawater. It did not seem to me that I was drowning or unconscious. The ocean felt like a remembered world that pulsed and flowed, nurturing me. I was completely happy, at home.

My father did not bring me back. It was the sea herself who gently lifted me up on a huge wave and lay me tenderly back down on the beach where suddenly many screaming relatives pumped my arms and blew harsh air into my mouth. My mouth and eyes streamed saltwater and the heavy air weighed on my tiny chest like grief.

"My daughter drowned," my father always finishes up his story with an expression of dismay and amazement. "She went all the way through the drowning process and no struggle. So she's not afraid of water, like some that are saved while fighting the sea. Instead, she fell in love with water. Go figure. Nowadays they call it 'near death.' And maybe that's why she was so peaceful. But back then in the fifties we just thought the sea bringing her back was a gift from God. That maybe she'd seen something she mistook for heaven. But after that she was so quiet and shy, except in water. And," he always finishes with a grin and a shrug as if long ago he gave up trying to understand his eldest daughter, "she's kinda strange since she drowned . . . like a changling."

I *was* changed after returning from my near death by drowning. What changed most were my animal dreams and my mourning for the forest. At sea level was another wild world of sea and anemone, of porpoise and seal, of kelp and shell and chambered nautilus. My devotion to animals expanded to include not only the forest creatures of my birthplace, but also sea creatures—from the pulsing ballet of translucent jellyfish to the far-off dolphins streaking across wild Pacific whitecaps.

When my father landed a fellowship at Harvard, we Forest Service children discovered that the ocean made as fierce and fond a neighbor as had the wild woods. I had just turned eight, more used to camping than to the cramped, hallowed halls of East Coast academia or the crowded apartment house in Revere Beach, Massachusetts. My siblings and I were grateful that my father settled us in a tenement right across the street from the Atlantic Ocean. We did not know we were living in a slum because every night ocean waves accompanied our dreams and we wandered windswept, seaweed-strewn beaches searching for soft-shell crabs and secret human lovers hiding in the rocks. Every day on our way to the tiny schoolhouse—in my class there were only eight other kids and only one other girl—we passed a ramshackle amusement park in which we spent our meager weekly allowances. My favorite was the roller coaster, which was always surrounded by a halo of lofty, crying seagulls.

It was here in the shushing shadow of winter waves and beach life that my love of the sea at last met and married my bond with the forest. That entire New England summer while my father was lost in the university library and my mother was lost because she couldn't find a Southern Baptist church in all of Boston, we kids lived on the beach. We trusted the tides, more reliable than most adults, to baby-sit my tiny brother, Dana, and toddler sister, Marla; they were playfully contained in tidepools more fascinating than any crib. Meanwhile, my adventurous sister Paula and I spent entire days floating on the gentle swells of our second mother, the ocean. We'd found a battered air mattress in the super's basement and took turns lying on our backs, wiry arms crossed beneath our heads to study the clouds in that pure summer sky. We believed the clouds, like the constellations, were animals watching over us as surely as God, as knowingly as our first forest creatures.

To this day I have navigated my way between ocean and forest like the true North and South of my physical compass. If it is true that character is shaped by landscape, then mountain forest and sea, with their very different wildlife, are what orient me to know who I am and where I can find home. After my father's year of graduate work was finished, the Forest Service called us back again to the mountains and the Western Rockies. The sea and her rolling surf, her whales way off shore, her scuttling crabs and thrilling storms were again, like the womb, just a memory.

THREE

~

GRANDMOTHER,
GRIZZLIES, AND GOD

MONTANA, 1959

THE MAKESHIFT GARAGE in Missoula, Montana, in which
my parents and ten or so other families met for church service
might as well have been a tiny ark. Its old wooden rafters held us
together in a vast Western wilderness, an ancient sea bottom of wide
prairie lands with no other Southern Baptists. I was nine years old, but
to this day I remember the musty, sweet-mash smell of horse or chicken
feed and the engine oil that stained the cement floor under our folding
chairs. Staring at the oil spill patterns in this garage floor, since there
were no windows, I'd concentrate on the birdsongs outside—any natural sound to escape the sermons, which were always too loud and
frightening.

Every time I did tune in to the minister's Bible stories, something
terrible was happening to humans or animals: Adam and Eve cast out
of their Garden and God's wise serpent condemned to crawl on its
belly, demon-possessed pigs stampeding off a cliff, Abraham raising a
knife over his own son and slaughtering a ram instead. It was strong
stuff for a child whose imagination had first imprinted on animals.

The problem with those Bible stories was that they felt so vivid and visceral, so dangerous to children and other animals. I well remembered crawling, serpent-like, on my first forest floor, where sharp pine needles pricked my skin and palms. What if, like that admonished Biblical serpent, or the one my own father had killed, I was never allowed to walk upright? And when I imagined Isaac trembling naked under his father's upraised knife, it was a terrible mixture of relief and remorse to hear the bleating of the ram, which I knew would have its throat slit for my sake. Hadn't I watched beautiful deer leap in the woods and later seen their skinless bodies hang in the shed awaiting our appetites? Everyone in the Old Testament seemed to be at war with God the Father, with offending armies, with themselves and Satan, and with the other animals.

There was one salvation for me in that Montana garage-church. It was not the fundamentalist religion—although my parents expected that soon I might offer myself up at the minister's weekly invitation to be saved; it was a fur coat and the first sermon I ever truly loved. Mrs. Ashworth was an elderly churchwoman whose husband had died in a hunting accident; some said she was a wealthy widow, for she wore real gold-hoop earrings and expensive rouge, which made her look like an old gypsy. But what people envied most was her cavernous bearskin coat. It was huge as a mountain man and she joked that it was like wearing her husband to church. It didn't seem strange to me that Mrs. Ashworth equated her thick, black bearskin coat with a lifelong mate. I'd seen pictures in her wallet of her husband and he did look like a bear, with luxurious tufts of black hair from the top of his head to his fuzzy arms. My own father wasn't as furry as Mr. Ashworth, but then my father limited his hunting to moose, elk, and the like. Maybe to hunt a bear, I reasoned with my child's logic, a man had to somehow be recognized as bear-kin. Then the bear would let the man close enough to shoot or wrestle or embrace in a bear attack.

My father had long ago taught me what to do if I met a bear in the woods: raise myself up to my full child's height, wave my hands above my head to look taller and fiercer, and scream out, "I'm a human being! I'm a predator, too. I'm as big as you!" Sometimes when we camped or hiked we'd tie silverware to our mess kits and that percussive clang and clatter let the bears know it was our turn on the trail.

One year, camping in Glacier National Park with my grandmother, we'd had our first close grizzly bear encounter. My three siblings and I had seen grizzlies only at Forest Service dumps, where we'd watched from a safe distance. But the past winter had been especially cold and the ravenous bears coming out of hibernation coincided with our spring camping.

That May morning while my parents and Uncle Clark were hunting for kindling to start a breakfast fire, Grandmother Elsie laid out a picnic table with fresh bread, thick bacon, campfire skillet–blackened scrambled eggs, and her famous homemade apple butter. Grandmother's apple butter, along with her recipes for Wolverman's relish, chowchow chopped pickles, black-walnut divinity, and cherry fudge, was her finest legacy. My grandfather even had a word for Grandmother's culinary delights: "larrapin" he called these delicious foods. And we did lap up Grandmother's cooking, especially the luscious, darkly sweet and tart apple butter, which had the slow consistency of molasses with succulent chunks of bright apple flesh and skin.

This homemade jam brought us kids to the wooden picnic table more surely than any breakfast call, for although we were all finicky eaters, we followed our noses to Grandmother's apple butter the moment we heard the whoosh and pop of the Bell jar wax break open. Other noses must have quivered at the scent of such a sweet treasure, too, because while we kids were saying grace with our eyes open, heads bowed over the apple butter, I saw a big blurry shape out of the corner of one eye: a gigantic grizzly bear was raised up on hind legs and lumbering toward us while we said grace.

Not one of us did what we had been so carefully taught by our forester-hunter father. At least we did not cower. We froze like possum in the glare of flashlights, standing absolutely still in the presence of such absolute animal power. This grizzly was so splendid in his reddish-black shaggy fur and paws the size of my little brother's head. We were more awestruck than afraid. Our paralysis was as ancient as if our reptilian brains had memorized this image: giant bears hovering over barely human beings. There was no talking to this creature, no bargaining or boisterous argument about sharing top predator status. We were in thrall and insignificant to this big bear. Eerily human-like, he walked on strong back legs toward our table. He did not roar, perhaps appreciating our sudden silence while Grandmother continued grace. I remember clearly being impressed by the bear's black, sniffing nose raised high with a surprising delicacy, as if this bear, too, understood the joy of homemade jam.

I also remember the familiarity and fascination I felt for this grizzly's great body. I'd slept as a child with Smokey Bear and still had a collection of stuffed animals in my bed. As my father later rose through the ranks to at last become chief of the U.S. Forest Service, people would give him Smokey Bear memorabilia—from hats to carvings to a huge painting of Smokey Bear with a shovel in one giant paw and a Bible upraised in the other. In this painting, Smokey wore blue overalls, belt, and hat as in all the official Forest Service posters, but his face was the familiar, round, half-bear, half-human face of my own father.

That morning in Glacier National Forest as a grizzly lumbered toward Grandmother's apple butter, it did not seem odd to feel complete reverence. Smokey had lived in my crib, in my first forest, and now he was coming to breakfast when we called him by saying grace. That was my child's logic, and it made more sense than trying to pretend I was as tall and as fierce as this gigantic grizzly hovering above us. It was my grandmother who lifted her head after a firm "Amen" and shook her finger defiantly at the bear.

"You! Shoooo!" she yelled at him as if he were one of her grandchildren stealing her apple butter. Grandmother was so possessive of her recipe that she hadn't even passed it on to my mother. She was darned if she would share her jam with a bear. "Shooo, shooo, shooo!" With each admonishment, Grandmother flapped her flowered apron at the bear. She was about half the size of the grizzly, but her fierceness was impressive. "This is my last batch of apple butter," she argued with the bear, "and it's not going to be gobbled down by any big bear! Go on with you now! Git!"

I closed my eyes then, expecting the bear to decapitate my grandmother with one massive blow from those paws whose claws seemed huge as rakes. Poised over my grandmother and her jam, the grizzly gave one last, almost longing sniff and then, with a huge harrumph and sigh, turned around and fell down on all fours. The grizzly did not run away, but strolled pigeon-toed nearby and shook his massive head back and forth. I wondered if we had hurt the grizzly's feelings by not sharing our sweets.

None of us, including my grandmother, felt endangered in the presence of that mighty grizzly, who now slowly lumbered a distance from our picnic table. In fact, we didn't say much about it, just dived into the apple butter with our own animal hunger. It wasn't until Uncle Clark came back, waving his arms and telling us to hide under the picnic table from the grizzly, that it occurred to us we were in grave danger.

"You can bet that bear didn't get my apple butter, by gum." Grandmother came the closest to swearing that I'd ever witnessed.

Uncle Clark stared at his mother in disbelief, then turned pale as we told him about grandmother's flapping apron. He quickly packed us into the station wagon so fast we didn't get to finish eating. As we waited in the car for my parents to return, I looked back and saw several grizzlies turn the picnic table upside down, licking the wood where I'd spilled some jam. I was very pleased to see that the bears had at least gotten a taste of Grandmother's glory.

Later in that Glacier Park trip, we pulled up to another campground at night and saw grizzly bears banging trash can lids against trees and crushing the metal containers like soda-pop cans. It was very dark, and when my mother saw the grizzlies she complained of a migraine, so I had to sleep in the tent with my father while all around bears crashed through the forest.

"They won't eat much," my father joked. "Just as long as we keep all the food in the car and not the tent." All day he'd been teasing me about eating M&M's on camping trips. "The bears will sniff that sweet chocolate smeared all over your mouth and they'll chew your lips off," he warned me.

Now I *was* frightened of bears, and I suppose that had been my father's intention—to instill a little terror in his children, who during the breakfast incident had seemed much too open and curious about these other creatures. "It's *good* to be afraid of bears," he'd said. "Smokey Bear is different. He's tame. These grizzlies are wild animals and they'd just as soon tear your heart out as look at you." He said this so cheerfully, I knew he was happy to have taught us healthy fear. "Sometimes people who don't know any better worship animals," he'd say. "Why, just until recently in Japan people were worshipping monkeys. And in India they have sacred cows and elephants."

This did not seem to me like such a wrongheaded instinct. If wonder and reverence inspired human worship, what child wouldn't feel a spiritual instinct toward such animal power? Awe and terror of an animal's divinity were absolutely real to me as I lay awake at night in the tent while the monster-shadows of grizzlies danced in silhouette around our campfire. My father snored contentedly in his sleeping bag while I lay wide awake worried about my lips being chewed off by a grizzly who smelled the sweet, telltale scent of M&M's.

I wanted to wake my father and ask, *Did Smokey ever attack children who ate chocolate? Why didn't we ever say grace to thank the animals we ate for supper for our survival?* I did wake my father up, but not with these questions. I awakened him after watching those grizzlies rear up on their hind legs and move together in bear embraces like giant dance partners. These bears had no interest in me. They were caught up in something bigger than me, maybe even bigger than themselves. Even I, who had been raised in a Southern Baptist Church that forswore dancing and drinking—even I recognized what my early primate ancestors must have witnessed when they came upon bears dancing in the woods.

Here was some kind of ceremony, maybe even an animal way of worship. The grizzlies were no longer banging trashcans, they were raising their shaggy heads and paws as if to greet the tall, ancient trees. They were circling around each other making pleasurable snorts and harrumphs like some kind of bear-song or celebration. I recognized a power and primitive joy that I rarely saw in humans, even in church when they sang the fast, military songs of salvation. I'd witnessed my mother's capacity for this rapture when she played her ragtime piano; I'd seen my father actually leap and shout when he'd brought down a stately elk on a hunting trip; and I'd seen siblings and friends my age do circle dances in snow or autumn leaves out of sheer pleasure. But I'd never seen animal ecstasy of this magnitude before and I will never forget its growling, physical happiness.

"Dad, do you think a bear would really kill us while we were praying?" I whispered. "Don't you think the bear would know we were talking to God?"

My father tossed about in his sleeping bag and unzipped it as if he were burning alive. This was exactly the kind of question he loathed. He never enjoyed philosophical dialogues, preferring the practical and reasonable realms of what he called "good horse sense." "Listen, you don't waste time wondering what's on a grizzly's mind! If you are bowing your head or you go down on your knees—it doesn't matter if you're praying or scared stiff—the grizzly will think you're dead and come investigate what he believes another animal has killed and left for him. But if you stand up and wave your hands and scream out that you're a human and his equal, he'll think twice before he attacks. Now, that's that. Go to sleep."

"But I'm not as big as a bear. I'm not his equal no matter how much I flap my arms. Grandma could do it because she's bigger and besides, it was her last batch of apple butter. Even a bear could understand that."

"Bears are not as smart as human beings," my father said wearily. "They don't have minds and souls like you and I. They're just animals and we have to respect them. But that's it. Don't go giving them what belongs to human beings."

"If animals don't have souls," I asked, "why do you put a slice of apple and a pine sprig in the dead doe's mouth after you've killed her for us? Isn't that so the deer can find her way back to earth in afterlife?"

My exasperated father threw up his arms. "Oh, honey, don't attach any spiritual significance to it. It's just something I learned from my own father and some other hunters I grew up with. More like respect."

I was very confused, as usual, whenever my father told me things that seemed at odds with his actions. Like the way he hoarded his animal skins as if they were more precious than money. Every Christmas Eve we were given carefully measured-out pieces of deer or elk skin to make moccasins for the New Year. And he never parted with his animal trophies, which adorned every fireplace like shrines in every one of our houses. In fact, the only falling out my father ever had with a friend was over a magnificent pair of moose antlers that one of his hunting buddies tried to claim for his own mantel. If this behavior didn't show some signs of spiritual practice and worship in my father, what did? Certainly not his calm and practical calculations of the church budgets or the chores of pulpit and finance committees that his status as deacon required of him.

Unlike my mother, who played the church organ and piano like a crazed saint—her upbeat tempo and enthusiasm so high-spirited they'd had to put potted plants in front of her to keep her zeal from distracting the whole church—I'd never seen my father inspired by church service or a minister's sermons. He never sang out "Hallelujah" or "Amen, brother!" like some of the other fundamentalists. The only time I'd ever seen my father really guffaw or give out belly-laughs was telling his hunting-buddy stories, and the only times I ever saw him truly happy and caught up in something obviously greater than himself was first when he was in the forest and later when he'd come home from the office and tend to his Tennessee Walker horses. The first time I'd seen my father cry was when his mother passed away. Decades later in Virginia, my father would weep for the second time when his favorite filly—the one he'd helped midwife—lay down in the snowy pasture and couldn't stand up again. My father would weep when he told me how he'd pleaded with Starlight to get up on her trembling legs, and when he saw she couldn't anymore because of her degenerative spinal disease, he'd called the vet and put her down because she was already so far down on the frozen ground.

But that night in Glacier National Park my father's favorite filly had not died; she had not yet even been born. That night I would ask the question that decades later I would know enough not to ask when Starlight died: "Do you think animals go to heaven? When you kill animals, Daddy, don't they go to heaven with us?"

"They go to sleep," he mumbled grumpily by way of giving up this midnight conversation. "Bears don't go to heaven. But they do hibernate in the winter and then in the spring they keep us awake nights with all this racket. They're not dancing, they're not in heaven. They're just—well, maybe they're playing, like you do." He reached over a paw to pat me on the head, then said groggily, "You go to sleep now. That would be some kind of heaven for me."

~○

FOUR

BUILD ME AN ARK

MONTANA, 1960

S INCE THAT MIDNIGHT with the dancing grizzlies I had been obsessed with the question of animal afterlives. It seemed like every deer trophy in our house, every hunting story my father's buddies told at dinner, every venison steak and elk stew and mooseburger I ate begged the question, Where do animals go when they die? I knew exactly where humans went because every Sunday the minister reminded us of heaven and hell. In that Montana garage I could see deer heads and rifles stored behind the piano and the pulpit. Our congregation was full of hunters and foresters who fed their families the sweet, lean game of Rocky Mountain wildernesses. If we were eating animals and wearing their skins to church, why weren't the animals allowed inside to worship with us? Some of the churchgoers even rode horses to service, but no one ever asked a horse into this garage the way the Nativity scenes showed Christ's birth surrounded by oxen and camels, sheep and cattle.

I would sit next to Mrs. Ashworth in the sheltering arms of her great bearskin coat and hibernate during sermons. This bearskin coat and adopted grandmother were my beloved sanctuary—and my first real maternal memory. My own mother also had a fur coat; it was leopard skin and sleek like my mother herself. It was from the time before she'd gotten saddled with marriage and children. Sometimes I'd sneak into her closet and wrap myself in its luxurious, perfumed folds. But like my mother, the leopard skin was too high-strung to be comforting. So Sunday sermons snuggled inside the wide, maternal arms of Mrs. Ashworth in our little ark of a church were my weekly refuge. Mrs. Ashworth let me doze in her kind and elderly way; I suppose at times she snoozed, too, because I'd hear her breathing deepen and that hibernating sigh and gurgle come from within the huge folds of her fur coat.

And then one Sunday service I woke up from my deep bearskin sleep to a sermon that galvanized my slumbering soul. As usual, the world was ending in the minister's sermons, but this time, instead of firestorm Armageddon's rapturous armies or the sinful fall from the Garden of Eden, there was someone trying to save everybody—and with God's help. " 'Build me an ark!' the Lord told his faithful servant Noah. 'Gather every beast of the field. Save the animals two-by-two. Make this great ark of gopher wood.' " The preacher told the story in his best Sunday breathing-as-bellows booming voice. "And Noah built himself an ark with God's directions, 30 cubits high and 300 cubits long, and 50 cubits wide. Maybe there were windows so the animals could look out on the forty days and nights of the wildest waves God's world had ever witnessed. Waves that deluged the whole world until the skies were black with thunderclouds and the rivers and oceans rose up so high all of creation perished!" The preacher eyed everybody in that small garage and his eyes rested on me with some surprise.

I was wide awake, sitting up straight in my folding aluminum chair, electrified by his story. The preacher nodded at me and took up again. "I say, people, *the rain fell down!* And the waves rose high! And all

God's children drowned those forty days, all except Noah's family and all the animals in that tiny ark floating up and down, and up and down on God's great flood."

Closing my eyes and rocking with the rhythm of the preacher's sermon, I saw it all: Elephants and tigers asleep in the same straw-strewn stall; orangutans and grizzlies on their furry hind legs in a graceful, grateful dance of survival; serpents and shy possums snuggling deep in the great ark's lower berths; wolves and wildcats making dens in stored firewood stacks that still held the dense smell of must and earth; and finally, coupled herds of deer, elk, and moose—not just their staring heads, but their whole sleek bodies leaping from every deck like guardian angels.

Imagining all the animals safe in this divinely directed ark, I felt a kind of security and happiness no sermon had ever inspired in me before. This ark was like my first forest, when the scale of human to animal seemed just right: animal presence far outnumbering the few human families. And in the ark, like in that deep forest, the animals belonged alongside us. Maybe these animals had souls that, like ours, were worth saving. And that's why God gave Noah such careful instructions on how to carry all the animals with him into the next world. As the preacher told his Noah's ark story, I realized that here at last was Biblical proof of what I'd always secretly believed: God so loved the animals. He didn't always sacrifice them; He wanted them to survive with us. And He wanted them with us when the world was ending.

"Forty days and forty nights, Noah's ark floated on God's great flood." The preacher's voice rose and fell in a trance-like syncopation. Perhaps he thought I was hibernating again in my bear skin and wanted to wake me up. "Listen! There was no Earth left. There was no day and no night! There was only the rocking of the waves and the creaking of the ark and all the people and animals in God's great hands."

I wondered about this wooden womb of an ark, which held every beast of the field. In that floating refuge the animals were Noah's only link with his lost world and with God, who was talking only in tidal waves. Inside the ark, I imagined Noah gazing forty days and nights into the almost human, ancient eyes of great apes. As Noah's family huddled together in the cavernous hold, elephants caressed each other with long, supple trunks and wept with happiness to be saved together. Outside, God's angry waves lifted Noah's ark only to drop it into pitiless valleys. But inside that blessed ark, Noah was calmed by the patient stillness of hibernating serpents and the quiet construction of inchworms making new earth. In this floating animal kinship, Noah's family found comfort and grace—knowing themselves all in the same boat, when before the Flood they had all believed they were on separate planets.

As the ark rose and fell those forty days and nights, Noah knew at last a great truth: He and his family were never alone. Aside from God, there were always the other animals. This was the new covenant with all that was living. And like the chorus of all the whales of the world, this newfound faith accompanied Noah's ark. Dolphins leaped reassuringly at its bow, tender gray whales guided its stern, and echoing from depths beneath, the sonorous singing of humpback lullabies soothed even the oceans.

"People, when God says 'Build me an ark!' He means 'Save yourself and all other creatures.' " The preacher closed his sermon, smiling down on me. I had never seen our preacher more radiant or reassuring. He seemed to reach beyond himself, certainly beyond his usual, darker visions. Looking benevolently down on me inside Mrs. Ashworth's bearskin coat, our preacher raised his arms and sang out in triumph, "Listen, people, we are all Noah's with our little arks, our spiritual lives. And whether we know it or not, we are floating on divine waves."

I was not afraid anymore of all the worlds ending in every sermon. Now I believed I was floating safely on God's own waves, as I had when I once drowned in the Pacific, as I had that summer in the Atlantic. At last I had an answer to my question about whether animals accompanied us into our afterlives. Noah's ark was a story that saved us all together. With his kindly beard and wide ark, Noah became synonymous with my invisible God of the heavens.

⁓

AND SO BEGAN my early childhood devotion to Noah and his generous ark. I began collecting colorful miniature plastic animals and constructed my own tiny ark of a balsam wood body and Popsicle sticks for a roof. I stole a book from the school library that had an illustration from a medieval Book of Hours in which scarlet snakes and gilded griffins intertwined their gleaming bodies with sacred texts as if the holy story of God and animals still belonged together. And I began my still-unsatisfied search for paintings or illustrations showing the inside of Noah's ark.

In every illustrated Bible story and even in the books at the Harvard University library I once was allowed to visit, all the animals were depicted entering or leaving Noah's ark. But none had shown what it must have been like *inside* that creaking, holy boat. I was left to continue envisioning it myself. In fact, whenever I was frightened or troubled I would find myself not only imagining the safehold of Noah's ark, but inviting myself inside the ark as well. Sometimes I nestled against the shaggy wool comforters of satisfied sheep; sometimes I shared the straw bales of my favorite palomino, paint, or Appaloosa ponies while contemplating the cacophony of raven caws, wolf howls, grunting piglets, and purring tigers. On balmier days, I'd venture outside the ark and sun myself on the battered deck, while in waves below I searched for the company of curious seals and breathing sea turtles.

All of my earlier drawings were preoccupied with this peaceable kingdom inside Noah's ark. These art works I kept to myself, even though my younger siblings often found me sprawled on the floor studying *National Geographic* to make my animals anatomically correct. Hippos, leopards, elephants, and giraffes were the easiest to draw, even though my little brother wanted me to color them pink or purple.

"There are no purple hippos in *National Geographic*," I pointed out pedantically, as if this magazine were itself another Bible. Although I had little patience for my siblings' lack of scientific rigor, as a fourth grader I was still open to their more fanciful suggestions to draw certain magical animals that might have escaped extinction by finding Noah's ark. Unicorns and griffins, and especially dinosaurs, were popular add-ons whenever my siblings discovered me populating my ark.

But one day my middle sister, the pragmatic Paula, doubted the peaceable kingdom. "Daddy, why didn't the lions just gobble up all the lambs?" she demanded at the dinner table, where we were eating a typical supper of venison steak from a doe my father had shot.

Paula was my father's favorite daughter for her beauty and zest; a "high-spirited filly" my father would dotingly call her. We other children always knew where we stood in my father's Linnaeus-like system of naming. He never called his horses by any other animal or vegetable name, and Smokey was always Smokey Bear—full title, full dignity.

So that one day when my seven-year-old sister dazzled my father with a question that begged the issue of the predator-prey relationship, one of my father's favorite themes, we were all more than usually jealous of her.

"Noah's ark was a magic boat, stupid," I snapped, even though I knew this would pull my father into the protector role and another of his favorite poses, what my mother wearily called his "Devil's advocate delight".

"It's God, not magic," my sister shot back with a toss of her palomino-colored mane. My father, the family hair-tender, had finally decided to let Paula's hair grow out, no longer cutting it with kitchen shears and a bowl over her head.

She and my sister Marla were the blondes in the family; my little brother and I had my mother's features and my father's darker hair. We all had my mother's gray-blue wolf eyes and my father's lanky, long-legged stride. Whereas I was the student, Paula even then had all the social graces in the family and this awareness often made her toss her head like fine horseflesh and trot from time to time in polite company. A Native American friend of mine once told me that horses have an innate striving to be beautiful. Perhaps this was also my sister's instinct.

When she entered my territory of science and the quest for spiritual knowledge I was instantly confused and on the alert. Scientific discussions were usually reserved for me and my father, whereas politics or social manners caused lively debate among my sisters. My brother never got to say much of anything until he was at least ten. He learned to be such a good listener that by the time he was in high school he had girls chasing him in droves.

"Your sister has a point," my father corrected me with a smile that showed us he was warming to his subject, "and she's asked an *interesting* question." My father rose to the occasion like the stately educator that he would one day become in Congress. But for now in that Montana outpost of what the Forest Service called "the field," my father practiced his lectures on a smaller, rapt audience.

"It says in the Bible that there is a time when the lions will lay down with the lambs even though in the wild, of course, lions devour lambs . . ."

"Are there any lambs for lions to eat in Africa?" I interrupted, a cardinal sin at our dinner table. We could interrupt anyone except my father. And if he were delivering himself of a lecture, it was a dire mistake. But I was emboldened by having recently devoured an entire issue of *National Geographic* devoted to the Serengeti. Nowhere had I seen evidence of sheep on the savannas. "Don't lions eat gazelles and antelope?"

Perturbed but not put off, my father turned his full attention to me— which was, after all, the point of my insurrection. "In the wild, of course, lions eat gazelle and antelope and even zebra," he said. "But let's get back to Noah's ark and your sister's perplexing question: Why didn't the predators eat up their usual prey, especially in such close quarters?"

I knew better than to interrupt again with any attempted answer.

This question belonged to my father's adult intellect and authority. It was a world, I'd noticed, where God the judge hung out a lot more, giving rules and such. In my child's lower atmospheres God, like benevolent Noah, was more buffeted about and involved with earthly emotions and events such as fire and floods. But from my point of view, God was still more involved with nature than in laying down the law. Even the Ten Commandments had been scrawled in lightning. Water springing from stone signaled the true way, burning bushes singed into prophets' souls told the lost tribes what to do next.

"You see, kids," my father leaned back from the table. This was in the days before he smoked sweet tobacco, but his leisure and contemplative manner were the same ritual with which he would later prepare his pipe. "Sometimes when God is involved, our human or animal natures can be reversed or redeemed: A killer repents and is saved and does good for others the rest of his life. Or, in Noah's ark, a lion who would usually rip into a lamb for dinner will instead lie down in peace with its prey. Why? Because they are being fed by a higher source. So all the animals and humans are one family—this is just the way of Noah's ark."

"But what did they eat, really? Those big lions?" my little brother asked, a question we all knew was too literal, but still needed answering.

My father considered this for a moment with a frown. We could see him locked in a familiar inner debate between divine logic and scientific fact. As a forester and civil engineer, science was my father's passion, but as a believer in the Bible as God's word, he was also devoted to finding a bridge between human faith and nature's wisdom. This bridge was perhaps my father's greatest engineering achievement. And, at least as children, we happily crossed his thoughtful constructions spanning deep and treacherous chasms of doubt, despair, and disbelief into which other children fell.

At last, my father nodded to himself and announced, "Big predators like lions probably ate rodents or small rabbits, which were multiplying faster than the ark could hold. Plenty of small prey around so the lambs could be safe nestled right there next to their former predators."

This satisfied us all and besides, there was no dessert that night so no use lingering at the dinner table for another lecture. We were all up and away. But I was never as easy again in my mind after that meal that had so satisfied my sister's curiosity. *What were all those animals in the ark actually eating?* I began to wonder. And if some of them were eating each other, then was Noah's family also eating some of those animals, even though God told Noah to save them for a new world?

These early doubts did sometimes get in the way of my imagining the inside of Noah's ark as a safe haven, though as with most religious doubts, I relied on faith and my lively inner life, which was still, like the ark, more populated with animals than with humans. Most of the humans in this Montana town only underscored the close predator-prey bond of the mountain frontier. We were never very far from our food, which was wild, not store-bought. There was no ark to be found perched atop these Rocky Mountains.

My peers, children of farmers and ranchers, were at this advanced age of nine presented with their first guns. Animals were their targets: first nervous jackrabbits, prairie-dog towns, and rattlesnakes; and then the acclaimed graduation to game—the deer, elk, and moose my own father still brought down out of the Rocky Mountains every hunting season to feed his family. But my schoolmates did not eat the small prey their BB guns and .22s brought down. The hallowed predator-prey relationship my father spoke about with more reverence than any church sermon was missing in my schoolmates' relationships to other animals. Montana kids saw animals as just food—or worse, target practice.

I could not fathom the neighbor girls who raised sheep for their 4-H projects. Lambs like living, delicate doll babies were loved, adored, even dressed up in silly fake flower hats. Then at the 4-H shows, these seeming members of the family were judged, awarded blue ribbons, given a tearful last embrace, shorn, and often slaughtered. I kept my distance from these neighbor girls, knowing their affection and loyalty could never be trusted—especially in the daily treachery of the school playground. Then there were the Montana mountain boys who bragged about how many rabbits they shot down in cold blood. They also committed the sacrilege of not eating their prey. For the first time in my life I realized that the human instinct to kill was not simply a physical hunger. Something else inside us was satisfied.

My grandfather had hinted at this when he told us with fierce pride his story of killing a "Kraut" by hand. "My bayonet sank into his belly," Grandfather said, his one eye, as always, running with what most would think a tear. In fact, a World War I battle wound had torn his tear duct so that it leaked even when he was perfectly content. Only later would we learn that his heroic injury was not from shrapnel but from a German guard dog biting his face. Though Grandfather didn't really cry when he told his hand-to-hand combat stories, I felt his sadness welling up inside me, and whenever I wept, my grief and confusion seemed to ease him slightly.

"And the horses," he'd add with a shake of his grizzled head, "Whoooey, girlie, it was the worst for them. Poor, dumb creatures. Horses and war, it's always been this way since the first early man broke down a horse's spirit and climbed up on top with spear or sword, bow and arrow, or rifle. In Germany, as we advanced, we didn't know it was almost the end of the war. All we knew was there was nothing to eat but cabbages unless we hit some little *frau's* farm and could slaughter her sheep. But in the trenches, it was all gunfire and grenades, mustard gas, horses breaking their legs in the gutted-out earth, hauling caissons full of dead men. And the smell—it was horse and human sweat, it was bitter smoke, burning skin, fire, and fear. We all smelled it at the front, that animal fear."

My grandfather's stories of the war that was to end all wars, but was really the beginning of another world war and now this Cold War all the newspapers warned about, were hardly a respite from the Old Testament. Unlike the Bible, these wars to end the world were started by humans, not God. So maybe no one was in control, not even God. Naturally, there was no Noah around to save us or make all sides sit down inside the safety and divine mediation of an ark. Besides we were on high ground, landlocked, no saving sea in sight.

In fourth grade, we studied these world wars, all the battles and grainy black-and-white photos of soldiers, maps with crosses symbolizing Allied losses and gains. We'd even seen some old film footage on our school's wheezing projector. Everyone whooped and hollered when our side won, but all I saw were people and horses dying, just like in my grandpa's war stories. In our American history textbook, one drawing of a World War I battlefield captured a horse's horrified eyes as it reared up, a hand grenade exploding like a cyclone of smoke beneath its hooves. This was not the horse's war, I reasoned, just as it was not the animals' fault when God punished humans by destroying our whole world with water.

This was the year I began to regard other humans around me in that Missoula frontier town with a new wariness and a more somber eye. Human history, I realized, was hard not only on us but on animals as well. In my forest birthplace the animals were wild and even though we ate them, the forest animals still had a better chance at survival than did these domesticated cows, hogs, and sheep whose lives were lived for the slaughterhouse or did the heavily burdened, often broken horses. Now I understood: Living so close to people was more dangerous than living in the wild.

While my schoolmates nurtured their 4-H lambs and picked off wildlife for sport, not survival, I said nothing. I was afraid that they would all discover something terribly wrong with me—that my love and alliance with other animals was something I should have outgrown by now, as they certainly had. If I had been a skinny, studious child of today's schools, I might have found my grief and passion met in an ecology class. But in 1960 in Missoula I had no inkling of the growing chorus of voices questioning this frontier mentality.

One day walking to fourth grade on top of three feet of snow hardened by the Montana winter into a solid glaze, I watched a schoolboy casually draw out his handgun and shoot a jackrabbit sprinting across the snow. The rabbit didn't stop at once but continued hopping just ahead of its own bloody tracks on the blazing white landscape. Then it paused, jerked convulsively, and lay itself down to die. I ran over to it just in time to feel its last terrified heartbeat through my heavy mittens.

This was the first time I had ever witnessed an animal's death, though I had seen many dead animals in the forest. The flutter of that rabbit's heart is still in my hands; it made a first and indelible synapse in my own skin. And then I knew what all my Noah's ark meditations could no longer protect me from—I was a predator and here was a prey. Sometimes humans killed just because they could, not for food or shelter but to satisfy another appetite, one that burned in soldiers like my grandfather. This hunger to prey on others, especially animals, was a human hunger that even God could only put to rest, like during an entire world flooded or for a brief ark-time when lion lay down with lamb.

As I carried that jackrabbit, already stiffening with rigor and the intense winter cold, to a snowbank that was soft enough for burial, I thought that animals were always in the trenches, in harm's way. Unless somebody, somewhere could find a way to build a new ark. It had to be bigger than my balsam wood toy. It had to be big enough to carry us all—again.

⌒

FIVE

THE REAL SMOKEY BEAR

VIRGINIA, 1961-66

WHEN I WAS eleven, my father moved us completely away from his regional forest fieldwork in Montana as he ascended the administrative stratosphere of the Forest Service national headquarters in Washington, D.C. Now we found ourselves in the domesticated though not yet suburban woods of northern Virginia.

We left behind in the vast forests of the West everything I loved. And in the place of ponderosa pines, wild rivers, or elusive white-tailed deer, there was an intruder my father called "History." Instead of listening to strong winds above timberline or studying daily dramas of Rocky Mountain silhouettes, everyone in the nation's capital watched the horizon as if any minute History would rise or set like another sun—a star more stellar because humans placed it in motion.

"We're living American History," my father would inform us when he came home, not from fighting forest fires or watching wildlife in the woods, but from what he called "the hallowed halls of Congress" where something called "committees" controlled what my father respectfully referred to as "the great events of the day."

At the supper table we'd sit stone-still as he told us, "We're witnesses, you might say, kids. Witnesses to History!"

To me, History was an unwanted and garrulous guest in our family circle, which once had included the more welcome and shy bears and badgers, bobcats and coyotes. Now all my father talked about were people who didn't even have names. They were just "undersecretary" or "senator" or "Congressman so-and-so" and they stood up in white buildings I'd endured two school field trips to see, to proclaim their politics of position and power.

All I loved was powerless here—the trees and forest animals, the fast-flowing rivers and gracious seas. After a year of living near D.C., nature was almost eclipsed by History, by the daily dramas of only human beings. Even the Virginia landscape seemed worn away by our history, the Blue Ridge Mountains beaten down and humbled by so many battles, Civil War markers everywhere. It was as if this land were important only because some general had died here. We searched for bullets in the ground, the way in Western forests we once had scouted for animal tracks.

The millions of acres of my childhood forests were reduced here in northern Virginia to fifty acres of piney woods bordering our old-fashioned red-brick home that was remarkable because it actually had an outside staircase leading nowhere. Sometimes that's how I felt about this History-saturated Southland—every stairway or monument a man could climb really led nowhere. How to compare the Washington Monument's cement spire to a giant sequoia forest whose wide-girthed trunks had watched over us since before the time of Christ? Or so one of my Montana Sunday school teachers had told us.

Even though these Virginia woods were second or third growth, the slender, new trees only a fraction the size of the tallest D.C. monuments, I found deep solace in our neighboring forest. It was to these white oak, sweet gum, and sugar maple trees I turned whenever the rigors of witnessing History overwhelmed me. Those days it was still safe for children practically to live in nearby woodlands, leaving their leafy green shelter only for sleep and school. My sisters, brother, and I conjured wild animals to repopulate these woods—cougar and wolf were our favorites. We named ourselves Eagles or White Wolf Clan, roaming the woods with neighborhood kids, always at war with other clans. Our weapons were chestnuts in the fall and snowballs in winter. Summers we hid out in our elaborate three-story tree fort with its rope ladder and the neighbor boys exchanged miniature Sugar Daddys for our kisses.

In that northern Virginia hamlet, there was a junior high hierarchy more dangerous than any animal pecking order I'd ever encountered. So in self-defense and a search for my own place, which was to be an invisible observer, I was secretly at work on my first real book—a series of sketches about animals based on my real-life colleagues in the school symphony. I was mimeographing anonymous sketches, inspired by George Orwell's *Animal Farm*. These stories about our closed musical society of tyrants, prima donnas, and teen trysts were passed around like precious *samizdat* throughout the symphony.

These early animal stories kept alive a relationship with all that I had lost when we left the forest. And they were my way of remembering that my first people and family were animals, even if now they were enslaved by History. Someday maybe when I was grown up, the animals would also rebel and ask for their civil rights. They would stage sit-ins in the Western forests, howling and calling out not only for their own restoration, but for mine.

Even though I was in exile here where human monuments towered over trees, I still believed that one day my forester father would weary of walking what he called "the corridors of Power," and his holy grail of "current events" to return full time to the field. Often while luxuriating in my backwoods tree fort, I'd imagine our return to the great Western forests of my birth. The mighty trees, those abiding Standing People, would welcome us with wide branches outstretched. It would be as if we'd never left—our absence a blip of tree-time, a few circles swirling inside massive trunks.

⁓

BY 1963 HISTORY had taken its human toll—interracial riots in our junior high cafeteria and gym, Kennedy's funeral parade with those symbolic boots turned backwards in the stirrups of a riderless horse, and meeting the real Smokey Bear for the first time in Washington National Zoo.

I was stunned and shocked at my first sight of Smokey Bear. Shaggy and antisocial after years alone in a cramped, concrete zoo exhibit, this shambling black bear—who was rescued the year I was born, whose wise image I'd trusted more deeply than any preacher or teacher, whose round, reassuring bear face was the guiding spirit of my childhood—was so obviously sad and forlorn. Smokey hunched over in the farthest corner of his concrete grotto away from human visitors. One big paw slapped the artificial mountain over and over like some drugged drummer. As I watched, both hands gripping the zoo bars to steady myself from a dizzying despair, I said softly to my father, "The last thing he remembers of his forest is that it all burned up. He must think all the forest homes in the world are gone now."

I felt heavy inside, as if my feet were sinking in cement. My heart actually hurt, pounding and painful. I wondered for a moment if pre-adolescents could have a heart attack and then I realized this was what adults spoke about when they sighed and said, "Heartache . . . it's just a heartache." Certainly I'd been sad often in my thirteen years, bewildered and even grief-stricken—especially over our many cross-country moves, leaving my forest birthplace and loved ones, seeing my mother's often wild or depressed face. But I don't remember such heartache as this that hit me during my first meeting with the real Smokey Bear. His tragedy took my breath away. I watched Smokey shake his head from side to side, his dull fur matted and his expression vacant. Even the dead deer trophies who first guarded my cabin crib had more life in them than this captive, broken-down bear.

Suddenly the door of the bear exhibit opened and another bear ambled in. My heart eased a little. So Smokey hadn't been alone all these years, after all. He had bear family.

"That's Goldie Bear," my father rested his hand on my shoulder and whispered so as not to disturb the newcomer. All around us, people were shouting out and clapping, so I barely heard my father explaining softly, "She came to be Smokey's mate from another New Mexican forest. We hope they might breed a healthy bear cub," my father said. "That would be full circle, don't you think?"

I knew nothing about bear breeding, barely having braved my own shy puberty waltz of courtship and mating. But somehow for all my lack of worldly experience with mating, I doubted that Smokey and Goldie were in love. "He acts like Goldie's not there at all," I told my father. "He didn't even glance her way when they let her back in with him. Maybe she's not his type." I had heard this said in the locker room of my physical education class and thought it was a diplomatic catchall for broken love bonds.

"Well, honey, this is the second spring Goldie Bear's been with Smokey." My father shook his head with a frown I recognized as worry. "She's in the mood to mate, but you're right—he's not. Some of the vets think Smokey is still suffering old injuries from that fire the summer you were born when the rangers found him. Some people think Smokey's just too old or he hasn't had any other bears to teach him how to properly breed with a female."

"It's sad, isn't it, Dad?" I breathed, counting the years. "Smokey Bear's been alone for as long as I've been alive."

"Yes," my father answered, again in his unusually soft voice. He reserved this voice for animals more than humans. This was the tender voice with which he soothed horses and cows when we visited his father's Ozark farm every summer. Sometimes he also talked like this to very small children, especially baby girls. My father didn't sing out grandly like my grandfather in a triumphant tenor, but he had a murmuring way with animals that hushed babies and horses. My father was speaking tenderly about Smokey Bear when no one else in the crowd was quiet or respectful of this once-wild animal. He knew only too well what I didn't.

Like human predators, official managers were determining what this living bear symbol should do: Without any training or conditioning, this bear was supposed to love another bear and make a baby cub so that Americans could preserve our illusions of Smokey Bear as founding father and protector of the forests. Gazing at a depressed adult bear holed up in a corner of a stone grotto, I remembered Forest Service photos my father had shown me when I was very little. One picture was of a bear cub, so tiny he was all eyes and a bandaged front paw. Another photo was of a small girl, no more than five years old, with the real Smokey Bear cub sitting on her lap, no bigger than a pup, nose-to-nose with her. He certainly hadn't chewed her lips off. There was such trust and curiosity and dependence in that cub's posture, and the little girl gazed down at him with equal devotion.

Who had cradled Smokey since his cub days, I wondered as I watched his adult bear self in the zoo? How could Smokey make a bear family if he never had his own animal traditions? On public display with five million visitors a year, how was the real Smokey Bear going to keep symbolizing the Protector of the Forest when he was so lost and alone?

Any child could see that it was this bear who himself needed protection. Even my own father, who hated to talk about anything sad or troubling, who expected in his children a stoicism he'd learned in his own poverty-stricken, backwards Southern childhood—even my father knew Smokey was suffering. He just didn't say it aloud. His face showed it, that same worry and concern as when he watched a horse limping or my mother wincing against the light when she was in the tightening vise of a migraine.

What my father didn't say then as we stood watching Smokey huddle in a corner, eyes lowered, turning away Goldie Bear, was that Smokey was falling from national grace. This year was a decline for the living Smokey Bear. The poster bear still enjoyed national popularity, but this was the beginning of the living Smokey's downhill slide.

It's riskier to slide down a concrete mountain than a real one. There was nothing alive or strong like a tree to catch and save Smokey Bear this time. In his descent from popularity, the Washington, D.C., press was vindictive about Smokey's refusal to father an offspring. Here was an animal who had borne the burden of superstardom. Many fans had first worshipped at Smokey the Cub's scarred paws. But as Smokey grew into an adult bear, his disposition was described by his zookeepers as sour and decidedly not showy. In the biography *Smokey Bear 20252*, by William Clifford Lawter, Jr., the last years of the living Smokey are described in sad detail.

In 1962, when Goldie joined Smokey for a reproductive match made by governmental decree, National Zoo director and veterinarian Dr. Theodore H. Reed worried about Smokey's inability to breed. Dr. Reed explained that the animal had imprinted on humans and perhaps "Smokey didn't know what bears were." Trapped in a very small, stone grotto exhibit that Lawter said some described as "a slum," Smokey Bear suffered the stigma and loss in status that is all too often associated with humans "living on the wrong side of the tracks."

As the poster-bear Smokey enjoyed a reverence and fame so spectacular that in 1964 the U.S. Postal Service gave Smokey his own zip code, 20252, to receive more than a thousand letters a day, the real bear (whose official income was several hundred thousand dollars a year) shambled around a small stone slum so pitiable that schoolchildren mailed in $4,000 in pennies to contribute to a new home for him.

As we stood in the zoo, watching Smokey Bear slap the concrete mountain replica in his grotto, I tried to make eye contact with this living symbol of all I had loved about the forest and wildlife as a child. It was like seeing God cast into animal form, a divinity held captive and conquered by the very men who had first honored him as protector of the vast American forests. Those forests, like Smokey, were now beginning their long, tortuous fall. I did not know all the statistics about the increasing use of clear-cutting, that more and more Forest Service managers were expected to understand that their top priority was not forest but timber management. Their performance would be judged mostly on their timber quotas, their willingness and ability to "get the cut out." Never had wildlife in national forests been given such a low priority as in these postwar boom years of prosperity, new housing, and cheap federal timber. From the 1960s through the 1980s, the official Forest Service motto of "multiple use" was quoted with an emphasis on the last word—*use.*

Like Smokey Bear, the forests were in trouble. Watching Smokey Bear deteriorate in the zoo my first faith, like the forest, was finally broken.

That day when I met the captive Smokey Bear for the first time, I looked up at my father, who was not even trying to smile. Haplessly, Smokey slammed his great-clawed paws against the cement mountain. What could a thirteen-year-old do about Smokey Bear, about his native forests, not burning now but being cut down? And what was my father doing about it, I wondered.

I watched my father's troubled face and recognized something new in him that in my adolescent self-involvement I'd missed before. My father's face told me that somewhere along the way he'd lost some of his characteristic certainty and regal rightness. It was almost more than I could bear, to witness Smokey and my father's slow-motion descent. Mrs. Chopskie, my English teacher, often lectured about her favorite Shakespeare characters, "a man—or woman—in conflict with himself." She loved King Lear and Cordelia the best. She also doted on Caliban as a "true tragic hero." To Mrs. Chopskie, the crawling and misunderstood Caliban symbolized "the animal within us all."

Standing before this tragic Smokey Bear, I recognized in my father a man in conflict with himself. Like King Lear, he still commanded his three daughters' complete attention. But he also sometimes seemed troubled and distracted by the Forest Service kingdom in which he was a rising power. There was some hidden cost to him—a complication and moral dilemma I was too young to fathom. Then I could only sense it, like an inner weather that was rarely revealed, even to him.

My father was keenly perceptive, but his introspection was mostly hidden from us. Standing before Smokey's cage, my father seemed suddenly reduced, the mythic man dismayed by his own unexpected vulnerability. He had lost something, too, I realized, once he'd left the forest for the city and life in these corridors of power. He had left something of himself behind with the trees and the animals. But at least then, he could never admit it. He was King Lear only dreading the heath, still monarch enough to forestall any self-reckoning.

"Some people in New Mexico on his native national forest are working to bring Smokey home," my father told me, but he had dropped his lecture tone. There was an unfamiliar hesitation in his voice.

I recognized this tone. It was the subtext of uncertainty that underscored statements meant to give us some qualified hope. It was the way my father would assure us that there was no more moving in sight. *Oh, I think we'll be here for a while longer,* he'd comment with just the hint of doubt that implied that soon he'd be moving us again. I wished that like Smokey, someone in my native forest were working to bring me home. This was a longing for roots and the wild that would only increase over the next years. My father's popularity with the Forest Service administration moved us relentlessly back and forth across the country, so that by the time I stood there in front of Smokey's cage, I had already attended seven different elementary and junior high schools.

I did not know that another—the most traumatic—move, from Virginia to California, was just three years away, that I would run away from home to escape this move, now fiercely claiming Virginia as my homeland. Yet it would be this Western move, back to my native state but not to my childhood forests, that would determine my future cross-continent separation from my family. When we would return to the West in 1966, it was not to the field but to the chaos of Berkeley, California,—a time of Peoples' Park, antiwar protests, and an environmental movement. All of these battles would divide my father and me.

But for now, standing together before Smokey Bear's concrete exhibit, I felt as if I still belonged to my father because, unlike Cordelia, I had not yet told my truth. And like King Lear he had not yet demanded of me what it was I loved the most.

"Maybe they'll bring Smokey home when he gets too old to be on show like this," I ventured. "He can't even hibernate here during the winter." This was the cruelest of solitary confinement, I realized, to be alone and adored, stared at by millions who saw not a real bear, but a symbol.

After a long silence, my father said, "Smokey's got a job to do here. When people see Smokey Bear they'll want to protect the forest from fires."

"But who protects Smokey?" I asked and then strode away from my father so that he would not see my tears. I did not ask, *And who protects me?* because I knew then that this was a child's question. And, as my Sunday school teacher had taught me, I'd put away childish things.

My father rested his arm lightly on my shoulder. It was not the correcting touch he used to direct a high-stepping Tennessee Walker. This time, his hand did not ask me to move this way or that. There was no

will in his touch, just affection. And the simplicity of this made me surrender all my adolescent defenses. My shoulders sagged.

"He's a sorry sight," my father whispered, "our Smokey."

I leaned against my tall, slender father as I might a forest tree. I
rested on him for a long time in silence as we both stared at Smokey
Bear. Not for decades would I again rest like this in my father's presence, as if we shared the same blood and beliefs, as if we still trusted
each other. And not for many years to come would my father trust himself and me to show his sorrow over the wild we were losing.

"Smokey will stay here until the day he dies," I said finally, flatly. I
separated reluctantly from my father's arm and stood on my own. I was
the tallest of his children, already almost reaching his shoulders.

"Probably so, honey," my father murmured. "Probably so."

Slowly I walked away from my family to blend in with another
crowd at Smokey's cage. I felt a despair that to this day still haunts me. I
could not at the time name my sadness, but now I recognize it as a broken treaty between my kind and the animals. Gazing at this forlorn real
Smokey Bear I knew that for the rest of my life whenever I saw the symbolic Smokey I would feel this tension of childhood trust and growing
betrayal.

In the midafternoon lazy light, Smokey Bear lay lethargically near
his small, stagnant pool. Unmoving, his shaggy back turned to the zoo
visitors behind bars, Smokey looked like he was sleeping or dead. It was
hot that day and most people in the crowd were bored by this bear who
did not perform, did not admonish and instruct them like some minister of the forest. Disappointment was palpable in the crowd.

"He's just a plain ol' bear," one of the kids dismissed him.

"Yeah, that's not Smokey. Where's his shovel and big hat?"

A teenage boy scoffed, "Stupid bear! He doesn't even know how to
make babies!"

I was outraged. How could these kids not see the real animal surviving in this captive bear? Hadn't they ever seen a wild bear crashing

through the forest, or a mother bear ferociously tall on her hind legs raised up to protect her cubs? Hadn't they ever listened in the dense night woods to the sound of bears dancing, their great paws thundering the ground, which trembled under us in our sleeping bags?

Then a terrible thought gripped me as I gazed around at my peers and gauged their adolescent contempt for Smokey Bear. They were becoming adults and putting aside any childhood love for or devotion to other animals, which to them was now something to be ashamed of, to disavow, just as the real Smokey Bear had been abandoned by a nation.

"He's just trapped here!" I cried. I tried to rally the other kids to Smokey's defense or perhaps to my own. Never in my life had I felt so alone, so in between the worlds of animal and human, of child and adult. "Smokey Bear is just *lost* without his woods. Maybe he doesn't even know he's a bear anymore." I was on the edge of tears. But when I saw that my pleas for this black bear I believed was a brave survivor, an animal who was never really rescued, whose story had never been truly told—when I saw the utter indifference with which the boys met my words, I let go my grief and instead rose up to my full height. This was how my father had taught me to face another predator, a bear in the woods. Raise your hands high over your head and cry out, *I am human. I am a predator like you. Respect me!*

I had never exhibited this survival behavior with a bear, even the grizzly over my grandmother's apple butter. Never had I felt the need for such fierceness before a bear. But before these teenage boys, such survival skills seemed appropriate. For though I was not in danger of losing my life, I was afraid of losing something deeper—my soul, my connection to all that was living around me, my companionship with other creatures.

My face burned red with fury, my fists clenched at my sides. I had fought boys before and even won a few times. My neighbors, the Parker boys, had taught me how to wrestle and play baseball with the best of them. I knew I could hold my own. "You don't understand what this bear's been through," I made my challenge in a low, growling voice. "*You're* the stupid ones!"

To my surprise, none of the teenage boys took me seriously. I wasn't much of a physical threat, with my gangly beanpole body and thin arms. "Ectomorphs," one of the scientifically inclined Parker boys had called my sisters and me. Two of the neighboring Parker boys were, of course, mesomorphs, with compact, muscled bodies. But even the Parker boys had learned to respect my pensive, subversive nature. I could usually outsmart them, especially when it came to protecting our tree fort from roving gangs of neighborhood kids. It was I who had come up with the device of a rope ladder entrance to our fort, rather than wooden slats up the tree that would have meant access for any stranger.

One teenage boy turned to the others. "She's just a girl," he shrugged, "and that's just a dumb bear. Let's go see the snakes!"

I stood there, dumb with rage. I wanted to shake those boys and make them pay proper respect to Smokey Bear. But I didn't have the physical power and I didn't have the words.

"Let's go now," my father called over to me, corralling me back into the family pack. But I turned back for one last glimpse of Smokey's supine body. Except, to my surprise, he wasn't lying down on the concrete mountain any more. Perhaps it was my loud display, or perhaps he sensed the connection to me that I felt to him. With one fluid motion, Smokey Bear stood up on his hind legs. In that instant of surging power I saw all that he might have been had he not been "saved" as a symbol in this zoo, but instead returned to his wildness, his woods. Ursine eyes gleaming, he pawed the air several times. To this day I believe he was staring straight into my soul.

"Animals watch us, too," my father had always taught us. "You walk through the woods thinking you're all alone. But you're not. You're never alone. Animals are always watching. Sometimes they see us better than we do ourselves."

What was Smokey seeing outside his prison bars? Did he still remember who he was, the forest of his birth? Did he remember a time when humans ran from his kind, when they didn't casually stand around eating popcorn and peanuts, without awe?

My earth science teacher had told us that once our human ancestors had worshipped bears, borrowing their abandoned caves to live in. In fact, he said, the words "to bear" children first came from humans' worshipping the Great Bear. Long ago we even named stars in the heavens for the Big and Little Bears.

As Smokey Bear stood in his small cage, I could not help but cry out his name. Then I fell silent, as he held my eye one more minute. With an audible sigh, Smokey at last collapsed on all fours. He shambled toward one corner of his grotto. There he slapped his great paw again and again on the concrete.

To be captive is to die while still enduring the semblance of life. I heard the words in my head as if listening to a Shakespeare lecture by Mrs. Chopskie. *Here is an American tragedy.* Smokey Bear's great body and soul had been captured and enslaved by what History and human need required of him. This shambling, isolated black bear who had first inspired my sense of the divine now sparked in me a crisis that still troubles me. Though I didn't fully understand it at the time, seeing Smokey Bear in the zoo would mark the making of conscience and a search to understand my own responsibility and right relationship to other animals.

"Let's go home," my father called over to me. "No dawdling now."

"Home," I murmured to my father as he finally strolled over and took my arm to pull me away from Smokey's cage. I closed my eyes and let my father lead me away. But I could still see Smokey Bear. I would always in my mind see him in jail, in the nation's capital, while far away the vast forests were falling. There was no place for either of us to return.

⌒

SIX

PROMISED LAND

NORTH CAROLINA AND GEORGIA, 1972

I T WOULD TAKE me eight more years to find my way back to the forest and to encounter other bears who helped balance my despair at Smokey Bear's long descent. After graduation from the University of California, Davis, I happily took a job in the Pisgah National Forest, nestled in the gentle, misty Blue Ridge Mountains high above Asheville, North Carolina. Though this was not my birthplace of West Coast long-lived conifers, the Douglas fir and ponderosa pine Standing People, it was a lavish hardwoods wilderness of oak, hickory, elm, persimmon, and the lofty evergreens of white pine and soft-needled Fraser fir. Mt. Pisgah towered over the surrounding Bible Belt. It was named after a famous ridge in ancient Palestine from whose summit Moses first viewed the Promised Land.

For once, my father and I agreed on my life's direction. I had turned down a scholarship in English to a graduate school in the East to "go back to my roots," as he proudly explained to his colleagues in the Forest Service, where he was now Regional Forester in Atlanta, Georgia. And even though my job was as a waitress in a mountain hotel and restaurant, my father and I both believed the forest offered its own higher education.

To find myself sleeping in a ramshackle, two-story log barracks that housed all the "help," as our backwoods boss called us, was strangely calming, after all the political upheaval of my anti-war activism at Berkeley and U.C. Davis. Even as President Nixon was making more History with his Watergate shenanigans, I found myself retreating more deeply from any human dramas into the woods, my long-ago sanctuary. For the first time since childhood I was living amid millions of acres of wilderness. Again I lay listening to the prowl and scuttle of wild animals every night: feasting raccoons, dainty deer prancing single file through slim forest trails, feisty elk who in this summer lull ventured near our cabins, one even knocking his antlers against my windowpane. And around every hairpin turn or switchback was the familiar bear face of Smokey on official signs admonishing humans to "prevent forest fires." I was home at last, returned from wandering to my own long-promised land.

Rarely did any of us have time to "come down off the mountain," as locals called it, because we worked daily shifts with no weekends off and our pay was beneath the minimum wage. This restaurant was not actually on federal land, so we were paid eighty-eight cents an hour, which although way below minimum wage was considered fair by the management because they also provided us room and board. A college friend and I were the only "outsiders"; the other staff were local mountain people, some of whom had worked in the restaurant for several generations.

Even though I was bone weary, my ankles blistered and bleeding, and I never got enough sleep, I spent every waking, off-duty hour in the woods. Walking down mountain trails, I learned to lean into the wind and let its warm updrafts support me. If the wind stopped blowing, I'd topple forward. Once I actually fell onto the forest floor. It felt so familiar to be on all fours, again crawling along the pine-needle carpets, my palms imprinted with twigs and fragrant bark.

But other things about the forest were not familiar, and it was not just that I was returning to the wilderness as a young adult. Clear-cutting had changed the forests. Mt. Pisgah was a patchwork of felled forests, like a threadbare, tattered Appalachian quilt. It looked like a gigantic rake had uprooted and slashed a symmetrical gash through once-tall trees. In this brutal wake was left a litter of stumps and tangled limbs like the careless and crazed aftermath of a massacre. Once the forest had been logged, a thundering iron drum rolled over and over like a mechanical earthquake, tamping the broken woods down. Small animals, red fox and weasel, squirrels and deer ran in terror from their forest homes only a little ahead of the fires, this time set by the Forest Service, as official planes dropped napalm from helicopters. Where was Smokey to warn the woodland creatures away or to remind the foresters that this was a precious place, not a battlefield? And what was to replace these slashed, pummeled, napalm-scarred forests? The precise pine plantations of tree farms.

It was on Mt. Pisgah that I fully realized that my forest birthplace was not considered valuable, except as a crop, a commodity. *Beauty is powerless*, I told myself with a despair that I hadn't felt since my first glimpse of the real Smokey Bear in the zoo. It was on Mt. Pisgah that I beheld a Promised Land—the future of my own and this country's family trees—ravaged. The gracious, sky-touching Standing People had fallen down. And all the animals, like myself, were left homeless.

In 1972, only twenty-two years into my lifetime, huge tracts of old-growth forests of the West were also falling at an alarming rate, until by the 1980s, only 10 percent of old growth would remain. In the Western forests of my birth, the ancient redwoods, sugar pines, red pines, Jeffrey pines, and Douglas firs were valued more as prime timber than as living treasures. Great trees, some with diameters as wide as twelve feet, standing as tall as twenty-story buildings and dating back to the time of Christ, were relentlessly chopped down as hostile, corporate takeovers forced out of business family-run timber companies with some historical or generational connection to the land. All across the country, private-land timber supplies boomed; as if in competition, the Forest Service more than ever felt the pressure to "get the cut out" and manage national forests as corporations that must show profits.

In the Southern forests like Mt. Pisgah, I bore helpless witness to the effects of a national forest system dominated since 1945 by clear-cutting. The Forest Service had gone from its pre–World War II true conservation ethics and selective logging to allowing the official cut to escalate from 3.5 billion board feet in 1950—the year I was born—to 13.5 billion board feet by 1970. This industrial forestry was raising disturbing questions among those who believed the U.S. Forest Service was failing in its stewardship.

Mt. Pisgah National Forest was a mirror of forests across the country. Since the early 1900s, when conservationist Gifford Pinchot had made Pisgah the base for his "scientific forestry," the emphasis on timber production had become so pronounced that it seemed cutting down trees had replaced mining in these "hollers" as the primary occupation. In another part of this forest, Katcuah, the Harmon Den Bear Sanctuary, which was established to protect the forest's bear population, was surrounded by so much devastation from clear-cutting that even the sanctuary's bears were now threatened.

The 1970s and '80s would be the very worst decades for America's trees, an epoch in which environmental journalist Mike Fromme, a longtime Forest Service critic and chronicler, would say of a 1970 Wyoming coalition of sportsmen, dude ranchers, stockmen, and others, "They argued that the Forest Service essentially was subsidizing, with public funds and multiple-use lands, a lumber mill operated by an out-of-state firm." It broke my heart that this out-of-state firm was my father's business. And I railed against him in letters home.

Years later, when my father retired in 1986, he would become obsessed with genealogy, tracking our family trees back on both sides to this Southland—his own family dating back to Virginia in 1720 and my mother's to Tennessee in the early 1600s. Sometime around the turn of the twenty-first century, my parents and I would walk the twenty-five acres of their own Blue Ridge Virginia land and my father would proudly point out all the windbreak trees, forty-five of them, that he'd planted in the late 1970s. But there was one special tree he didn't plant. Gnarled and great-limbed, this tree was more than 350 years old and had weathered not only the Civil War but the Revolutionary one as well.

"Trees stand witness to all sorts of wars," he would tell me, "human and natural. This big beauty is an oak, a mighty tree." He'd touch its rough-hewn black bark. "Hit by lightning here," he'd breathe. "Still standing. Been here longer than any of our people in the South. Even after I die, it stays on." Then he'd turn to me and I'd see how he had aged, his face wide and sun-battered, his thin, silver hair curling at the neck. "Never cut this oak down," he told me. "Call it our 'family tree.' "

BUT THAT TURN-of-the-century truce would be two decades in coming, after my parents and I had struggled long to make some peace, and when there would be tentative movements by the Forest Service toward reforestation and a new concept of "ecosystem" and "biodiversity."

Back in 1972, all I could do was mourn the national forests to which I had finally returned. All I could do was rebel with the wildness that was left in me from my first forest. At times on Mt. Pisgah, walking in the woods, I wanted to get down on all fours and howl like the forest child I had once been, like the wolf so long silenced in these territories. Most of all I wanted to grieve and never again let go of the Standing People, my first tall guardians, who now needed guarding.

One evening on Mt. Pisgah at dusk, I lay in a small meadow where I hid out whenever I was not scheduled to work. It was a warm night; flowering dogwood and honeysuckle scented the mountain winds. I raised my head to better catch the sweet drift when I heard a thump-thump as two small bear cubs scampered into the meadow only yards away from me. The cubs had not yet caught my human scent downwind, but their mother would as she lumbered along behind them, her snout also raised to sniff the honeyed winds.

The cubs looked about six months old; in bear age that was about the equivalent of a human teenager, my father had taught me. They were long past the "terrible twos" and were on the threshold of adolescent discovery and testing. I lay as flat and still as a boulder, ignoring all my father's forest-skill teachings to stand tall and proclaim my human stature and rights. I knew this was wrongheaded, especially if the mother bear thought me tasty carrion.

I was so exhilarated to see wild black bears, imagining that the cubs were cousins to my Smokey, who still languished in that Washington, D.C., zoo. But these cubs were free and curious, tumbling over one another and locking furry forearms in a somersault that was so playful I almost gave myself away by laughing out loud. If I could remain hidden, there would be no trouble. But as the mother casually approached her cubs, I clearly saw that I was in the most dangerous position possible—between a mother bear and her beloved cubs.

Oh, to not be human, I thought at that moment, to be so much a part of the forest that I would not be recognized or feared or afraid. To be even welcomed back, the way long ago that rattlesnake had settled on my tiny, two-year-old chest as if I were a warm stone.

Suddenly the mother bear stopped, let out a growl, somewhat like a guffaw or a harrumph, swung her shaggy dark head from side to side and signaled her cubs to disappear, which they did with startled snuffles and no looking back. I would have to show myself, I knew, or she might mistake me for an enemy or a prey. Ever so slowly, my heart pounding, I stood up to my tallest height. Like a slim tree I lifted my arms even higher above my head so that I was probably 6'2", my father's height. But I could not speak with the gruff self-definition that he had taught me. Not when I saw the mother bear's face, so protective of her own, yet purposeful and perhaps, I thought, open.

She was sizing me up, her eyes golden and alert, her black nose sniffing, her head lifted to take in my full height. Only twenty yards from me, she seemed so close and considering. Her gaze I can only call contemplative.

Our eyes met. "It's just me," I said in a soft voice, not the bold declaration I'd been grilled to do whenever faced with a wild bear. "And you."

Her gaze wavered as she watched her cubs retreat in a circle behind her, crashing as they came through the underbrush. I could see them each take up a position just behind her ample rump. One even ventured around her to sniff the air and me. *What did I smell like to them?* I wondered. *Herbal shampoo and human sweat, Pond's cold cream and carnivore?* The thought suddenly occurred to me that I must smell like food, since I'd been serving pan-fried mountain trout, sweet potatoes, and German chocolate cake all afternoon to ravenous tourists. Maybe I even smelled like their favorite garbage dump. If so, then I was in trouble.

With a reprimanding roar, the mother bear cuffed her curious offspring back behind her protective bulk and it took all my courage not to bolt and run—the worst thing I could do when facing another predator. But I was still more amazed than afraid, because not since Glacier National Park and their midnight dance had I come so close to wild bears. If I were mauled and died, that might be what I had been born for—a life taken in memory of Smokey's own lost life.

These were ideas contrary to my body's instinct for self-preservation, but in that meadow it all seemed strangely right. And I realized then that it is always when in the woods or the deep canyons, by the sea or in the mountains that I feel reassured that death is all right, natural. I was young, but back where I belonged. So the bear could take me, if that was what was necessary.

But she didn't. She did something that seemed so sensible it made me smile at all my philosophizing. With a plop, she sat down on her back haunches, yawned, and pulled one of her cubs toward her in a brief embrace. I took a few steps sideways, still facing her, then I quickly slid behind a boulder, where I could better watch her with her cubs.

They gamboled and grabbed at her, then loped away. She lay back, another yawn, stretched out her full length, and then amazed me by closing her eyes. She knew I was still there, but apparently had decided I was not a threat. It was a time when black bears were being all but wiped out around national parks and forests by poachers who killed them for their gallbladders, lucrative on the black market for Oriental medicine. And in a territory of mountain people who still in their poverty sometimes poached bears for sustenance, the bear's trust was touching to me. It was as if she knew I belonged here, too, that I could come back home. Perhaps I had not taken on the stench of the Other or the world outside the forest.

I watched from behind my stone shelter until it was so dark I could only hear the family noises of bear life—snorts and snuffles, whimpers and a few maternal growls. The mother bear's eyes seemed to glow in the dark as I showed myself tall again and then slowly moved sideways out of the meadow, facing her. I felt my way along the trail back to the cabin. With a little light from the moon rising above Mt. Pisgah, I backtracked to my own room, expecting it to be quiet; my roommate was working night shift.

But there was a light in my room and I could make out the agitated shadows of several people inside. Up the stairs I bounded, eager to tell my black bear story to my mountain friends. But when I opened the door, several pale faces and angry voices greeted me.

"Double shifts for all!" my college friend groaned. "And only one meal off a week. They've got us trapped up here."

As I listened to the fiery young voices raised up against our bosses, I found myself thinking about Smokey Bear, held captive all his years in the zoo's stone grotto. He was trapped, just as these mountain people were trapped in jobs that would wear them out and give so little in return.

"First you work, then you die," one of my co-workers was fond of saying with the wry drawl and pinched expression of so many of the mountain people.

When I at last joined the fray, I found myself telling them the story of Smokey Bear and his capture, his long captivity. Then I told them about the mother bear and cubs who had abided with me all afternoon.

Everyone had a bear story to tell and that was the first time I realized that storytelling could make a difference—not only for oneself, but for others. Stories shared could lead to action. Soon our talk turned from bosses to the loss of forests and habitat not only for the animals, but also for the people whose families had lived here for almost two centuries.

"We can't let what happened to Smokey Bear happen to us!" someone suddenly shouted. For a long moment all of us squeezed into that tiny wooden lodge exchanged glances. No one had protected Smokey Bear or his forests, and no one would protect us or our habitat, either. Not unless we fought them.

Our strike was the talk of every holler for miles around. "Shut 'em down," we whispered while leaning on the wind to support us as we refused to fill salt shakers, debone trout, or cater to Blue Ridge tourists who were passing through. Here we staked our claim to dignity and respect and something more—a commitment to protecting people, animals, and land.

On the third day of our strike, the boss called the North Carolina State Patrol. By nightfall we "pinkos" were escorted off the mountain and told if we returned, we'd be arrested. My last memory of leaving Mt. Pisgah in the back seat of a squad car is the sight of several of my mountain friends raising their fists, one with a sign that said for all the national forest tourists to see, "Me and Smokey Bear Are Not Your Slaves."

I returned in shame to my family in Georgia. I was at a complete loss about how to make my own living. Even though I'd worked much of my way through school as a short-order cook and secretary, I had few worldly skills.

"Even ditch diggers have your Phi Beta Kappa," my father told me after another job interview in which all my university honors mattered not one whit. He was appalled at my union-organizing activities. "I'm so ashamed of the ruckus you raised down there with those poor mountain people," he said. "Imagine if you didn't have us to come back to. What would you do to survive?"

Survival was much on my mind those humid, summer days. I worked as an engineering secretary in an Atlanta firm. Though secretly I was writing my first novel, at the age of twenty-one I felt that perhaps my life was as limited and downward-spiraling as Smokey Bear's. My father had told me that Smokey Bear was now so disagreeable toward zoo visitors that they'd moved him and Goldie Bear to a smaller exhibit and identified them only as "American black bear." Maybe he and Goldie had also gone on strike.

Every day I'd glumly commute with my father from our rural home to downtown Atlanta. At last my father had realized his dream of raising horses like a Southern gentleman farmer. He had just bought a Tennessee Walker named Sandy. She stood tall and elegant, true to her plantation bloodlines. In the late afternoons when we came home from work, he and I would stand in silence in the back pasture. Watching his mare in wonder, I saw in my father the small boy who once believed, like the North Carolina mountain people, that he might never escape his backwoods fate.

But he had, and here was proof in this thoroughbred who galloped, her golden-red mane glowing like a halo as she outran any fate, disregarded any fence. Our whole family shared in one great expectation: Sandy was pregnant, her foal due any day. Dad kept us in the dark as to when Sandy would actually foal; he was more nervous about this birth than those of any of his own children, Mother said. Every morning and evening he'd check his mare's swollen teats for the telltale leak of milk that would signal she was within a day of giving birth. We'd clamber after him into the pasture and stand in awe of Sandy's gigantic belly, swinging low as she grazed.

One August dawn in that summer of 1972, a few days before my birthday, I woke to see that my sister Paula was missing from her bed. In an instant I knew she must be down in the pasture with my father and that this was it! Grabbing a robe, I almost ran into Paula, who was breathless.

"Quick, we need a gunnysack! There's a foal lying on the ground next to Sandy but she isn't moving."

We grabbed a gunnysack, a flashlight, and a pail of water, which sloshed as we raced back down to the pasture to discover my father on his haunches a respectful distance from his mare. Sandy stood dazed, her lovely chestnut tail raised high to let a flow of bloody afterbirth slide down. She seemed unaware of her foal, lying several feet behind her absolutely still on the grass.

"Either the foal is stillborn or stunned from the fall out of its mother," my father whispered. "Y'all stay back here."

Tucking the soft gunnysack under his arm, making the clopping sound between his teeth that he used to soothe his horses, my father ever so carefully approached his mare. "Easy now, girl," he murmured. "Just let me see your baby."

Sandy allowed him near and he first lightly ran a practiced hand over her rump. "Good girl," he reassured her. "You did good." Then he bent down behind her even though she could have killed him with one kick. Lifting up the dark heap that was a foal, he revealed a perfect, miniature horse.

Tenderly he opened the foal's foaming mouth and cleaned it, all the while speaking nonsense sounds under breath. Then, more vigorously, he rubbed the little foal's wet sides, her thin belly, and endless legs. Suddenly with a popping sound and a sigh even we could hear on the other side of the pasture, the foal took her first breath and squirmed, little legs flailing.

"A filly," my father called out and his deep voice was almost a song. "With a perfect star on her face. She's the spitting image of her mother."

There was only a thin blaze of light over the piney woods glimmering across the green pasture, but the moon still hung in its elegant sliver, and stars seemed to fall over us all.

"Starlight," my father told the filly. "That's what we'll name you, little girl." And then he proceeded to perform what I can only call a parental dance with his new foal. He'd bodily lift her up to balance on all four spindly legs, but the moment he let go, Starlight would wobble crazily as if on ice skates, then plop to the ground, collapsing so completely we worried she might break a leg before she could even walk. Lifted up, falling down. Over and over, my father and his filly danced in the pasture. He would lead and she'd fall.

As I watched, tears easing from my eyes, I did not know I was also crying for myself, that this birth stirred in me a primitive hope that one day soon I would be able to make my own way. Like this new filly, I would try over and over to stand on my own; it was natural for me to fall down. My father did not have the faith or patience in me that he had in his new filly. In that way my father and I were alike — we both had more hope for animals than for people. In his own way, he had tried to help me. But I had failed him, and others, in falling down off Mt. Pisgah and being cast out of the Promised Land.

Seeing Starlight's struggle to stand, I slowly realized that I was also young and had so much before me. The feeling of being trapped lifted as I wiped my tears away and was left with only wonder. What new worlds awaited me, as they did this new filly who gazed around her, seeing everything for the first time: the lush and sweet-scented meadow grass, the silhouette of piney woods running like a backbone along the horizon, these humans who were like family members welcoming her home? And if this Southland did not feel like a home to me, that only meant that somewhere, perhaps far away, I could search for and find my own home.

But I did not know all of this that dawn in the pasture. I only knew that this was a turning point and, as often in my life, an animal had shown me the way. Starlight again toppled, but at the very last moment she righted herself and stood, legs quaking, yet at last locked. I knew then that just as this filly was arriving, I could leave. I was free to go, free to be born again. I shouted out with more joy than I'd felt since first returning to my forest. Newborn horses stood on their own, even without my father's help, I reasoned. And his filly would stand as she did now, her withers wet with sweat from the strain. Though her thin forelegs buckled with this new weight that was herself, Starlight stood tall, all seven hands of her. She let out a sound, half-neigh, half-yodel, then shimmied sideways, her tiny tail flickering, toward her mother.

Now we could see her clearly. Dawn light lent a golden aura that gleamed off her thick baby coat, still matted with placenta. She was the color of chestnut trees, the kind that had suffered long blight and no longer grew in this country, the trees my father loved the most. And she was the most beautiful animal I'd ever seen, in her curious and somewhat comic seeking of my father's chest for a teat. He gently guided her to her mother.

The moment her filly found Sandy's swollen, milky teat, the mare seemed to return to herself. With a low snort she turned and recognized her offspring as if seeing her for the first time. Only now did her ears lay flat back, a warning to my father to give them privacy and retreat, which he did with a sigh of his own.

Sandy did not keep her filly to herself for long, only a day or two, before she let my father and later us keep steady company with

Starlight and herself. This new horse mesmerized us. During that long summer we often cooked out, eating all our meals in the backyard, the better to lovingly eye our new sibling.

⌒

IT WAS AS hard to leave Starlight as it was my own family when that fall, a U.C. professor of mine recommended me for a job as an editorial assistant at *The New Yorker* magazine. At the interview I proved only that I could type at the speed of someone dictating copy, my credentials to enter their hallowed, shabby hallways. Before catching the bus back to Georgia to gather my belongings, I took the Staten Island ferry and studied my soon-to-be-home of Manhattan, its imposing skyline so far from the timberline of my birthplace, its human animals so foreign and unpredictable

I left for New York City without my father's benediction. "Everything will turn to mud in your face," he warned me. "And just remember, if it doesn't work out up there in that awful city, you can't come home this time. You'll have to find your own way now."

I did not tell him, as he stayed back in his study, letting my mother drive me to the bus station, *This is not where I'd come, if I fall down again.* Instead I promised him what I was unsure of myself: "It will all work out."

This was my mantra, repeated to the thunder of the wheels as the Greyhound sped toward a city of skyscrapers taller than any tree. *It will work out.* I closed my eyes and held my backpack in my lap. In it were all my real possessions, since I didn't yet possess myself—my battered Smokey Bear poster and stuffed animal, and an 8 x 10 inch photo of my family proudly planted in the sweet grass pasture, all of our hands resting on a blazing chestnut filly named after the stars and the light she lent us.

SEVEN

⌒

DOMESTIC HAPPINESS
WITH DOGS

WHAT I REMEMBER most about my five years in the human wilds of New York City was the domestic contentment of finally finding a canine companion of my own. Kasaluk. If I couldn't have a wolf or live in the forest, then the closest I could come to restoring the wild in my tiny Manhattan apartment was a Siberian husky. All those years of being denied more than a handful of domestic pets in my family home were redeemed the moment my eyes met the blazing blue-wolf gaze of a pup that the breeder called "a keeper."

"She's a watcher," the breeder added as I held out my hand to the rigorous sniffing and scrutiny of this perfect miniature sled dog. With her elegant black mask around eyes so newly opened and bright, the pup studied me intensely then plopped back on her tiny haunches with the certainty of decision. Her posture seemed to say that she would never move again until I reckoned with her. This pup's stare demanded that I forget the heaving mass of her littermates, all in a milken stupor rolling atop their mother's belly. *I am here*, her regal expression said.

"Is she the oldest pup?" I asked the breeder, certain that I recognized in her a keen awareness and sense of lifelong responsibility.

"Oh, yes," he said. "And don't you forget it. She's the first and the most curious. Nothing gets past her."

I was not looking for a watchdog; I wanted a companion who still had the memory of wilderness in her genes. I well knew that Siberian huskies were known more for their sense of play and independent natures than for their loyalty. Siberian huskies were the last canine breed to be domesticated, and the black thatch on their tails shows just how close they still are to their wolf cousins. I identified with Siberians, believing myself barely domesticated, certainly more at home in the woods or by the sea than in this city.

As if to prove her alpha animal status and mark her territory, the first thing Kasaluk did when she dashed into my apartment was pounce onto my futon bed, seize her sharp baby teeth into the worn, woolly fur of my stuffed Smokey Bear, and rip him apart. Triumphant amid the swirling cotton stuffing, Kasaluk raised her small snout and let out a surprisingly haunting howl that called all the dogs in the apartment house to community. Mournful basset hounds upstairs and yipping poodles down the hall, operatic Airedales and anxious terriers, all joined in my husky pup's howling. Her prey vanquished, her place in the den of home assured, Kasaluk promptly raced across the tundra of my scuffed hardwood floors then stopped in her tracks. With a satisfied yawn, she toppled sideways and within seconds slept the sound, legs-splayed rest that belongs only to puppies.

I lived at the tip of Manhattan island, near the 500 acres of Inwood Park, and Kasaluk and I found solace from the stress of city life by bounding through these lush hardwoods. She ran off leash and I tried to keep up with her as we loped through the domesticated forest to the Hudson River. Here, ice floes cracked with the great, groaning sounds of glaciers calving. At night we walked under safe streetlights in this old, brick, Puerto Rican, Jewish, and Irish enclave. The Spuyten Duyvil

Bridge between Manhattan and the Bronx curved over cold waters; its lights shone like a human constellation, since we could see no stars.

Though I was living with a lover at the time, it is Kasaluk's companionship I most remember. My partner was not unkind, just distracted and driven, as most city people seemed to me. But the quality of canine attention I observed daily in this little pup made most people seem like sleepwalkers. Kasaluk was a born observer. She could patiently watch an anthill, as if each tiny insect were unique and compelling, as if the drama of drones and scuttling workers was the most fascinating event in the entire universe. Rarely did Kasaluk pounce by way of exploring; she always scrutinized first. And if she did engage, it was with a certain detachment.

Though doting dog owners and the camaraderie of sniffing canines mobbed her on the city streets, Kasaluk rarely paused in her steady, sled-pulling prance. I was the sled and she the lead dog. To this day my arms seem just a little longer because of her headlong instinct to pull weight. And it was her keen and wary wolf senses that saved my life one night.

Our Inwood neighborhood seemed safe back in the 1970s, and even the elderly Irish McHallfey sisters down the hall or Mr. Edelstein, the Jewish widower downstairs, often strolled late to walk their dogs. There was courtliness and the old-fashioned manners of a small village in our block of 1920s red-brick apartments all bordering the park and the water. We'd all nod pleasantly to one another, let our dogs do their business, and sometimes linger a little to visit—news of the day, weather, the pleasurable drawl of our shared dog stories.

One winter night when the windchill off the river felt like an arctic blast, I walked bundled in an ankle-length down coat and hood. Visibility was nil. A blizzard lashed snowflakes sideways as I trusted my now-juvenile pup to steadily pull me along. In the dimmed streetlights, I was mesmerized as a mantle of snow shimmered on Kasaluk's back, flocking her proudly raised husky tail. In the privacy and embrace of this blizzard, my imagination soared, as if this city had been returned by weather to wilderness. The last thing I remember thinking before bending double from a blinding blow to my temple was, *We could be anywhere, even Alaska.*

Wild hoots and fierce barking as Kasaluk ran straight into a pack of young men circling us. Through a blurred eye I saw a man in a red coat pick up another rock, scoop up soft snow to make a missile, and prepare to hurl it at me. Egged on by the shouts of his fellow gang, the young man grinned and reared back to throw. Stumbling, I cowered, realizing that the first blow had brought blood that was warm and sticky, matting my mitten. I was woozy, struggling not to faint.

As I dropped to my knees I saw what happened next in slow motion. Illumined in the soft spotlight of street lamps, a small, six-month-old Siberian pup leapt as gracefully and high as an antelope. Her fangs bared, glinting, and her growl belonged to some ancient canine lupus ancestor as she clamped down on the man's upraised arm. His surprised howl and her own wolf cry almost harmonized as Kasaluk let him go and then attacked his vulnerable ankle. Howl and lunge, howl and bite, Kasaluk attacked the man with the ferocity of an entire wolf pack bringing down prey.

The gang was so shocked that such a small pup could be so fierce and ferociously smart in her feints and bites that they scattered. Someone launched one last snowball-rock and I had enough consciousness to duck. It landed with a menace meant for me in a nearby snowbank. Then I must have fainted, because the next thing I remember is Kasaluk's warm tongue lapping my face and Mr. Edelstein, who was himself quite frail, struggling to lift me to my feet.

First the pain in my head, then the loud sound of what seemed like hundreds of dogs howling. Kasaluk had summoned them with her wolf howls, an entire neighborhood awakened, dogs and people.

"Who wouldn't recognize *her* howling?" Mr. Edelstein asked as he helped me back to our apartment house. "Who else thinks all our nice little apartment dogs are still wild?"

"Oh, dearie, do come in for some hot chocolate," the Irish sisters with their basset hounds pulled us all into their large apartment. "We'll spike it with Peppermint Schnapps. Then we'll call the police."

"What can they do," Mr. Edelstein said and lavished attention on Kasaluk who sat next to me like a sentry, "that a dog like this can't? Give me a dog over a cop any day."

Perhaps it was that mugging, my third in four years, that convinced me it was time to leave New York City. Perhaps it was the next summer when Kasaluk in our morning walk came across my private pea-patch vegetable garden in Inwood Park. Vandals had ripped up ripe tomato vines, stomped on sweet peas, and hurled my white corn like small rockets against nearby trees. Tousled corn silk like pale, torn cobwebs was strewn everywhere. In that garden trashed by any one of the growing gangs who now roved the park like adolescent soldiers, I stood with my husky and knew that I had to find a way off this concrete island.

When I moved out West to fix up a farmhouse my parents had inherited, my co-workers at the magazine pleaded with me, "You must not think of yourself as a failure." They called my move to Colorado's Rockies "downwardly mobile." But when Kasaluk and I arrived at the family farm, she took one look at the railroad tracks and the impressive ridge of mountains rising up from the prairie and raced off after a freight train. I had never seen her run that fast. We were home.

The farmhouse, set right next to a railroad underpass and at a crossroads of two dirt streets, was a rural antidote to my city life. Even so, I would sometimes find myself jumping from bed and running for the subway only to find a dusty railroad track and a real locomotive rumbling twenty feet from the house. I did miss the dark waters of the Hudson River, though there was an irrigation-ditch lake to stave off the claustrophobia of feeling landlocked.

Disrepair was hardly the word for my great aunt and uncle's farmhouse. The picket fence was listing every which way, the white paint on the sideboards was streaked with grime and sun-gouged, the roof leaked, the well ran dry weekly, and the furnace was a behemoth that sent the whole structure shuddering when it randomly decided to do its winter's work.

In my sleeping bag on the filthy living-room floor, I lay looking up at the luminous moon over the Rocky Mountains and at last felt safe. No screams from streets below, no shattering glass to accompany my insomniac city nights—just the staccato symphony of crickets and hum of summer mosquitoes. Kasaluk curled in a contented ball in the crook of my sleeping bag, her soft snores syncopated to the comforting chug of the nearby night trains.

Though the farmhouse was a shambles, I loved how this prairie land was upended into raw, red-rock mountains. In the rural stretch between Denver and Boulder, this farmhouse had been in my family for half a century, ever since my great aunt and uncle ventured out West from southern Missouri. A formidable schoolteacher and coach for Colorado state spelling bee champions, Great Aunt Mary had turned her farmhouse into a home for abandoned animals. Great Uncle Harry was well known for his hunting skills and inventive ideas; his wooden vending machine for worms to supply local fishermen who sought our irrigation ditch for trout still stood, although crookedly, in the front yard. Scrawled across its gap-toothed front was the black, block-letter invitation, "Worms: One Nickel."

In my great aunt and uncle's farmhouse, worms were worth more than many of the other animals routinely abandoned there. Like so much living refuse, crippled cats, blind dogs, broken-winged chickens, and bullet-ridden raccoons were left to die on my relatives' property. I'd visited this Colorado homestead as a child several times on cross-continent moves. I'd been terrified at the attack of chickens and two dogs that leapt toward me, teeth bared, but no bark.

"They got nothing but a growl left in them," Great Uncle Harry had told us kids. "Vocal cords cut out in some laboratory experiment or a breeder who thinks dogs sit better with folks without their bark."

Great Aunt Mary had cheerfully shooed away the assault chickens with a big broom and a fond smile meant more for the chickens than for us children. "Since the dogs can't bark, these chicks take over guarding us. They do a mighty good job, let me tell you! And they don't ask much in return."

We watched her gently sprinkle chicken feed on the dusty ground. Some of the chickens, though blind and flightless, were spectacular in their blazing scarlet feathers and bright yellow or orange breasts. "I got chicks from all over the world right here," Aunt Mary would boast and tell us about her fancy breeds—from Japanese Buffs to Sultans to Silkies with their feathers just like white raiment. We stared in wonder at the exotic breeds with their orange and scarlet feathers, their black skin and bright orange combs. "Why people abandon their animals is a mystery to me," Great Aunt Mary told us. "Never do it, children. It's not human. And it's not animal, either." She paused to pet a small dog, part daschund and part beagle. Along with a hound called Dirksen, after the famous senator, this small mutt named Bowser was one of her all-time favorites.

It was Bowser and Dirksen, the only dogs still able to bark and the only survivors of my relatives' death, who formed Kasaluk's devoted pack. Though they were much her elders, she was their leader, their alpha female, at five years of age. Even though the condition of the farmhouse made me sit down and cry on the sunken front steps, the sight of these three dogs sleeping on their porch den together softened my shock at finding the farm so rundown. And as I swept the chicken dung out of the living room, I discovered the first of several mysterious gifts my great uncle and aunt had left their heirs. In a tin bucket, under chicken feed and white bird dung, was a sack of Indian-head nickels worth almost a hundred dollars. Another time, I'd found a 1936 hundred-dollar bill buried in burlap feed sacks in the chicken coops. These legacies came in handy, since I was unemployed and living off my meager savings while I worked on the farmhouse, grew my corn crop, and finished my first novel.

I settled into a rural rhythm that slowly healed my shattered city nerves: up early to work my five acres, labor on my book, then as the sun eased into cool mountain sunsets, I'd paint the wooden siding, oversee a new well drilling, prime the temperamental pump, and scour the house. At night I'd irrigate the cornfields using my red irrigation-ditch pump and gaze out over luminous rivulets of water running alongside corn growing taller than me.

When I ran out of money or could no longer like a dowser intuit my relatives' money stashes, I took a job in a Boulder typesetting factory on the nightly swing shift, working on newspapers such as *Cattleman's Gazette* and *Rodeo Sports News*. My friends back at *The New Yorker* couldn't believe I found contentment having left their literate editorial department to descend to blue-collar status and type rodeo results or cattle prices. But the truth was, I was very happy, if a little down-at-the-heels. A revered editor at *The New Yorker*, Rachel MacKenzie, had agreed to read my first novel. And in that book I'd created a character who was carving a Noah's ark bestiary to save his wondrous animals from extinction. In my rundown family farmhouse, surrounded by my own animals, I sometimes felt we had found our own little ark, too.

That first fall in Colorado, Bowser, the bouncy little mutt I'd inherited with the farmhouse, ran off mysteriously. As if in mourning, his dog pal Dirksen grew withdrawn and irritable. He began biting neighbors he'd known so long; they reckoned he must be senile. Soon after, the dear old confused hound died. As if to confirm that death comes in threes, I got a call from my parents informing me that Smokey Bear had also died at last. On November 5, 1976, at the age of twenty-six, Smokey Bear died in his sleep, in a concrete den where he'd holed up to avoid the pain of moving and fighting off the birds from his food. Goldie, the female companion who long shared Smokey's cage but never his sexual affections, was "weaving her head, muttering and grumbling," reported Dr. Theodore H. Reed, Smokey's longtime veterinarian. "She let us know she wasn't happy."

Though there were rumors about hijacking Smokey's funeral flight, he and his official coffin were unloaded like routine cargo back in his New Mexico homeland. The media recorded Smokey's coffin's arrival in Albuquerque but were not informed as to his exact burial site. There had been some threats that Smokey Bear's body might be stolen, so the Forest Service, under the guardianship of the New Mexico State Police, whisked Smokey's coffin to a private spot in the Capitan National Forest, where Smokey had first been discovered as a cub. As night fell, in the faint circle from their pickup truck headlights, a handful of Forest Service employees dug Smokey's grave. They lowered the casket, used a backhoe to cover it with dirt, then parked the heavy equipment atop the grave so that no one could dig up Smokey's body.

Although Smokey's burial was unrecorded and unceremonious, his memorial, or "dedication," as it was called at the Smokey Bear Historical State Park in Capitan, New Mexico, was a small media event. At the time of Smokey's death the park was little more than a vacant lot. According to Smokey's official biographer, William Clifford Lawter, Jr., there was only one "legitimate" tree on the property. Park officials chopped down a few live trees and planted them in the ground for effect.

From all over the country, people sent flowers and letters to Smokey Bear. Children and adults alike poured out their affection for this bear, who lived on as a symbol with his own zip code, even as his body was at last buried in his homeland. At Smokey's memorial service a local preacher was asked to give an invocation, but he refused. The minister did not want to preside over the funeral of a bear. At last, the preacher was convinced when he was told that this wasn't really a funeral, it was a "rededication to a cause."

To this day I am haunted by this fact: that a minister of God refused to give a funeral or say a prayer over an animal who was not only my first childhood divinity, but who for millions of other children was the spiritual protector of our country's once-great forests. That preacher believed an animal could not possess a soul. Perhaps one of the reasons humans can live with the increasing extinction of so many other animals is that we don't believe they have souls, so they are in some eternal way dispensable. And by locating our immortality as separate from Earth, we have defined the natural world and all other animals as mortal. But what if we accepted the spiritual parity of other animals? Could we suffer so many extinctions? Or would we *bear* them as sorrowfully as if they were directly related to our own fate?

What was Smokey Bear's life except an unacknowledged form of animal kinship and authority? Like an inspired guide, Smokey Bear instructed us in how to live within nature, and he taught generations of children that the forest and wildlife were essential to us and therefore sacred. His symbolic presence is still teaching our children. Smokey Bear's simple challenge, "Only You," stays with us like a mantra as we walk through our country's brave and beloved forests.

I have never visited Smokey's grave with its simple boulder and plaque. I saw the real bear only once, in a zoo. But almost every day of my life, I've felt the symbolic Smokey Bear staring out at me from my own family's most treasured heirlooms—Smokey Bear wall portraits, posters, stuffed animals, woodcarvings, and even my wristwatch. I have learned to locate Smokey's borrowed spirit in these human memorabilia. I still believe his soul was always within his great black body.

Someday I will make a pilgrimage to Smokey Bear's grave in New Mexico. I will stand before his modest monument and tell him that I was born the summer he was rescued from the wildfires and that I will always recognize a kinship between us, between our species. I'll tell him that on my fiftieth birthday in the new century 2000, the worst wildfires since 1910 consumed many millions of acres in the national forests of my Western homeland. That my parents journeyed West to spend my birthday with me. They presented me gifts—a Smokey Bear pen set, bed sheets, and a small sculpture of Smokey teaching young cubs to fight fires. Days later, my father phoned from the Bitterroot Valley in Montana. He was coughing from the smoke, which hung like memory over forests in flames.

"It's real bad here," he choked.

"What's happening?" I asked. "Aren't people listening to Smokey anymore?"

"Not enough, honey," he said hoarsely. "And can you believe it? They're wrongly blaming Smokey Bear for these fires."

All through my childhood my father would say softly, "You'll probably outlive the real Smokey Bear. But his legacy will outlive us all."

When I make that pilgrimage to visit Smokey's gravesite, the summer fires of 2000 will have died down, and I will say a prayer there as well for all the wild animals who lost their lives, the people who lost their homes. I'll tell him that I am sorry for his life and grateful for his sacrifice. Then I'll confide in Smokey Bear what surviving him by a quarter of a century has taught me most—to bear whatever it is life brings us. Fire and ripe fruit, service and freedom, fame and the refuge of deep forest.

THAT SAME WINTER of 1976, when I heard about the death of Smokey Bear, Kasaluk gave birth to two pups. It is comforting for me to trace patterns of birth and rebirth in the animal companions who accompany me through life. As I grieved the real Smokey Bear's death, Kasaluk would curl up beside me, her blue wolf eyes watching and waiting her own pups' birth.

One freezing night, the old farmhouse furnace barely puffing heat, I heard Kasaluk's wolf howl. She began pacing in tight circles in my study. The moon was full and my five acres were fallow. I had just come off the night shift at the Boulder typesetting factory and desperately needed sleep. But Kasaluk's labor was hard upon her and neither of us could rest.

Sometimes she would stop her circling and gaze into my eyes with a kind of panic and I felt so inept, too human. Where was her pack, the

elder alpha females to midwife her first birth? I'd called the vet and she
told me to be patient and not interfere, only support the birth process. I
reassured myself that this was not the first time I'd seen an animal give
birth. Along with kittens in my childhood, I had a keen memory of the
birth of my father's filly Starlight, who entered the world so shyly.

As I held Kasaluk in those rare moments when she settled from her
pacing, I remembered the night Starlight was born in Georgia—how
welcome was that new filly with her frail legs and strong spirit, how
long it took for her to stand on her own. I'd been standing on my own
now for seven years since I'd left home, and though I hadn't amounted
to much in my family's eyes—having published only one short story,
having left the low-paying but high-prestige job at *The New Yorker* for a
ruined farm in the middle of a mountain-shadowed prairie, I was still
making my own way. And now I had the help of my ancestors, my family's land. Every day that I wrote, worked as a typesetter, and came
home to these irrigated acres convinced me I belonged somewhere on
earth. Here I stood on the shoulders of my own people, who had lived
half a century before me. This bond, my relatives' treasure-stashes of
cash, my own dreams, and Kasaluk kept me strong.

I was in fact dreaming when Kasaluk welcomed her first pup into
the world. Awakened by small snuffles, I started up to see a miniature
Kasaluk by her side: black mask, wolf mark on tiny tail. The pup with
its closed eyes seemed stalwart even at birth and already sought his
mother's full nipples. But then Kasaluk began circling and she seemed
in the worst pain that I'd witnessed all night. Yelping and whimpering,
she could not settle. I saw something poke out from her and realized to
my horror that it was a tiny paw—a breech birth. She was in trouble
and so was the second pup.

I called the vet, who sleepily said, "You'll have to reach in and turn
the pup around inside her. You can do it. Otherwise, the breech birth
will harm them both. Just feel your way and turn that pup!"

My heart was pounding and I was terrified of hurting Kasaluk, but I eased one hand into her and closed my eyes, better to see the hidden shape of pup inside mother's body. At last I felt a tiny skull, then a paw still sheathed in slippery placenta. With a painful twist of my wrist, I turned the pup upside down and then pulled with all my might. With an audible whoosh, then a stream of watery blood, the pup plopped out in my hand. I marveled at his blazing white forehead like a tiny dolphin melon and his black mask streaked with blood. But the pup was completely still, not breathing.

At that moment I remembered my father calmly cleaning and rubbing Starlight when she first lay so quietly in the pasture. Dad had refused to accept stillness as stillbirth. So would I. Holding the pup, my finger feeling for a heart pulse, I quickly realized the blue-white birth cord twisted around his tiny throat was cutting off his oxygen. As I had seen my father do, I grabbed a small knife and slit the umbilical cord. But still the pup did not breathe. He lay too quiet and perfectly formed in my hand. To this day, I don't remember exactly how I did it, for I'd never performed artificial respiration on anyone except in seventh-grade health education class—and even then I'd flunked. But that night some maternal instinct took hold in me.

I opened the puppy's tiny mouth and breathed in, then pumped his slick and furry chest. With a little puff and snort, the pup finally drew his first breath. It was deep, clear, only a little rattle from some mucous plug that had also prevented him from getting any air. Immediately Kasaluk began licking her second-born and that pup went from first breath to teat in seconds, a sure sign of a healthy appetite.

But I sat on my haunches, stunned. My hands were covered in placenta, my mouth tasted of blood and wet fur. I had given my own breath to another animal and it had come back to me with such life force it took my whole body and soul to receive it. This little pup, whom I would keep and call Inouk, the Eskimo word for "my people," had given me back more than I had given in that first breath. He had, in an instant, reconnected me to animal life, the vitality and visceral power that always live right alongside us.

No one can tell me a great soul was not born that midnight. Inouk would grow to be a huge half-husky, half-malamute mix, with a gleaming white forehead, an unclosed mask, and wolf-blue eyes. At night he would rest only if his forehead were under my hand and his daintier mother's protective paw draped across his neck. We were a family pack and sometimes, in the farmhouse of my ancestors who had made a life of adopting abandoned animals, I howled with happiness, right along with my huskies.

EIGHT

⁓

WOLVES IN THE DESERT

I N THE WINTER of 1980, I found myself traveling across Arizona desert backroads so luminous and otherworldly that it seemed we glided across an alien red-gold planet of towering stone spires and petroglyph-scrawled cliffs. I was a writer in residence at Arizona State University. Except I wasn't exactly in full residence. Since 1978, I had been commuting three days a week to Tempe, Arizona, from my Colorado farmhouse. My first novel had been published that year and I'd accepted a teaching job to escape the swing shift at the Boulder typesetting factory. In Colorado I shared my farmhouse with a family who doted on Kasaluk and Inouk while I commuted to Arizona.

In the desert I enjoyed the company of other writers. One of them was Jo, a poet, dance instructor, and university-colleague who often accompanied me in exploring the Arizona backroads. "I'm not saying we're lost," Jo said wryly, "but half a day driving without another car or building might make some suspicious."

I laughed and turned up the country-western radio station. As we sang along at the top of our lungs, only prairie dogs and rattlesnakes heard us. One of Jo's favorite antidotes to university life was to read aloud to me tidbits from the *National Enquirer* or *World Weekly News* as if they were prose poems—the wife who finally shot her husband after twenty years of his snoring, and missed; the man who chose his pet pig over his wife, the "wild child" raised in India by a pack of wolves.

"Here's one up your alley," Jo teased as we rounded a dusty curve on the Navajo reservation. "Noah's ark discovered atop Mt. Ararat."

We drove on in companionable silence and I reflected that Jo's was the first friendship I'd ever had with someone who distinctly did not like animals. Even in New York City my friends had been devoted animal lovers. I didn't quite know what to make of her, and instinctively kept my distance.

How lonely, I often thought, watching my new friend. Jo believed that humans were alone here in the world. How brokenhearted someone like Jo must be, I thought as I tried to fathom her separation from other creatures. What dance might she exhilarate in if she included partnership with the animal kingdom?

Suddenly I leaned forward, my eyes squinting against the sun. Was that a small building ahead? "It's nothing," I said with a sigh, dropping back in my sweaty seat. "I thought it was a store or something. Maybe it's a mirage."

"It is like dropping acid, this desert," Jo said. "How does anyone live out here for so many miles without at least one store?"

No sooner had she mentioned it then the car turned a bend around a tower of red rocks and there, nestled in a crook of the canyon, was a tiny trading post, swirling in its own private dust devils. It was so small and ramshackle that it looked more like an abandoned shed. There was no gas, but there was warm Coca-Cola and a very old desert rat who sauntered out of a rusty delivery van that was half-buried in sand, like a car wreck. It was impossible to tell if he was Native American because his skin was burned black, wizened by wind and sun. He and Jo struck up a desultory conversation—it was too hot for much else—and he offered her strong Scotch. Soon they were singing Broadway show tunes such as "I'm Gonna Wash That Man Right Out of My Hair" and 1940s torch songs like "Am I Blue?"

I poked around inside the trading post, which had a few glass cases of modest Native-made jewelry and wrinkled postcards from the 1950s. How did this old man survive way out here? I wondered. Did anyone who wasn't lost ever stop and give him business? I was startled when a woman appeared from a back room. She eyed me silently from behind the dusty counter. By the look of the heavy turquoise and silver bracelets encircling her forearms, I guessed she was Navajo. Soon I found out she was related to the old desert man by distrust and marriage.

"I make him live in his old heap-car," she told me right off, in case I supposed he still shared her bed and her beauty. She was very striking and stately, in her early sixties with black, oval eyes. We said very little, but I felt at ease with her. She showed me an exquisite Navajo blanket made for her marriage. We talked about how easy it was to get lost in the desert. During our slow conversation, she kept watching me—not warily, but carefully, as if giving herself lots of time to take me in. Her scrutiny did not disturb me. I was simply happy not to be so lost anymore.

I was surprised then by a sudden sense of dread and dizziness as I moved toward the end of the glass counter to study more closely some Navajo earrings. This was a disturbing vertigo that sometimes strikes out of the blue. I've learned to associate it with premonitions of earthquakes. My sister has these dizzy spells, as well. For decades, with her medical training, we tried to figure out whether it was a genetic disorder or family illness or even panic attacks. The spells come swiftly—unsteadiness from the feet to the head that lasts only seconds and then it is over. But within the next twenty-four hours there is usually a big earthquake somewhere in the world. For example, the 1989 San Francisco earthquake knocked me off my feet six hours before it struck, and my sister fell off the couch one night in Florida before a giant quake hit Afghanistan. The closer the quake is, the worse the physical symptoms.

Perhaps it's because Paula and I were born in the wilderness and imprinted first on animals. Yet we've both met other people who are extremely sensitive to earthquakes, like those animals—particularly snakes—who suddenly abandon cities before big quakes. Perhaps in our bodies we feel the earth's subterranean trembling; perhaps we are simply sensing subsonic rumbles that roar with the same deep bass frequencies of blue whales, elephants, volcanoes, and tidal waves. Once in Italy, while visiting a spa built over an underground volcanic lake and grotto, my feet felt vibrations and shifts so intense it was like walking on a rocking boat.

My sister and I used to call each other every time we sensed an earthquake, trying to track scientifically and even develop this intuitive sense as a skill, if only to give ourselves the illusion of more control. But the fact is that we forest-born, with feet that listen to what our ears cannot hear, have come simply to accept our earthquake premonitions as we would any other evidence of our senses.

What I could not accept that day in the desert was the fact that the dread and dizziness didn't subside in seconds, as they usually did. In fact, as I placed a hand on the glass counter to steady myself, the vertigo intensified. For a moment I thought I might faint and felt the nausea brought on by a sharp blow to the skull. It wasn't pain, I recognized even then. It was some kind of power emanating from the earth herself.

"I'm sorry," I managed to say to the Navajo woman. "Maybe I'm allergic to something here . . . the dust . . ."

She said nothing, simply watched me closely. And then for no logical reason, I suddenly knew something I didn't dare say: I knew there was something buried right below my right hand in that dusty glass case. It was so powerful that it touched me long before I ever touched it.

I was both curious and frightened. In a small, unsteady voice I asked,

"Is there . . . is there something here—underneath, I mean?" What I meant was, beneath the layer of modest earrings. Even as I asked, I did not want to know the answer. Most of me wanted out—out of the strong pull of this place and whatever was hidden here that had the power of an earthquake. But my feet were riveted to the trembling floor.

"Nothing there," she said, and kept watching me.

I was silent, not wanting to press her. I did manage to take a few unsteady steps away from the case toward the door. It seemed miles away, slipping into the hallucinatory waves of a heat mirage. I wondered if I'd gotten a heat stroke in the desert and that was why I felt so dizzy.

To this day I do not know what possessed me to speak up again, but I heard myself saying, in a very faraway voice, "Something's there. I feel it." Then I was at last released from the dizziness and dread. I had done whatever it was I was supposed to do—acknowledgment or recognition of a power beyond me. I was free to leave. Taking a deep breath, I was about to thank the woman and leave when she looked directly at me and nodded.

"Yes," she said softly, "something *is* here."

She lifted up the dusty glass counter and reached beneath the fake velvet drawer of earrings. Reverently she held up the most beautiful necklace I have ever seen outside a museum. Spider-web turquoise and silver strung with strange, smooth animal teeth. "Here," she said, "maybe you don't need the poison."

I was frightened as she placed the necklace in both my hands. The animal fangs did not frighten me; how often had I fingered coyote teeth in my first forest? No, my fear was for this necklace, which lay in my hands with all the sleeping authority of a coiled cobra. "Poison?" I asked in a tremulous voice.

She shrugged. "You don't need it."

Didn't need the poison or the necklace? I wondered, but kept silent. The woman seemed to speak in riddles, and I was obviously out of my depth. I was twenty-eight years old and this necklace seemed much my elder.

"My father made it over forty years ago, for protection," the woman told me. "For someone who never came back for it."

I didn't ask why—world war or despair or any number of white men's maladies her people had fallen prey to for generations. I felt unworthy even to hold this art that had survived what its maker and true owner had not. I stood holding the necklace as if it burned my hands. But by habit my fingers began fingering the animal teeth, seeking comfort—the way as a child I'd abraded the animal fangs my father found for me on the forest floor. Over and over I'd fingered those teeth like a rosary until they shone as if polished.

"Wolf teeth," the woman said with the same reverence that she'd shown the necklace itself. "Wolf was here once in this desert."

How fierce and strong these predator teeth felt against my fingertips. A ferocious spirit still clung to these wolf teeth, because for one instant I had an image of bared, bloody incisors and a terrible growl too low to really hear, much like the warning growl and rumble of earthquakes.

Alarmed, I respectfully handed the necklace back to the woman. "It's still so alive," I whispered.

"It is awake," she corrected me and turned away without taking the necklace.

I didn't understand her meaning, but my body knew she spoke truthfully. She meant alive not just as the Buddhist concept of higher awareness or enlightenment, but also as a raw and visceral life force. The necklace was awake and alert in the way that wolves are wary and always aware of what is around them. Such complete consciousness frightened me.

The Navajo woman busied herself with rearranging the earrings atop their dusty velvet board. I sensed it would be impolite to simply set the necklace back down on the bare glass case. This necklace needed skin—animal skin of deer, elk, or moose to sink its teeth into. It should have ceremony and sage surrounding it.

"Thank you for showing me this . . . this wolf thing," I said lamely. I also longed to ask her why she kept it hidden beneath trinkets. Why did she not, in Navajo tradition, wear it proudly on her dark, green velvet bosom, letting it partake of her daily life and work—attending every ceremony as an honored guest?

I said none of this. Instead I held the necklace warily, waiting for her to take it away from me. When she crossed her arms and frowned at me in silence, I shifted uncomfortably. At last I broke the quiet to inquire, "What kind of wolves used to be here? Mexican or red wolves? Didn't they all go extinct after the bounty hunters? Are there any returning now?"

I knew from my own reading and wildlife studies that wolves, like Native Americans, once had bounties on their heads. When I was a child, my father had told me that the Forest Service had its own hand in helping rid the Southwest, as well as most American forests, of wolves. In fact, when one of my father's heros, the wildlife conservationist Aldo Leopold, was working in 1909 in the Apache National Forest in Arizona he, like other forest rangers, routinely shot the wolves that were common then in that area. By 1915, Leopold had proudly put together an alliance of hunters and ranchers in the Southwest who practiced zealous "wolf control." Leopold called them "varmits."

In thirty years, the U.S. government decimated the Southwest wolf population from 300 to 30. This was before Leopold would look into the "fierce green fire dying" in the eyes of a female wolf he had just killed and forever change his heart, his life's work. He wrote in his essay "Thinking Like a Mountain," which influenced a new generation of human-wolf predator-prey relationships, that "only the mountain has lived long enough to listen objectively to the howl of a wolf." As he gazed into the eyes of this female wolf, dying by his own hand, Leopold recognized, "There was something new to me in those eyes— something known only to her and to the mountain. I was young then, full of trigger-itch; I thought that because few wolves meant more deer, that no wolves would mean hunters' paradise. But after seeing the green fire die, I sensed that neither the wolf nor the mountain agreed with such a view."

"No wolves left here now," the woman told me. She didn't have to add *and not as many of our people left, either.*

"Thank you for showing me," I said and awkwardly handed the necklace back to her.

But she held up her hands and wouldn't take it from me. Then she explained to me very seriously, as if explaining some important rule to an outsider, "My father said to hide it until someone knew it was here. It's waited a long time and maybe," she paused to study me intently, "maybe you don't need the poison."

I was terrified now—of her, of the wolf necklace. Why did she keep talking about poison? Would this necklace poison anyone who handled it without proper authority or respect? Did it carry evil spirits? It was obvious to me from my museum trips that this was a medicine necklace of great worth and power and not for the likes of me to possess.

"It's not mine," I protested. "It belongs to you, your people, your children. It's way too big for me . . . not made for me." At last it occurred to me to try and explain to this woman, who lived so close to the Earth, what I rarely talked about with my own friends. "Look," I began, "the only reason I felt it there was because it was like . . . like an earthquake."

This made the woman laugh, and I realized it was the first time she had smiled. "An earthquake," she repeated, as if this gave her great pleasure. She was silent for a long while, then said simply, "Yes, it's an earthquake. It's wide awake. You take it."

"Oh, no!" I said. Then I did put the necklace down on the bare glass. It clattered loudly and I saw immediately she read my gesture as disrespectful. But I couldn't help it. My terror was increasing by the moment. The dread I felt now was much worse than any earthquake premonition; it was deeply personal. I felt myself in grave danger. So I planted my feet on the slanting floorboards and tried to calm myself.

"Thank you, just the same. It is the most beautiful thing I've ever seen in my life. But I could never afford it." I took a great breath. "And I'm not just talking about money."

"No money," she said, and very patiently held it up to me again. "It was not made to be sold. It was made for something else. It has its own work to do."

"Please," I asked her, "it's too powerful. Keep it here with you." And when I saw her stony look of disappointment again, I added, "It really scares me. Doesn't it scare you?"

She looked surprised, then admitted, "When I was little and it was so awake—yes, it did." Pausing, she reached out for my hand and gently laid the necklace in my palm, then she closed my fingers over the animal teeth and turquoise and fixed me with a meaningful look. "But that was when I was a child. I was afraid of wolves then, too."

"Now you're not?" I asked.

"No," she said. "I'm older now."

Her words braced and calmed me. Somehow I felt protected enough from the power of this medicine necklace to see down to its spirit. I knew then without a doubt that this medicine necklace had been made with love, a gift to protect someone deeply cherished. It was like the wild wolf—fierce to outsiders, but devoted to its own pack.

"My father made this. And I can give it," the Navajo woman finished. "You saw it without the poison." She folded her arms over her chest. "Goodbye, now."

I stood absolutely still. It would be a terrible insult, after all this, not to take her great gift. But I must give her something back. "I know this is beyond price," I began. "But I have a small savings account. It's all the money I have."

"Yes, it's worth all you have," she said, and again there was just the shadow of a smile. We knew we were not talking money. We were talking about something of much more value, which was harder to give and receive. We were talking about my deep and whole attention, which I've always believed is the purest form of prayer. "It will protect you," she concluded cryptically.

From what? I wondered.

"I'll lend you some more money." Jo startled me from the shadows of the store. When had she entered? I wondered. How much had she observed of all that had passed between the woman and myself and the necklace?

"No more money," the Navajo woman said and her face closed, along with the subject. She gave Jo a fierce look, then abruptly turned away. Whatever had gone on between us she did not want to share with my friend. As I wrote her a check that emptied my account, the Navajo woman dusted her glass counter. Without knowing why, I slipped the wolf necklace into my pocket, burying it deep before Jo could see it closely.

It would be many years before I would discover more about the meaning of this wolf necklace. My instinct then was simply to place it reverently on a deerskin my father had sent me by way of a birthday present. And there the wolf necklace sat for the next two decades, wherever I wandered. It may have been wide awake, as the Navajo woman assured me, but I went soundly to sleep—still scared and overawed by its power, its purpose.

It would not be until the deep winter of 1993 that I would at last take the wolf necklace up from its resting place on my altar and carry it somewhere wild wolves still stalked: through arctic Alaskan woods. It would not be until late 1999 that I would again encounter Arizonans who dreamed of wolves coming home to their deserts. Then I would meet another grandmother who was working to bring back the Mexican wolf—under the threat of bounty hunters and menacing ranchers—to these lands so long silent of the howl of any wolf tribe.

BACK IN 1980, in that blazing Arizona desert, I thanked the Navajo woman and told her that one day I would visit her again. But I never have. Many times I have tried to find that reservation road; sometimes I even drove into the Navajo or Hopi reservations, trying to get lost. But I never did.

For the next dozen years I buried that wolf necklace. Once I wore it to a powwow a Native American friend took me to in Arizona. It so overwhelmed me and all who saw it that I quickly took it off.

"It's too big," my friend said and nodded when I took it off and hid it again. Even she didn't want to look at it for long. "It's not my tribe," she murmured.

To this day very few of my friends have ever seen it. But in 1992, a dozen years after the wolf necklace passed into my shaky hands, I told my story and showed it to a Cherokee friend who is a museum curator of Native American art. Hoping that she might at last take the necklace off my hands for her museum, I was nevertheless not surprised when she examined it gravely and gave it right back to me.

"You keep this," she said. "It's not meant to be locked up in a museum exhibit. It has work to do in the world."

"But I can't imagine what this necklace wants with me, what I'm supposed to do with it," I sighed. "All I know is that it's the most beautiful, most powerful thing I've ever . . ." I laughed mirthlessly. ". . . well I can't say 'ever possessed.' Because obviously it possesses me more than I ever could it."

"That's the way with true power," my Cherokee friend said softly. Then she explained. "Do you know what the Navajo woman meant when she said, 'You don't need the poison?' "

"That really scared me," I confessed. "I thought it was a kind of Navajo riddle that as a white person I wouldn't take on the poison of hatred toward whites that her people surely felt. That there might be something evil in the necklace that could harm someone who wore it without a sense of its full power and sacred work."

My friend laughed with a certain reserve. It was obvious she was also discreetly laughing at me. "The poison the Navajo woman referred to was literal poison. It's from a hallucinogenic desert plant called the sacred datura, which is often used in Navajo spiritual ceremonies. Datura is very dangerous, hypnotically beautiful with its white flowers that glow in the dark. Navajos use the datura for seeing into other worlds, but only the old ones know how to ingest it properly without dying. The plant's poison can be fatal if one doesn't have the wisdom to use it well." My friend paused, and studied me for a long time. I was much younger than she, and it was obvious she was trying to discern how much or how little to explain to me of the mysteries of a people not hers or mine.

At last she continued. "So when the Navajo woman said, 'You don't need the poison,' she meant that for some reason you recognized the power of this other world—and make no mistake, it is a dangerous world of spirits and lost souls and witchcraft—without the poison of the sacred datura plant for vision." My friend looked down then said in a low voice, "Of course, you can't know this, but from my experience with such things, the necklace looks like those used to protect people from skinwalkers."

"Skinwalkers?" I said in a tremulous voice. Now I was truly terrified.

"The Navajos believe that there are human witches, called skin-walkers, who disguise themselves as wolves or coyotes and work evil against those they dislike. You see, the Navajos in the Southwest are more ambivalent about wolves than tribes in the Northwest, where you come from. The Northwest tribes see wolves as strong spiritual allies, whereas the Navajos believe there are real wolves who are part of nature and therefore good, but there are also humans who disguise themselves as wolves and do witchcraft. You never know who you're dealing with, really, so the wolf necklace with its real wolf teeth can protect someone from the human wolves, those skinwalkers who prey on other humans."

"Is there someone else I can give this necklace to," I said in some desperation, "if you can't take it?"

My friend looked at me a long time, pondering my request. At last she said slowly, measuring her words, "Have you ever considered," she said quietly, "that maybe it is you this necklace is trying to protect?"

I sat back, stunned in my chair, and without thinking I reached out to the wolf teeth to rub them between my middle and index fingers. "No," I said, "I've never thought that. I'm not Navajo."

"You're human," she said simply. We both fell quiet for a long time. Then she concluded, "Well, think about it." She placed her large hand on mine as if to reassure me. "These sacred artworks rarely make mistakes. It's the humans who don't know how to use them correctly. Like the sacred datura that can open up one's vision to the spirit world—or kill you if you use it unwisely."

I took the wolf necklace with both hands and held it more reverently, with even more fear than before. But at the same time I also accepted it, as if for the first time. It was like trusting something beyond my understanding, even deeper than my fear. "All right," I said at last. "I'll sit with it and give it a place of proper honor for as many years as this wolf necklace takes to reveal itself, and its work, to me."

My Cherokee friend smiled. "It may take all your life. All I can tell you now is that it is deep protection and it chose you. Maybe back in that Arizona desert there was a skinwalker next to you and you didn't even know it. You could recognize the necklace without the plant poison, but perhaps you couldn't recognize the human poison the real wolf spirit was protecting you from. And then again, you must ask yourself, why are the wolves protecting you? Do you owe them some debt?"

Today I understand at last my Cherokee friend's words, and I acknowledge the profound protection of the Navajo wolf necklace with great sadness and a sense of indebtedness. But all I knew back in 1980 was that I had stumbled on a rare gift of the Navajo spirit and that I must safekeep this wolf necklace until the time came for it to protect another.

Oddly enough, though I showed it to very few people, I did feel drawn to present it to my animals. When I showed the wolves' teeth to my huskies, I was not surprised by their reactions. Kasaluk sniffed the old teeth warily, then jumped backwards, her tail straight up in the air. Raising her snout, she howled her wolf call as if she'd just heard a siren or another wolf. Her son, Inouk—by now two hands taller than Kasaluk—didn't dare approach the necklace, but did join his mother in a howling session. I had to keep the necklace on high bookcase altar so that Inouk did not spray it to mark his territory. And I marveled at how my domesticated dogs could still sense the wild wolf clinging to these teeth after death, after decades of human handling.

Perhaps it was the same way I can still smell the clean fur scent of my Siberian huskies long after I have lost them. For I did lose my dogs, though not to death.

One night in 1980, after two and a half years of commuting between the desert and my Colorado farmhouse, I got a late-night phone call. It was Amanda, the woman who shared my farmhouse and cared for my huskies when I was away. She was hysterical, screaming about her cat and new kittens. "Your goddamned dogs killed them," she yelled. "All of them. All at once!"

I was shocked. How could my huskies, who were kenneled in my garage-sized back porch, break into the farmhouse to attack the cat and her six kittens? Somebody must have left the kitchen door open. But I couldn't question Amanda. There was no point in blame: the deed was done. And it was terrible.

"There's blood everywhere," she sobbed. "I'm leaving. Taking my kids and leaving. You can fly back here and clean up yourself!"

"I'm so sorry," I said over and over. But it did no good. She was about to slam the phone down when I asked, "Where are the huskies?"

"You're lucky I didn't shoot them!" she snapped and hung up on me.

I cancelled my classes for the week and took a redeye plane. When I walked into my farmhouse six hours later it was such a horrible sight—a small massacre from the kitchen to the living room. Blood smeared on linoleum and white walls. I felt sick and miserable as I heard my huskies howling their greeting on the porch. They greeted me with abject friendliness, blood still smeared and dried on their snouts. Inouk, the proud predator, happily lay a small matted fur body at my feet.

"No!" I said loudly and put his snout in the bloody mess. "Bad dog!" But it was a useless punishment, about as useless as reprimanding a human for eating a hamburger. As I stood there surrounded by the animal carnage, I knew that if there were any fault it was not the natural predator-prey instinct; it was my own fault for leaving my dogs in the care of someone else. I was not caring for my own animals as well as I should have—half the week gone, half the week here. As my huskies clambered happily over me, I tried to clean up all the bloodstains.

I had seen the kittens only once and I deeply mourned their mother, a tabby who was as affectionate as she was a fierce mouser. She used to hunt mice in the chicken coops and proudly display her kills on the couch. It had been a long time since I'd witnessed an animal hunt. I had forgotten the brutality. And I couldn't understand why my dogs had gone after a cat they'd lived so amiably with for years. Perhaps she had died protecting her kittens, whom my dogs saw only as prey. Or perhaps my dogs were, in my absence, frustrated at being locked up for too long and not exercised enough. This destruction might be their canine way of showing distress.

I knew then that I would have to make a terrible choice: leave my job to return to Colorado or give up my dogs to good families who would take better daily care of them. It was one of the most difficult decisions I've ever made in my life. Moving the dogs down to the desert with me was not an option. Once I'd seen a Siberian husky on a leash in the Arizona summer heat. Panting, her tongue hanging out, she looked even more miserable than the humans did in the 102-degree weather. Already I'd gotten heat stroke three times just walking to teach my classes. Having grown up by water or rivers, I was drying up in the desert. I was allergic to the dust and had contracted a fungus in my lungs called Valley Fever, which was like walking pneumonia. But I was still under contract at the university, so my time in the desert felt like a kind of prison sentence.

Soon after the huskies' rebellion, my parents decided they wanted to rent out the family farmhouse so they could cover their mortgage payment. Now I had no job in Colorado and no home. All I had were my two dogs. For almost a year I'd been half-heartedly looking for homes for Kasaluk and Inouk. But the prospect of really giving them up for good left me with a desperate sadness. I just couldn't give them up, even though I could see they were no longer happy. I was not there daily to walk with them along the prairie or play wolf pack or howl alongside them at every train whistle and siren. We no longer rested side-by-side in the moonlight, running our irrigation-ditch water through an acre of tall, bright corn.

Through the want ads I advertised for a family to take in Kasaluk, who was now nearly nine years old and a little weary of her son's rambunctious devotion and demands for play. A sweetly affectionate elder who had always loved small children, Kasaluk found a home with a kind couple who had a toddler and another baby on the way. Since Siberian huskies are known for their fondness toward children, Kasaluk was an easy match for this growing family. For a while I visited her in her new home. Though I missed her terribly, I was satisfied to see her deep involvement with the family. I knew she was happier there than she would have been in the desert with me. She settled in with her new family so amiably that it eased my pain. Kasaluk was protective of their toddler and seemed very content. Perhaps she even preferred the human children, like a doting aunt, to the daily burden of mothering Inouk, a giant of a son who still related to her as a pup.

Finding a home for Inouk was not difficult, but it was excruciating. I found a family in Boulder through the university. They had two teenage

marathon runners, energetic boys who jogged every day along the moun-
tainous Flat Irons trail. When they saw Inouk, with his malamute-husky
passion for sled racing, his cheerful and amiable character, the teenage
boys adored him. Immediately they took him for a long jog, which so
delighted and exhausted Inouk that I knew he would be happy with
them. He would also be able to run free in a large, enclosed backyard,
instead of being cramped in my farmhouse outbuildings and back porch.

But I could not imagine myself not sleeping at night with Kasaluk
cuddled by my side and my hand resting on Inouk's broad, white forehead. "Dolphin-dog," I'd called Inouk, because his expansive and
gleaming brow was so wide it resembled the large melon of a dolphin.
It had been bad enough commuting to the desert and not having
Kasaluk and Inouk near me at night. But to imagine that both huskies
would disappear from my daily life altogether, that I would never hear
Kasaluk's life-saving howl or watch Inouk bounding ahead of me on the
prairie trail—it was too much to contemplate. Even after I'd assured
the Boulder family that they could come take Inouk to his new home, I
put off the exact date of our leave-taking.

Finally, I could delay no longer. I would soon be moving to the
desert full-time myself and leaving the family farmhouse to strangers
who paid rent but didn't have the love or history I shared with this place.
It was a bright summer day, and I was preparing for my stint teaching
summer school when the station wagon drove up to my farmhouse.

The Boulder family piled out of their big car with great happiness
and excitement. "There he is!" shouted one boy, and I realized with a
mixture of gladness and grief that the boys had been lonely for my
beautiful Inouk. "Here, boy!" he shouted and Inouk bounded up to
him in recognition. A run, a race—that's what Inouk saw when he leapt
the fence and into the boy's open arms.

Tireless boys and dog were off, running along the railroad tracks, while
I spoke quietly with the parents about dog food and my Arizona phone

numbers, about making sure if they ever had to give up Inouk, they'd call me first. Too soon, our conversation was over and we fell politely mute. At last their boys returned, faces bright red with exertion. Inouk was dragging one boy bodily along the trail Kasaluk and I had made.

"Please treat him kindly." I was barely able to speak.

"You can be sure of that," said one boy. "He's the best dog in the whole world! He should be on my track team!"

There was a very long and awkward pause. I had said my private goodbyes to Inouk the night before. Mostly I held his large, stalwart body, speaking tenderly in his soft ear assurances that I would always love and keep him in my heart. With his wolf-blue eyes and gleaming forehead, Inouk had held my gaze for a long time. But this was his usual way. He did seem restless during the night and howled several times at what seemed to me like nothing. I knew that howl—Inouk had not howled like that except when he watched his mother being driven away to her new home. It was plaintive and heartbreaking. I didn't sleep for the rest of the night, just listened to Inouk's sweet, bass snoring.

I did not know how to say a formal goodbye to Inouk before these strangers. He waited by my side for them to leave and when they all crawled into the station wagon, he looked up at me as if expecting water or food or play. "Inouk! Come here, boy!" one of the teenagers called him.

Inouk bounded toward the boy, but then stopped short. He did not hop in the car, as was his usual way. He was a big dog who loved to ride in cars, his huge head hanging out of the open window, tongue tasting the wind. "It's all right, boy," I said, barely able to keep hold of myself. "You can go with them now."

Inouk hesitated. Huskies are not as loyal as German shepherds or as possessive and protective as golden retrievers. Huskies, like their wolf ancestors, love to run away, far and wide, roaming their territories. They are also the friendliest of dogs, willing to go with almost anyone if they sense fun and food await them. But Inouk would not get in the car, even though the boy offered him a delicious real bone. He stayed by my side, glancing up at me. He was very still.

With a sigh, I walked over to the station wagon and gestured for Inouk to jump in the back seat, where the boys eagerly awaited him. He would not. I got down on my knees and looked right into his eyes. "I'm so sorry," I told him, holding back my tears. "I will always miss you." Then I buried my face in his warm, fragrant fur and felt a sob rising up. I steeled myself not to cry. Inouk would never leave me if he saw my weeping. Whenever I cried, he'd station himself next to me and stare out warily, growling into the air, as if grief were some invisible intruder he could pounce on. It was the only time he ever tried to protect me. Friends used to joke that someone could mug me and Inouk would think it was a game. But he recognized sorrow and he responded to it as a wolf would some interloper.

"Up you go, Inouk." I gathered all 135 pounds of him in my arms and lifted him into the back seat. It was the first time since he'd gained his adult size and weight that I'd been able to lift him more than a foot off the ground.

I pretended it was a game, but Inouk was not fooled. He watched me very carefully, those blue eyes tracking me. Then slowly, he lay down on the seat and let the boys stroke him, but he never took his eyes off my face. I closed the door. "You'll be happy," I told him. "Really happy."

"We'll take very good care of him," the mother, said and I could see the compassion in her eyes. "Call us if you want. Or come by."

But I knew I never would. I could never go through the grief of letting him go again. As I watched Inouk gazing at me, his snout pressed up against the station wagon's back window so intently that immediately the glass was fogged with his breath, I remembered that first night, when I'd lent Inouk my own breath and his came back so small and unsure. And at last I let go my own sobs, bent double with the pain of this leave-taking. I knew that if I ever got my hands on Inouk again, I could never let him go. And he needed a bigger life than I could now give him.

As the station wagon disappeared down the dirt road, I swore I would never again have another dog companion until I was settled down and would not ever have to give up my dogs again. Dogs needed a settled life and so did I.

PART TWO

RETURN

THE WILD

The wild creature has just as much right to live as you or I. . . . As in human life, there are tragedy, humor, and pathos; in the life of the wild, there are facts of tremendous interest, real lives, and real happenings to be written about.

—Loren Eisley

NINE

CATS IN THE RAIN SHADOW

I N THE TWENTY years I've spent settled in Seattle, I've migrated up and down one particular stretch of windswept beach on the serpentine Puget Sound. Here, on this abundant Northwest coast, gratefully hidden by marine fog and darkening showers, I have learned to live by water and share my backyard beach with apartment dwellers and other animals. It is not unusual to see river otters slide down our culvert to fish in the sound or witness the gathering of great blue heron, bright-beaked black-and-white harlequins, and several resident bald eagles who swoop across the waves in their search for salmon. The small park nearby is a shorebird and wildlife refuge, adorned with indigenous grasses and a gallery of gigantic driftwood. My apartment neighbor awoke one spring day to see a huge sea lion asleep on our backyard mini-plot of salt-drenched grass; the sea lion was using the rusted barbecue for a pillow. And one Christmas when I opened a present from my father, his best hunting binoculars, I raised them up to spy seven tall dorsal fins—a pod of orcas intent on their winter passage.

With its walls of salt-splattered windows, its wind-tunnel whoosh and clatter, its precarious perch several stories above the high-tide splashing of Puget Sound, my little waterfront studio is like the inside of an aquarium. Except here, we humans go about our daily lives encased in glass, while sea gulls, bald eagles, Dall's porpoises, harbor seals, and an occasional meandering, migrating gray whale are the observers—if they are interested. Sometimes I believe they are, since seals are known to fix on a familiar onshore landmark to navigate their deep fishing dives.

Perhaps marine mammals who surface to spy on our human activities through this waterfront glass believe that our shore-clinging structures are also alive, like an undersea city of coral. We land creatures slip in and out of our houses, hiding for long hours like moray eels or tropical creatures with our flickering bright yellow and red rain slickers.

My studio's battered teak desk is so sun-blistered and rainswept from summer winds blowing sea mists in through window screens that it looks like salvage washed ashore off some nineteenth-century shipwreck. On the glass-paneled porch where I work, there is no baseboard heating, so I wear a black knit cap, goose down vest, wool mittens with no fingers, and an afghan or Siamese cat draped across my knees.

Living so close to this vital, inland sea and all her creatures lends my home a double life and a balance. My waterfront studio's decor is an extension of the beach, designed as if by mermaids. Lining each long windowsill are seashells, driftwood, a chambered nautilus, black bejeweled barnacles, and binoculars for handy viewing whenever my resting eye catches sight of a seal, river otter, or eagle diving down for salmon. In the hope that passing marine mammals will recognize a land-legged ally, I hang small stained-glass medallions of orcas and dolphins in the window. And all my plants, from aloe vera to Norfolk pine, have somehow found themselves draped with dried seaweed.

There is a bond and a balance when one counts as neighbors the river otters, seal pups, and seabirds who also sunbathe on our backyard beach. Except for the nearby apartment owner who once hired an animal-control agency to trap several otters she found rolling too often on her lawn, most of the people who call this Puget Sound shore their home embrace the other animals who make our houses seem so alive, our families extended between species. Those otter traps were destroyed as soon as they were discovered, and we are all anxiously awaiting the return of our river otter neighbors.

Anxiety ebbs and flows with the tide when one lives so close to the sea. The wind, the water, and the waves are not simply a backdrop to my life; they are a steady companion. And that is the grace, the gift of inviting nature to live inside my home. Like a chambered nautilus I spin out my days deep inside another bright shell on the beach.

My daily spiritual practice includes this inland sound, these sea creatures, and of course my cats. Every morning my aging Siamese Manx, Ivan Louis III, hoists his frail body up on the bed to find his early nesting place on my chest as I perform my lying-down Taoist meditation. Then a second cat, Isabel, drapes herself like a Davy Crockett hat over my head, her purring a meditative vibration inside my skull, like cat plainchant. Surrounded so by fur and the faithful, it is easy to imagine that my bed is its own tiny ark floating in luminous seas as I listen to the wild slap and shushing murmur of Puget Sound outside my window. Like Noah, I imagine that I am finding refuge and spiritual retreat with the animals.

Ivan Louis III has been my constant feline companion since my first spring in Seattle, when I arrived from the Arizona desert. Ivan was born in May 1981, the week before my friend Jo died. Though I'd known Jo for only nine months, her tragic death by her own hand deeply shadowed my first years in Seattle's contemplative cityscape, which dwells contentedly under the drape of rain clouds off the Pacific. The Olympic Mountains catch these marine mists and blanket them over our city for most of the year, a moist, gray cloak that we proudly call the "rain shadow." To survive here, one has to have an inner life that is bright with what Rainer Maria Rilke termed "a dark light." Jo, after a lifelong battle with depression and a family history steeped in suicide, did not survive here for long. Only five months passed before she decided that the solace of death was her only release. I had never suspected the depth of Jo's despair or how her struggle with depression left her with only a half-life — like someone who was walking around inside her skin but just couldn't stay there. Perhaps despair made her a skinwalker, with most of her malice directed inwards. But for her friends, there was little protection or comfort after her suicide, only the haunt of questions and sorrow.

The week after Jo's death, my partner, believing that an encounter with animals might restore and cheer me, took us on a surprise ferry trip to Whidbey Island, north of Seattle. On a sunny sea cliff we met Carrie Bline, an ambulance driver and cat aficionado. Carrie's small bungalow sat on the cliff like a sentinel. In her cozy living room, small silver-gray balls of fur immediately surrounded my feet. The Siamese Manx mother cat, Maka, lay contentedly in her human companion's lap, licking the runt of her litter. Two of the kittens were in her image, with distinctive seal-point dark masks and paws and no tail; the other two kittens were dark gray and bob-tailed. Of the two tiny Siamese Manxes, litter twins, only one was spoken for. The adoptive owner planned to name her kitten Savage. We all smiled at such a silly name for these tender newborns.

Against my plans to resist taking a kitten, I found myself watching the tiniest Siamese Manx with complete fascination. "Will these Siamese twins have blue eyes like Maka?" I found myself asking Carrie. For the first time in weeks I was taking an interest in life around me. It was as if these newborn cats had the primal power to call me back into my body, my animal soul.

"We think so," Carrie smiled, seeing the color come back into my pallid face. "What do you think?"

My attention wavered from the kittens, and I stared out at Puget Sound, unaware that tears streamed down my face. I was remembering that, three days before she died, Jo had promised to take one of these little Manxes for her own. Now here they were, bursting with life, and she was gone. I did not see the tiniest Siamese kitten making his slow way across the woven-rag carpet toward my foot. Not until I felt tiny claws sink into my ankles did I snap out of my stupor. "Ouch!" I cried and then had to laugh as I watched this blind kitten pull himself up my pant leg as if climbing a small tree. Snuffling and sniffing, he hefted himself up over the cliff of my kneecap and tumbled into my lap with a startled squeak.

"Mt. Everest!" Carrie smiled. "He made it to the top."

I gazed down at this Siamese kitten, who fit perfectly in one palm. Scratching him under his velvet neck, I felt his contented purr pulsing up through my fingertips. For just an instant I had a flashback to the first moment I'd ever felt fur. Long ago in the forest, it was the smooth flanks of my first deer guardians I stroked for comfort and care. As I petted the kitten, I was startled to feel something kindling within me: I recognized it then as hope. Hope that I would soon see these lovely kittens open their eyes. Then I felt another stirring deep in my belly. I hadn't eaten much in the week after Jo's death. Yet this was the first time I had felt hungry.

"This is the one," I said softly. "This kitten found me even when he couldn't see me." It was like that wolf necklace that had found me in the desert when I couldn't see it. I kept that wolf necklace now on a pelt of rabbit skin on my private altar. More and more, it lent me a sense of safety and protection, though I was still in awe and somewhat afraid of its power.

"This kitten just knows you are here," Carrie said. "Animals recognize their real companions." Then Carrie gave me her fond lecture on Siamese Manxes. This rare breed was a cross between the fiercely protective Siamese temple-guardian cats and the Manxes, felines of the ancient Phoenician world, whose seafaring merchants sailed with these rat-controlling cats from the Far East to the Irish coast. "There are legends that the Manxes were late to catch Noah's ark and the big doors slammed on their tails." Seeing my sudden grin, Carrie continued, "This breed is loyal and sweet-tempered; they love routine and home. But you have to play with them every day."

"I'll take really good care of him," I assured her and felt a surge of unexpected happiness. The littlest Manx sank tiny claws into my blouse and would not let go. Blindly he raised his face to listen to my voice, then the physical trill of his kittenish purring reverberated as he tucked his chin into my palm.

"I'm sure you will," Carrie grinned. "And he'll take good care of you." She laughed as the kitten growled whenever someone else came near me. "He has a strong spirit. He will protect you. He will help heal you."

And he did. For eighteen years, this Siamese Manx, whom I named Ivan Louis III, protected and cared for me. For the first six months, Ivan gave me a daily reason to devote myself to life instead of the shadows of my friend's death. All his life, Ivan has slept soundly on my head and the wolf necklace has rested on my bedside altar. Between these two great protectors, I have learned again to feel safe at night when skinwalkers stalk the living and sometimes people die.

Through nearly two decades of living with me, Ivan proved himself a great hunter of shrew and forest mice. With their rabbitlike back legs, Manx cats can defy gravity and perform astonishing leaps. The first time I discovered this acrobatic genius I was standing in the kitchen talking on the phone. Suddenly I heard a whistling of air I thought was static on the line. But a graceful plop on my shoulder and purring into my free ear startled me. At six months, Ivan Louis had leapt from the floor onto my shoulder in a single bound. Then he proceeded to drape his warm body around my neck like a living, silver stole. My shoulders were Ivan's favorite perch and I grew so accustomed to his companionable clasp that when he wasn't riding around on my shoulders I felt that something was missing.

For the first eleven years of his life, Ivan Louis was a robust and stalwart companion. When we lived farther south on Puget Sound, renting a ramshackle house with 180 feet of beachfront, Ivan Louis was in his heyday. He'd patrol the beach, stalking seagulls and sometimes digging for clams, which he could never open. Sea anemones squirted him as Ivan strolled the wet sand like his Irish cat ancestors from the Isle of Man, who were said to have fished for their food after washing ashore in the 1500s from shipwrecked Spanish Armada galleons.

At night he'd roar through my housemate Lynettie's open window, hollering as he bounced on her bed and her boyfriend. Then he'd race upstairs to settle like a sentry on my head. Ivan always smelled of salt and kelp. Sleeping with him was like camping out in my own bed: he left sand and bits of seaweed on my pillow.

During the days, Ivan hunted trophies for me, always politely leaving them on the back porch. Lynettie and I were endlessly holding funerals for the multitudinous shrew and field mice Ivan sacrificed for us. "He's a good provider," Lynettie would say. Ivan's health was as legendary as his hearty appetite. And he was the only cat I'd ever lived with who would actually respond to my call. I'd holler out into the backyard in treble arpeggios, "Ivy, Ivy Lou, . . ." and from green space or water's edge, he'd meow back and then race home, a silver streak through the vibrant green underbrush.

Ivan's vocalizations were as expansive as any dolphin's. Friends teased me that Ivan Louis had his own daily talk show. The breeding combination of Siamese and Manx lent my Ivan Louis a personality that was at once imperial and chatty. Ivan had something to say to everyone. He delighted in punctuating long-winded human dialogues with eerie yowls, operatic squeals, and sonorous growls. Over the years I found myself relying on him as a good judge of human character. It is said that cats often seek out the one person in a room who dislikes felines and insist themselves on the allergic or wary or frightened visitor. But Ivan was the opposite. He'd study any newcomer with an unblinking blue stare, his posture like that poised and graceful wariness before a pounce.

It is difficult to describe how aloof and yet loving this Manx cat could be, but anyone who earned Ivan's fierce and protective friendship believed herself fortunate. And I was the most fortunate of all, because Ivan always acted as if I belonged to him. In some ways, Ivan's bond was more like the devotion of a dog. Compared with my Siberian huskies, Ivan was more loyal and possessive. He always slept vigilantly on my pillow, "still guarding the temple," as my partner said fondly. And he was an even lighter sleeper than I am: once when we thought there was an intruder, he attacked only to find he'd clawed a dear friend who, stalled in a Seattle snowstorm, had taken his skis off his car and slalomed down to our beach house.

After more than a decade of such vigorous and fond companionship, I was shocked to discover that my vibrantly healthy and burly cat had developed diabetes, just like his mother had. Over the next eight years and in combination with acupuncture, herbs, and chiropractic treatments, Ivan endured two insulin shots a day. He was diagnosed a "brittle" diabetic, which meant that his illness was unpredictable and more difficult to manage. In eight years, he almost died five times from either hypo- or hyperglycemic shock.

"Ivan has given me a healthy decade of love and companionship," I'd tell friends when they inquired about the rigors of giving two shots a day and the roller-coaster ride of maintaining a diabetic cat. "I can give him whatever he needs now to stay alive."

And stay alive he did. Ivan Louis III is on record in several veterinary textbooks as one of the longest-living diabetic cats. He astonished both my holistic and my Western medical vets. It is a statement of the devotion Ivan inspires in others that my holistic vet made Ivan's care her only house call, and my Western vet, Dr. Glenn Johnson, once took Ivan to his own house overnight when we thought he would not survive a hypoglycemic episode.

Both Ivan and, later, his companion cat, Isabel, taught me, like natural Zen masters, about survival and love. My pillow used to be Ivan's perch alone, but from years of diabetes and twice-daily insulin shots, his intermittent small seizures made it too dangerous for him to continue to sleep on my head. Without any training, he chose to sleep during the night at my feet, like a silver muff. And when my lover also joins me, there are several more animals in attendance on our bed, which floats us all into a watery rest as waves lap our backyard beach. Sometimes I lay awake at night listening to the sound of beloved breathing—my partner's soft snores, my cats' midnight preening and purring, a visiting dog's little asthmatic coughs. Then I imagine all around the world there are these dream-time Noah's arks—dogs and cats and other domestic animals all curled up together with us humans in an interspecies night vision. Together we animals and humans drift through unconscious worlds, still searching for new land, some territory we can consciously claim and share.

ANOTHER TERRITORY WE share sometimes more tenderly with animal companions than with humans is that of the passing from life to death. On the night of my birthday in August 1999 I came home from celebrating to find my elderly gentleman of a cat lying sideways on the floor, his front paw paralyzed. As always, Ivan was talking. But his cries were frightened and muted.

I knew Ivan had not suffered a stroke, because he was alert and loving. I managed to get him to Dr. Donna Kelleher, my holistic vet, at 3 A.M. Sunday morning. She confirmed it was a blood clot, common in diabetics.

"It'll be only a matter of hours before it reaches his heart, and he might die a terrible death," Donna said. "Bring him home and take the night to say your good-byes. Tomorrow, you'll have to let him go because it's his time. And that would be mercy."

I will never forget that long night together, with me cradling Ivan Louis and thanking him for his constancy, telling him the story of his long life's adventures as an ace shrew-hunter and stalker of bamboo plants, the way he guarded my weary head every night, his early morning ritual of tucking his face right under my chin, and the physical purr of his heart right into mine.

In the week before his death, Ivan had showed a new and haunting behavior: he would climb his staircase of blankets up to my bed and go to the very edge, next to the screen window opening onto Puget Sound and its incessant surf sounds. Balancing on his crippled haunches, he would lean so far out I worried he might topple, sniffing the sea air and listening intently to birdsong in the nearby elm tree. His entire body was rapt, posed as if between two worlds, this one and the next. In his posture and distinguished Siamese face was a longing so intense I could also feel it.

"Oh, I hope this is not a sign of his leaving," I had told a friend the night before Ivan's blood clot. "Doesn't it seem like his spirit is longing to be outside again—even if it's outside his body?"

"Maybe he's memorizing this world," my friend suggested softly.

On what was to be his last full day, Ivan had lingered longer on the sill than his arthritis usually allowed or was his habit. In the early morning, he draped across my chest, his blue eyes with their one brown dot (the first sign I had eight years ago of imminent illness—his diabetes) resting on mine. For some lazy reason, or perhaps because I sensed his insistent intimacy, I also lingered with him that morning and sang his favorite songs, all the lullabies I long ago made up with him as the hero.

I had no idea that the night would bring our vigil together and I will always be grateful to my vet Donna, whose early-morning diagnosis allowed me to spare Ivan the cold, steel examination table of the ani-

mal emergency room and a quick goodbye. That night of conscious love and comfort will always be one of my dearest memories, and a gift because so many other of my losses have been traumatic, with no time to "be still, and know."

What I knew that long, last night with Ivan Louis III is that there is a peace in calmly facing death with a loved one, animal or human. The grace animals give us is that we often can share a quiet, painless death, without struggle or stress. With our animal companions we sometimes have foreknowledge of their death. So simple kindness and intimacy mark their passing, rather than high-tech stress and life-saving insistence that gets in the way of the mystery, the communion, the surrender. That long night, as Ivan lay quietly next to me, letting my tears bathe his face and looking up at me without denial or fear, Ivan completed his life as he had lived it, close by my side. "Abide with me," I sang to him the old Southern spiritual. And he did.

In the late morning, about a half-hour to the minute of my birth 49 years earlier, the hospital vet confirmed Ivan's zero-recovery prognosis. She was very kind and told me we must euthanize him immediately or he would suffocate from a fatal heart attack, which was only minutes away. With a dear friend by my side, we made Ivan comfortable in his favorite blue wicker laundry basket and wrapped my red flannel nightgown around him. We lay sweet peas and catnip near his nose and across his silver-gray fur.

For the first time Ivan seemed to drift a little away from me, his eyes open but pensive. He still responded to my voice as I sang to him, between sobs. I thanked him for his great spirit.

"See you in another world," I promised him.

In giving Ivan Louis the final injection, the vet was gentle and kind; her assistant, a man who'd saved Ivan's life several times in diabetic crashes, stroked him and my friend's soft voice soothed him. I held the back of Ivan's head in those little indentations on the occipital ridge—

the acupressure points I was taught long ago to hold during birth and death, for a safe transition and passage. Within thirty seconds, the injection stopped his brain, but Ivan still breathed a few times, his eyes wide open to the world that he now peacefully left.

The hardest part for me was leaving his physical body, the rich silver fur and blue-eyed face I had loved for eighteen years. At last I clipped a few strands of fur, which I later put inside my favorite Hopi clay pot, the one with the butterfly designs symbolizing eternity. I planned to have him cremated and to hold a memorial service for all Ivan's caretakers. On the beach we would scatter his ashes everywhere Ivan lived and save the rest for a small, humbly woven willow basket, which is on a little altar for his soul's safe passage.

Everywhere now I see his great, bright spirit. He left at the age of 106 in human years, my father calculated. My meditation teacher tells me that cats, like some other animals including horses, cetaceans, and primates, individuate: their souls are distinct throughout every incarnation.

"I believe," my teacher said, "that certain feline souls come to us again and again all throughout our lives. It is the accumulation of loving we feel when we meet up with our soul animals all over again."

Surviving Ivan is just what he taught me to do, though it is so sad not to see him every day, only to sense his nearness, especially at dawn and twilight when the veils between the worlds are thin. He is survived not only by all those who were devoted to him, but also by his companion, Isabel, who mourns him as well. In Isabel's face Ivan's expression is mirrored. My loneliness for Ivan is more bearable because Isabel is still here with me.

Some part of me will always have my eyes out for Ivan Louis III. "Who are the first and second?" the hospital vet had asked as she tenderly injected him with his mercifully last needle.

"There was none before him," I answered softly. "There was only him."

IF IVAN LOUIS'S story is one of constancy and loyal alliance, Isabel's story is as amazing, for it is still a mystery. One winter my neighbors—whose idea of a good time is gathering up all the feral cats in the backyard green space, getting them spayed, then releasing them to the woods or good homes—called to say they had found another Siamese Manx they knew belonged with me. Joyce and her daughter Pamela are ex-New Yorkers, veterans of that city's cat shelter and animal-rescue volunteer work. These formidable women are persistence personified. Joyce is the St. Francis of our neighborhood and her daily rounds of animal feeding make her backyard like an urban wildlife shelter: boiled eggs and tuna for the wild fox and her kits; hummingbird, owl, and crow feeding stations; small cat houses and mountains of kibbles for stray cats and dogs; peanuts for the squirrels who now eat out of her hand. Lately several eagles have been eyeing her house from perches in woods high on the hillside above. In her daily animal devotions Joyce reminds me of my Great Aunt Mary's Colorado home for abandoned animals. Like me, she is active in neighborhood whale-watching groups, always on the alert when the orcas or an occasional migrating gray whale cruise down our beach. Joyce is also involved in cat and dog rescue and in foster parenting homeless animals—from baby birds to raccoons. For Christmas, her daughter gave Joyce a nightscope for watching all the animals migrating through her backyard refuge.

"Who needs looking up at the stars?" Joyce says. Though she is in her sixties, her trim body and energy and her bright green eyes give her the look of a much younger woman. "I've got an entire universe of animals moving through my backyard. Some people watch videos, I watch the animal world go by."

Watching and caretaking are what Joyce does best. One winter several years ago, she was taking care of her old home up the hill as well as the animals in her new waterfront home. Animal-feeding chores were running her ragged, and she is already as thin and graceful as a ballerina. When she called me, there was a certain desperation in her voice.

"This homeless cat is Ivan's twin. Come see for yourself!"

I had wanted another Manx for a long time, but they were very hard to come by. I'd read that cats and dogs live longer in the company of other animals (besides human beings); as Ivan grew more elderly I hoped to prolong his life, and perhaps some of his play, with another cat comrade.

The moment I walked into Joyce's house, which looks like an animal kingdom with its tall, shag-carpeted cat jungle gyms, its overstuffed chairs with clawed legs, its floors littered with cat toys, I saw the new-comer. She looked so much like Ivan Louis, it took my breath away. "She's Ivan's clone," I marveled as she settled companionably in my lap.

Instantly I knew her name would be Isabel. Whereas Ivan was hearty and every inch the hunter-feline, Isabel was delicate and petite. She also lacked all confidence and seemed almost fatally exhausted as she stretched herself across my lap. Sleeping, she looked like roadkill.

"Is she all right?" I asked Joyce. "Is she sick or something?"

"It's trauma," Joyce nodded with a sad smile. "The vet says cats who have been homeless for as long as she has often forget how to play or even be catlike ever again. They just need to rest after all the stress of surviving outside alone."

"So play is a sign of good health?" I asked Joyce, intrigued.

"You bet," she said. "My vet calls animal play one of the best indica-tors not only of good health, but also of an animal's chances for sur-vival. If Isabel here doesn't learn to play again, she may not ever fully recover from her homelessness trauma."

I looked down at this little image of Ivan Louis and wondered what her life had been like. "How long do you think she's been lost?" I asked Joyce. "She's not gone feral yet, not if she can trust me to hold her like this."

"No idea! All I know is that for the past month at least she's been liv-ing up the hill at our old house, peering out from underneath the back porch. Wouldn't let us come near her! When I'd go to feed the other animals she'd streak out, chow down some kibbles like it was her last supper, and then dash back to her hiding place. She was so sneaky and scared even I couldn't trap her and take her up to the vet to be checked. Outwitted me every time."

"If you couldn't catch her, she must be really wily," I laughed.

"Then one night everything changed." Joyce's face took on a musing expression. "You know how cold it's been this winter and I worry about all the homeless animals outside—exposure. Well Pamela and I pulled up into the driveway and heard this hideous yowling. It sounded almost human! Like life-and-death cat cries. We ran to the back deck and this ball of fur streaked out and right toward us. Before we could duck or move, this little cat hurled herself into the air and right smack dab into Pamela's arms. She was like a heat-seeking missile. Shivering, she curled into Pamela's down jacket and at last stopped crying. It was like she was having a kitty nervous breakdown and just couldn't stand it anymore. She had to seek comfort, even from us humans."

I gazed down at the sleeping Manx. She was like an Oliver Twist version of Ivan—the fate Ivan Louis himself might have endured if he'd gotten orphaned, lost, or lived homeless. As I gently stroked this little look-alike Manx's fur, my fingers found matted, greasy furballs along her belly and neck.

"I thought they were tumors," Joyce told me when she saw my concern. "But the vet said just cut them off, this is what happens when a cat is too freaked out to even preen and wash herself. It's like they're soldiers, always in the trenches. Every minute is red alert. They can't even sleep for fear of raccoons, dogs, or other predators who might attack them in the night. Like someone who's gone without sleep for too long or like Vietnam vets, this little one is just a bundle of shattered nerves."

Studying the sleeping Manx, I tenderly traced the black stitches inching along her lower abdomen. "Too bad you had to spay her so soon after the rescue," I said.

"That's the funny thing," Joyce interrupted me. "Vet went in to spay Isabel and couldn't find any ovaries."

"Someone must have spayed her in her other life," I shrugged and didn't think much more about it.

I was caught up in the next week or so with introducing Ivan to Isabel, keeping her in a separate room with a screen in the doorway so the cats could hiss and spit and study other before they shared any territory. To my surprise, Ivan accepted Isabel almost overnight, as if they already knew each other. "Maybe it's because they're the same breed and look so much alike," I suggested. Perhaps the Manxes' ease with one another was like that kinship humans feel when, in a foreign landscape, we come upon someone of our own tribe or country.

"Like seeks like," Joyce shrugged happily. "Usually takes my homeless cats a month before they're acclimated to another cat or home. Maybe Manxes like mirror images around. They're pretty enough to be that vain."

"Sometimes I can't tell them apart," I admitted, "even though Isabel is smaller. I've studied their faces and, you know, they look like twins: the same broad noses, and even their expressions are exactly alike."

"The mysteries of DNA," Joyce mused.

As the weeks passed, I realized that Isabel didn't look exactly like Ivan, but she was the mirror image of his mother, Maka, who had died of diabetes complications the year before. I called my old friend Carrie, who by now had moved from Whidbey Island down to Seattle. In fact, she now lived just up the hill, several miles from my beach. We rarely saw each other, but she had called me after the death of Maka and we commiserated about the dangers and difficulties of living with a beloved, diabetic cat.

"Come down and see this new Manx," I invited Carrie. "But be prepared. She's the spitting image of your cat, Maka—so it might be a little sad for you to see her."

"Might make me glad," Carrie countered. "I miss seeing Maka's little face."

Carrie quickly acted on my invitation, and when she opened the door to see Isabel, as usual, sleeping on the front bookcase, Carrie stopped mid-threshold and just stared. As an ambulance driver and medic, Carrie has witnessed her share of trauma and sights most of us never have to behold. I couldn't understand, then, why her face suddenly drained of all color and she almost staggered to keep her balance.

I thought her reaction was much like one who sees a ghost of a loved one returned to haunt them. "She is just like Maka," I murmured. "I told you to be prepared."

"Yes," Carrie managed to say, and tears blurred her eyes, "and someone else."

I couldn't believe Carrie's emotional reaction. In all the years I'd known her, I'd never seen her cry. Stoicism was her survival strategy. "Yes, she could be Ivan's twin," I murmured and reached out a hand to comfort my friend, as many years before Carrie had comforted me after Jo's death with the gift of Ivan Louis.

Carrie slipped past me and darted over to the bookcase where Isabel lay stretched out in the sun. For weeks Isabel had not left her chosen station high above the rest of the household. Gazing quietly out the window at branches filled with starlings seemed to be Isabel's only desire. I even fed her atop the bookcase. The only time she left this sanctuary was to use the litter box or to exercise what one of my cat-loving friends calls "kitty aerobics"—racing up and down the hall.

Carrie examined Isabel with all the tender and skillful scrutiny of a trained medic. Just when I expected her to pronounce some dire disease because Carrie seemed so shaken, she said softly, "This is Ivan's twin."

"Yes," I agreed blithely. "It's amazing, isn't it? They do look so much alike. I think of them as family, like siblings."

"Not *like* siblings," Carrie corrected me, exasperated. "They *are* siblings." When she saw my noncomprehension, she said slowly as if speaking to someone of another language, "They are twins. Littermates. Brothers!"

"No, no, Carrie, how can that be?" I stammered. "This new one is female. Look for yourself."

"I have," Carrie insisted. "This Manx just looks female because he's been, well, re-plumbed! What I'm trying to tell you is that this is Ivan's real littermate. There were two kittens exactly like Maka. Don't you remember? There were two Siamese Manxes. The twins, we called them."

"Tell you the truth," I shook my head, "I don't remember much about that time right after Jo's death, except that Ivan kind of saved my life. Taking care of him helped me through."

Carrie acknowledged me with a kind smile, then she held up Isabel. "You'll have to call this one—call him Izzie now. This cat was born male as Ivan's twin brother. I gave him to a Seattle firefighter who lives just up the hill. Remember now?"

I barely remembered a woman who had taken Ivan's twin brother and named him something unusual, something utterly unlike both these cats' natures and appearances. "What did she call him?"

"Savage," Carrie grinned. "Weird name. Anyway, the first year after she got Savage, the owner discovered he had a serious urinary tract problem and the only solution was slow death or to have this expensive operation in which he was castrated and his urethra surgically kind of . . . rerouted. This cat looks female, unless you really search and see the old scars from that kittenhood operation."

"I guess that explains why the vet found no sign of ovaries," I said slowly, still stunned. It was not easy to suddenly see my newfound Isabel as an Izzie. It was even harder to believe that this was actually Ivan's twin brother restored to him. "Isa . . .—I mean Izzie—looks so much younger. She can leap up where Ivan can't. And besides, how the hell did she—I mean he—ever find her—I mean his—way down here to me and Ivan? It's like some strange destiny, or kitty karma."

Carrie had to laugh. A rationalist and scientist, her forays into spiritual life are concerned more with studying evolution than theology.

She suggested, "There is a perfectly logical explanation for this all. You know how I always insisted that if any of my Maka's kittens' owners couldn't care for her litter they should call me and I'd take them back? Well, Savage's owner called after ten years and said her new partner was deathly allergic to cats. Sorry, but she had to give Savage up. I took him in gladly, but by then Maka had died and my other two cats were really mean to him. They chased him and ate his food—not a good life. Savage ran away about eight months ago and I looked everywhere, assuming he was lost or someone else had taken him in. It's been awful wondering whatever happened to him. But now," she turned back to the new Manx, "now I know he's right where he should be."

"You're sure this is not wishful thinking?" I had to ask her.

"Check the DNA, if you don't believe me," she said. "I've known this cat since his birth and as an adult. I lived with him for eight months and know every curve and characteristic of his body. Why don't you believe me?"

"I just can't believe that in all this world, Ivan would end up spending his last years with his own littermate," I said and shrugged my shoulders.

Carrie laughed. "It explains why your vet couldn't quite tell his age or sex, and why Ivan accepted him so immediately."

"Wait a minute," I said. "I'm not usually this much of a Doubting Thomas, but where exactly is your new house up the hill?"

She told me and then I had to sit down on the couch, at last accepting her story. Her house was two blocks from the old house Joyce and Pamela visited every day, where they had found my Isabel hiding under the porch.

"All right," I said laughing. "It's Izzie instead of Isabel. It's Ivan's long-lost twin."

Still, I decided to check out Carrie's story with my own vet. He listened very carefully and slowly nodded. "Well, it could be. Explains about the lack of ovaries and the fact that she—er, he—has teeth that seem older than this cat acts. Ivan's diabetes has slowed him down considerably. If this is his true littermate, you'll have to check often to make sure he—or she—hasn't inherited the family history of diabetes. The only sure way you'll know if they're twins is if you do a DNA test, and that's really expensive."

I haven't done the DNA testing. After studying my two Siamese Manxes I am just about convinced they are indeed twins. When strangers meet my cats they invariably comment, "Littermates, I'll bet." I hope they are right. I hope that this story of brother finding brother, of cat finding not only home but proper family is a true testament to some mystery at work in the world that isn't centered around humans. Years later my vet and I would conclude that all evidence does point to Isabel and Ivan as siblings, when Isabel also developed diabetes.

I tried to train myself to call Isabel by the proper male name of Izzie. I tried to call this new Manx "he" instead of "she." Sometimes when I spoke to the Manxes together, I'd say, "Hey, boys," and it felt right. Other times, it was "How's my little sister and brother," and I just didn't bother to correct myself. First impressions die hard. And to tell the truth, I kind of liked being the only one on the block to live with a transsexual cat. Lately I've taken to calling Isabel by the simple name "Isa," which could be short for Isaiah—a good Biblical name for a miracle cat. Other little cat miracles are more explainable, such as the symmetry with which Ivan and Isabel slept together, facing each other like bookends, their bodies in exactly the same stretch or graceful curve or tuck. It was literally like seeing double. And their synchrony reminds me of another species, dolphins, who actually breathe and leap together in perfect sync all their lives. These Siamese Manx brothers restored to each other's company did have one big difference: whereas Ivan chatted and carried on conversations with seagulls, waves, humans, and computers—anything that was nearby—Isabel is more reserved. She greets humans and escorts them out the door; she bares her tiny teeth and growls at seagulls peering eye-level with her as they zoom past her window perch; she coos like a turtledove when she takes her astonishing leaps, most often right onto someone's lap. These two tailless twins have been the true north and south of my companionable compass. Between them I have navigated my small home here by the sea. And because of them, I have never been lonely.

⌒

AFTER MY FIRST two years of living with Ivan and Isabel reunited, I faced the breakup of my own family, an eight-year romantic partnership, and a series of setbacks in my work. It was Isabel who taught me a lifelong lesson in healing my own heart during this, one of the darkest times of my recent life. Often I would find myself lying flat on my studio floor, face to face with my cat. As I wept over my many break-ups, Isabel would leap over me as if my prostrate grief were a posture to invite her kittenish pounces, her purring growls and tiny tiger attacks. If she were a kitten, I could have better understood her sudden playfulness—indeed, her mania for play. But Isabel had never played with me before. Why, when I was the most grief-stricken, would she mistake my sorrow for high-spirited cat games of stalk and bat-the-birdie?

As I lay snuffling on the old carpet, a desultory hand stroking this small, bobtailed cat who threw herself into dazzling cartwheels over my legs, I found myself smiling in spite of myself. And when Isabel growled and grabbed my socks, I had to laugh out loud. Soon I was checking out cat-play toys at the pet shop and brought home a feathered fake bird contraption tethered to a small pole. With a whistling not unlike birdsong, the black, pink, and bright purple "bird" whizzed through the air around Isabel, inspiring her to acrobatic leaps and midair somersaults shocking in their grace and complete abandon.

One morning I was, as usual, lying on the carpet, crying my eyes out. Already I had gone through half a pack of Kleenex. As I was blowing my nose, I opened my swollen eyes and saw Isabel's slanting blue irises. She stalked me with ferocious glee, her bobtail twitching and trembling in anticipation of her pounce—which she did, right into my nose, snatching the Kleenex and shredding it all over my face. This flimsy foe vanquished, she turned tiny tail and hunkered down next to me, awaiting the next fabulous threat.

It was only then I wondered if something about my grief had engaged my cat's imagination so deeply that her response was new behavior: this inspired play. For more than two years, Isabel had not remembered how to play, and perhaps I'd given up hope or decided it was just not in her nature. And when her unexpected, wholehearted playfulness coincided with my own wholehearted grief, it took me a few weeks to notice. But at last I recognized that, for some reason, Isabel's trauma was over, even as my own began. She was not trying to balance me, though she did. Perhaps she perceived my horizontal crying bouts as a delicious new game in which her human was at last on her own level and therefore she could reveal her many mysterious, ingenious, trapezelike talents. Whatever the explanation, her clowning was so serious that it literally eased my dark moods.

Just as Ivan had helped comfort me after a friend's death, Isabel's playfulness restored my own sense of humor and balance, easing me into a new life after divorce. Often I've engaged in lively dialogues with friends about why the companionship of other animals is sometimes even more healing than human kindness. I have always cherished the love and loyalty of my own kind, but our animal companions offer us a different quality of attention and presence.

The renowned primatologist Dr. Jane Goodall speaks of this in her recent memoir, *Reason for Hope: A Spiritual Journey*. After the death of Goodall's beloved husband, she sought the familiar beauty of her Gombe forest in Tanzania and the solace of the chimpanzees she had studied for decades. By returning to Gombe, Goodall was "hoping that contact with the chimpanzees, so accepting of what life brings them, would ease my grief." For Goodall, these chimpanzees had always "sustained the inner core of my being," and "gradually my sense of loss was purged of bitterness, and the futile railing against fate was stilled." In her healing after so devastating a loss, Goodall credits the chimpanzees: "I needed their company," she writes, "undemanding and free of pity."

In my own life, each of my Manxes abided with me in times of trouble. I have never felt pitied by an animal, or judged. As my own animal companions accompanied me through some of the most difficult journeys of my life, they offered a steady presence and playfulness, a curiosity that was never prying, only companionable.

"My dog got me through my divorce," one of my close friends always says. "He listened so intently, with such unceasing patience. I could tell my dog the same story of my breakup over and over again until I finally understood it myself. Bless that dog of mine—he never got bored, and how many times did he hear my sad tale?"

Because animals seem to dwell in the present moment, because their own presence is so instinctive, their attention so unwavering, they offer us a different kind of compassion than humans do. Anyone is lucky to have both human and animal comfort in their lives.

I shall always be grateful to my cats for their abiding companionship. Together we nurtured each other out of despair and into some daily delight in living alongside one another, here in the misting embrace of the rain shadow.

TEN

~

AN AFTERLIFE OF ANIMALS

E VER SINCE MY childhood encounter with the real Smokey Bear, I've been uneasy in zoos. My years with animals in the wild have taught me that most zoo creatures are a sad shadow of their wild relatives. Nevertheless, for almost a decade I've made pilgrimages to visit several beluga whales in nearby Tacoma's Point Defiance Zoo.

At their underground observation tank I place my hands against the glass as the luminous belugas swim in slow figure eights, an infinity of captive circles. Eleven-year-old Mauyak (whose name means "Soft Snow" in Inuit) and Shikku, the younger female, and Inuk, a beluga version of Herman Melville's mammoth sperm whale Moby Dick, all swim together in gentle, undulant glides. Their great, gleaming bodies float through the cold turquoise waters as if they are flying at the bottom of the ocean. When they see my palms pressed flat against the glass, they will curiously come to drift eye level with me, their extraordinarily sophisticated sonar sensing, as if they can echolocate and scan me even through glass.

Then we begin our ritual. I hum and whistle in my human attempt at a signature call, and these "sea canaries," as they are called for their intricate treble trills, clicks, squeaks, and twitters, converse with me. Our "singing" together in interspecies choir is as ancient as anything human. Though whales are millions of years older than our species, and as such are our evolutionary elders, I sometimes wonder if they are waiting for us to catch up, especially in our communication skills. Beluga sonar is so sophisticated humans cannot mimic it, even with all our sound technologies. And their altruism, their close social bonds and gentleness, are far beyond us.

Some of our earliest human petroglyphs show human stick figures calling out to the great-souled whales. Since childhood I've been fascinated by whales, ever since I fell in love with the other Bible story that completely captured my imagination: Jonah and the whale.

The story of a man running away from God and his own gift of prophecy to be swallowed up by a great whale obsessed me. In my own child's paintings I would draw the belly of Jonah's whale, complete with chairs, table, and lamp. I decorated the whale's belly with starfish and nets the whale had sadly swallowed. Jonah also ate krill and plankton, I decided in my drawings, and he slept right under the blue whale's huge heart, which I'd read in Earth Science was the size of a Volkswagen. Humans could walk upright through a blue whale's arteries, I'd discovered from my science texts; beluga whales almost never breached. One day a scholarly fifth-grade teacher told me about a well-known Irish monk named Brendan in the early days of Christianity, when everyone still believed that animals had souls. It seems my namesake had no sanctuary for church services, until one Easter a huge white whale appeared so that the people could all come celebrate mass atop its mighty leviathan body.

These great creatures were another ark, I believed, but Jonah's whale was alive and living in the sea. It could carry prophets safely while they explored their own hearts and agreed to go back to dry land and do God's will. And what was God's will? Listening to the divine prophecy that lived inside a great whale. This belly of the whale was not unlike heaven, I reasoned with my child's logic—and wasn't the whale a divine womb to birth better human beings?

As I grew older and moved from myth and child's drawings, my obsession with whales only increased with my science studies and my own cetaceous encounters in the wild. And spiritually I am still happy to trace in my mother's Irish heritage a saint who so loved whales. Rarely have I identified with my mother's ancestors, those Irish and British immigrants who settled in West Virginia and Tennessee in the early 1700s. My spiritual as well as emotional lineage has always felt more centered in my father's people, mixed-blood tenant farmers with wilder, more instinctive bonds of family, land, and animals. My father jokes that by the time my mother's immigrant ancestors got to the New World on the *Mayflower*, his people were already here, waiting to greet them.

My mother was a town girl who married a farm boy, believing he would do well. And he did. Her Southern manners and Irish/British ancestry hint at a bloodline of schoolteachers, fervent female poets, and preachers who fiercely held to a spiritual tradition of Christianity long separate from the Earth and its animals (or farmers). My mother married a farmer's son who would spend his career working with forests and wildlife. She is much more comfortable sharing the side of my father who shines in political circles while she plays the Southern belle and society lady. At home, she will help tend to my father's horses and cows, she will find imaginative ways to cook venison or moose meat from his hunting trips, but she will do so by cheerful rote, much the way a ritual becomes, with service and over time, a chore. Animals have never been for my mother what they are for my father and me—companions, guides, and mentors.

Once, after my mother had read an article I'd written on the brief life and death of a whale calf born to Mauyak, the Point Defiance Zoo whale, she dialed me up posthaste, happening to get me when I was in the bathtub. My article had been titled "Beluga Baby: An Afterlife of Animals."

My mother always shouts in her deep Southern accent, as if to make up for the long distance between Seattle and Virginia. "Brenda Sue," she called out, and I could hear her shaking her head—that curly, often dyed-red coif that in her youth had been a mane of black ringlets, the envy of all her girlfriends. "I have a bone to pick with you!"

I smiled and sank deeper into the bubble bath, sighing, "Yes, mother. What bone?" As an adult I have put a continent's distance between myself and my family; my father visits me most often on his forest or wildlife business trips. I am always slightly shocked to see that my mother has actually aged. Her eyes are still that wild, wolf blue and her voice is still vibrant and enthusiastic, especially when she is in a good mood. She can be playful and bright as an untamed animal herself. Whenever I anticipate her descent into the depressive side of her mostly manic moods, though, I have trained myself to withdraw.

But that day of her phone call, I sensed that I did not need to withdraw from my mother. She was engaging me in a kind of cat-and-mouse game I knew well, even enjoyed—except I always remembered my mother was feral. She was, as her leopard-skin coat had always warned me in my childhood, unpredictable.

"A really big bone, honey," Mother said. "I was *shocked*, just shocked to read that whale article about you someday expecting to meet up with that beluga baby in your own afterlife! You don't really believe that, do you? You think there'll be animals with us *in heaven?*"

"Are you admitting me now into your heaven, even though I'm so backslid?" I decided to play with her. My more mystical take on spiritual things seems a direct assault on her citadel of fundamentalism. But what was in my adolescence a Cold War between us has become, as we both have aged, a more high-spirited dialogue in which I tease her and she wistfully proselytizes me.

"Well," she said doubtfully, "I surely do hope you'll be in heaven with us. But there certainly won't be any animals there. We never taught you that stuff about animals having souls. You know we don't believe in that!"

"But I do," I said quietly, shifting my tone, noticing that the water in my bath was going cold. I didn't want to be impolite by running more hot water. "I believe in an afterlife for animals, especially after watching that beluga mother mourn her newborn."

"What do you mean, 'mourn'?" my mother demanded.

But she was interested. My mother has always been a wonderful listener, if the story is, Scheherazade-like, imaginative enough to hold her interest. Unlike my father, who usually dominated every discussion to the point where we referred to dinner as "Father's lecture series," my mother has a deep appreciation for a good story, even if it goes directly against her own beliefs. There is still a childlike inquisitiveness in my mother that is captured whenever she encounters another world or people utterly unlike her. Even though she has spent many years volunteering with her Southern Baptist church to help convert visiting foreigners to Christianity, she is also very impressed by their unique cultures. As an adolescent I'd often find myself sitting at the supper table with East Indians, Japanese Buddhists, Balinese and Hawaiian animists, or South African Zulus. Ostensibly mother was supposed to be converting them to Christianity by way of socializing, but mostly she was happily cooking their foreign recipes and listening to their tales of far-off places with a delighted curiosity that is her best talent.

I have always loved telling my mother stories, and this time was no exception. The trick was to tell her about this beluga whale without offending her own spirituality. "Mother," I began, "do you remember when Mrs. Norris lost her baby, how she wouldn't come to church and she shut herself inside the house for such a long time that your Women's Missionary Union finally had to take church service to her?"

"Yes, yes," Mother said. "She was a mess. Could hardly feed herself, much less her husband and kids."

"Well, that's how Mauyak, the beluga whale, was when she lost her newborn—before he even took his first breath."

"Was he a real whale—I mean, born with all his organs and everything?"

"That's what was so heartbreaking, Mother," I told her. "That newborn male was perfect, a little gray calf who looked so healthy and alive at 125 pounds. But when he floated up to the surface of the water to take his first breath, nothing happened."

I'd seen it on the news and heard it firsthand from my friend Alan, who worked on staff with the belugas at Point Defiance. "Everyone was clapping and waiting for that baby beluga to breathe," Alan had told me. The whale calf floated like a gray buoy, bobbing up and down, his bright eye wide and wondering as he looked around at all the humans making that clapping noise with their hands. How long did it take for that dark, newborn eye to grow dim, moist, and finally fix in a death stare? Alan said nobody could believe it at first. Everyone stared at that beautiful, newborn eye, waiting for the beluga's blowhole to spout its first stream of moist breath. But the eye stayed open; the blowhole never did. Divers jumped into the beluga tank to try and resuscitate the newborn, even blowing human breath into that blowhole they held open with their hands. *Breathe, breathe!* they cried out to the baby whale. But he never did.

"Why couldn't that baby breathe?" my mother demanded. "He wasn't a stillborn, he was born alive. What happened?"

"Some think the zoo tank was too small and Mauyak, the mother, had to thrash around in labor in such a tiny space that all the corkscrewing damaged the newborn calf's blowhole valve. It was broken." I paused, then told her, "You know, in the wild about half of beluga calves die."

"Why?"

"Well, they think it's because there are so many toxins in the oceans that get stored in the whales' blubber. In Canada when a beluga whale carcass washes ashore it has to be buried as toxic waste because it is so full of heavy metals and poisons from the ocean. When the mothers nurse their firstborn calves, they actually purge themselves of all these toxins. The poisons flow into their milk and the calves nurse on those toxins and die."

"That's terrible," my mother said in an unusually soft voice. "That's terrible to nurse on poison, just trying to eat and survive."

Never one for much empathy, my mother still surprises her children at times with the powers of her imagination. Sometimes she identifies with others, even animals, if their story is dramatic and compelling enough. But I was not looking for empathy from my mother in telling her the story of the newborn beluga; I wasn't even looking for acceptance or to persuade her to my spiritual point of view. I was simply trying to connect Mauyak's story with her own life and mine. Because it is a connection that, once lost, can be restored. And perhaps in a way, all of my animal stories are about restoring that connection, just as those zoo trainers instinctively tried to breathe life back into another animal, never hesitating because they were different species.

"What was really terrible was what happened after the death," I said.

"Well?" Mother prompted. "What happened? Tell me!"

And between us, mother and child, I felt a common ground that is rare and always a bit of a miracle in my family life. "You know, Mother," I began slowly, "whales will mourn their lost newborns like this: they carry their little corpses for a long time, until they disintegrate—that's how long they mourn."

Rarely have I seen my own mother mourn. Diagnosed bipolar, my mother's mostly manic swings can range from great, good fun to frightening descents into migraines and dark moods. And yet those very extremes make her more mesmerizing than most mothers. How many mothers have a complete electric train set at the age of 70? If she were one of my father's beloved, high-spirited horses, she would be called "hot-blooded." My mother is like the weather, and I have always been held in thrall to storms. Yet I cannot remember witnessing in her what felt to me like authentic grief. She cycles through moods so quickly and mysteriously that often she is lost to those of us who love her the most. So it is we who mourn my mother, because we cannot follow or fathom her inner weather.

But that day when I told her the story of the beluga mother and newborn, she stayed with me, at least for a while.

"Until they disintegrate?" she asked with a dismay that was not disgust. "That's a long time."

"A long, long time," I breathed. "Even in the wild, the whales will carry these little corpses. Isn't that grief?"

There was absolute silence that struck me as sad and ironic. Here I was asking my mother about grief—she who had been in a cyclical despair all her life. But I wondered if she ever felt the release of true grief. I had witnessed more grief in that mother beluga than I ever had in my own mother.

When my friend Alan called me to the zoo, he'd said, "Mauyak doesn't trust any of us staff who were there at her calf's death. And maybe she's right about that. You know, they decided at last to just take the newborn away from her. But Mauyak was so distressed that the zookeepers decided to ease her mourning with a surrogate calf. So they replaced the corpse with a rubber buoy that Mauyak can carry around while she lets go of her grief."

When I visited Mauyak there was no mistaking her grief. Slowly she swam the small circumference of the cement tank, her gleaming white forehead, or melon, all but hidden by an orange rubber ball. She pushed this buoy around the pool, using her melon to nudge the buoy as if it were a baby she were trying to keep afloat, instinctively trying to bring her calf to the surface to take that first breath. Like Sisyphus pushing a stone uphill only to have that boulder roll back down, Mauyak kept carrying that surrogate corpse around and around.

"She hasn't let go of that rubber ball since she lost her newborn,"

Alan told me as we both watched Mauyak from the side of her small pool. We were behind the exhibit where Mauyak's mate Inuk and the smaller Shikku swam in another tank, the one with the underground glass wall lined with zoo-goers screaming and tapping on the glass. "We've kept Mauyak away from the public," Alan continued, "because even the kids can tell there's something wrong with her. When we tell the children that Mauyak lost her baby, they get real quiet and say things like 'That baby's in heaven now,' or 'She's just so sad, isn't she?' They really understand her need to be alone now."

"How is she expressing her grief?" I asked, aware that Mauyak was swimming closer to us, but keeping a wary distance. She seemed to be curious about me, but careful not to approach Alan.

"She's not making eye contact with any of us. You know, whales use their eyes for a lot of their social interaction. That, and touch." He fell quiet and seemed troubled. He did not stretch out his hand to summon this whale with whom he'd worked for years. Instead he stood awkwardly with his arms as if plastered to his side.

"Do you initiate touch?" I asked. "Or will whales see that as a sign of dominance, like dolphins do?"

"Usually the belugas will come alongside and use their melons to actually lift our hands up, like cats seeking to be stroked. They love to be touched. Whale skin is at least twenty times as sensitive as our own. In the wild whales will embrace each other, belly to belly, and corkscrew through the water like a sensual ballet." He paused, then took up in a strained voice. "Mauyak isn't asking for us to touch her. She's lost trust in us, thinks we stole her baby from her."

"Do you think she knows her baby died right after birth?"

"She knows," he said simply. "She knows everything." Then he shrugged and stepped back away, leaving me alone beside the pool. "Maybe she'll come to you," he sighed. "She needs interaction, especially when she's so sad. We're worried about her."

Suddenly Mauyak raised her luminous body half out of the water and with a powerful thrust of her tail flukes she was across the pool and at the wooden platform that floated level with the water. Alan whispered for me to step forward onto the platform to meet Mauyak. My feet sloshing on the watery platform, I knelt down, balancing with one hand behind me, while I held my other hand outstretched. In one sleek movement, Mauyak's forehead slipped beneath my palm and I felt that familiar sensation of cetacean skin. It is as cool and smooth as raw silk, but so scintillant one can almost hear the sensitive vibrations along skin that feels like the rind of a honeydew melon. Then I was astonished. Mauyak's forehead began pulsing and actually grew larger beneath my hand, undulating like a belly dancer's strong-muscled stomach. Open-mouthed, I looked back at Alan and almost lost my balance. "It's . . . it's her head . . . it's moving, getting bigger and smaller all at once."

"Yes, yes," Alan called, "see how her melon is rounded?" I watched the beluga's luminous forehead visibly balloon out and flatten in that eerie pulsing against my palm. "We figure it has something to do with their sonar."

My open hand vibrated as if it were resting against a throbbing stereo speaker. It felt so alive, like encountering an alien intelligence resounding in my open hand, tingling up my arms, and actually singing along my bare skin. I could even feel Mauyak's high-frequency echolocation ricocheting inside my ribs and vibrating along my jawbone.

From my years of swimming with dolphins, both captive and in the wild, I well recognized the throb and tingle of cetacean sonar; what I'd never felt before was this burst of echolocation sounding from her skin right through my hand. Because it was ultrasound, I couldn't hear it, but my open hand heard it so loud, I wondered if the strength of it might shatter the bones of my hand. Then Mauyak let out a series of high-pitched blips and whistles like someone letting helium out of a balloon.

"Now." Alan coached, keeping his distance behind me. He seemed very pleased. Later he would tell me it was some of the first contact Mauyak had made with humans after the death of her newborn. "Let her take your hand in her mouth. Don't be afraid."

I was not afraid. I was in a state of complete surrender and wonder, my palm still singing with sound. It didn't occur to me at the time that I was offering my arm to a two-thousand-pound sea monster who could easily chomp on my hand and draw me to a watery death. All I felt was a deep sense of gratitude for this creature who honored me with her trust. After all, why should she trust humans? We had captured her, stolen her from her family and the wild arctic waters of her home; we'd denied her a territory and taken her newborn from her to substitute that pathetic rubber buoy. Why reach out to me or any of my kind?

"Go ahead," Alan said softly. "Lay your palm against her tongue and let her taste you."

Carefully I placed my palm inside Mauyak's gaping-wide mouth, and in a delicate movement not unlike suckling, she closed her jaw so that from fingers to forearm I was enveloped inside her mouth, my palm resting against her huge tongue, which was shockingly soft, like baby skin. Surrounding my hand was the semicircle row of tiny teeth, between which were tucked fragments of fishbone and herring. She smelled of the sea, of salt and fish, and when she held my hand, it felt like she had the whole world of me inside her body. Sensations on the soft underside of my palm told me there was something else extraordinary going on—something I'd never felt before.

"She's sounding you," Alan called out, as if to answer my unspoken question. "That's the way she decides just what kind of human you are."

It was as if Mauyak was taking a reading of my very soul—that's how deep her tactile scrutiny of tongue and echolocation felt. I found myself weeping, tears streaming down my face. Perhaps I was also registering her heartbreak in my open hand. This was real mothering and this was true grief. And here was a mother's grief.

Mauyak's deep, black eye caught mine and then very slowly she began to close her eye until it was half-open. Its expression seemed calm, as if we two were simply resting with one another. I'd read somewhere that when an animal blinks, one way to establish contact is to return the blink, so I half-lidded and finally closed my own eyes. Sightless, I was suddenly much more aware of my body. My outstretched arm felt endless, a physical bridge between mammal kin, as Mauyak's soft tongue clasped my palm. I was swallowed whole inside her and with my eyes closed, the darkness seemed to expand and I was back inside some great belly-womb where there was no time, only the watery pulse of my own surrounding sea-placenta. I felt dizzy and tottered on the dock, but Mauyak held and balanced me. I felt so small and encircled by a body so much greater than my own, by a mammal so much more ancient than my own species, by a being so much calmer and more conscious than any human I'd ever known. At last I knew what Jonah knew.

"She's mothering you," Alan whispered. "She has a need to nurture now after all she's lost. Just let her."

And I did. I let this great, brokenhearted whale mother me. I felt safer like this, eyes closed, arm and being swallowed up by a great whale's mouth and belly, than I ever felt in my own mother's unpredictable arms. Here in this whole world of a womb, I felt accepted and nourished.

Mauyak sang out a soft whistle through her blowhole and my eyelids involuntarily flew open. She was gazing steadily at me, her black eye wide open, so large I could almost see my own reflection. And I realized that this was profoundly familiar, this mirror of myself in an animal's gaze. I remembered all those years beneath the benevolent glass eyes of the deer faces. But this animal was hugely alive and her scrutiny was soul-searching. She was looking back at me. She was not the simple glass animal eye of my infancy; she was not a documentary video or a face studied through field glasses. Here was a wild animal watching me as steadily as I watched her. This was a two-way vision, and I only hoped I was equal to it.

"I know," I found myself whispering to this huge mother whale, "I know."

What I knew that day when a whale held the whole of me with her eye, in her mouth, as if I were deep within her recently abandoned belly, was that I was not alone here on this Earth. That I was connected to a larger kinship system than I'd ever really understood physically. Spiritually, since childhood, I'd felt a bond with other animals. But now I understood that my very body was connected to these other creatures by a mammal umbilical cord: we were warm-blooded, we breathed air, we nursed our young, we were both born from the primal seas.

Very slowly Mauyak's mouth opened and she raised her gleaming white forehead to rest my palm on the dock. It was a delicate movement and my hand still tingled, but not with the cold. It vibrated with her soundings and warm tongue. She turned on her side, her eye still holding mine. We gazed at each other for what seemed a very long time. Perhaps it was as simple as the fact that this whale needed a child and I needed a mother. But I think there was something else going on during that long exchange. And so did Alan.

"Whales want to connect," he said softly. "It's what they do best—so much better sometimes than humans." He managed a faint smile at Mauyak, who broke contact with me to glance briefly at him then swim back to her rubber buoy. "She can't connect to a rubber ball," he finished. We both stood by the side of the tank and watched Mauyak again begin her mournful circles, nudging the bright, lifeless rubber buoy. "She would have made a wonderful mother," Alan breathed.

"She *is* a wonderful mother," I said softly and placed my palm one last time atop her blazing white forehead, which pulsed again as she squeaked out bursts of sea-canary song. Her song seemed suddenly lighthearted and wild, echoing against my hand. And I found myself laughing out loud, even amid all the sorrow. As I laughed, Mauyak lifted my hand higher and closed her eyes as if in pleasure, singing her ultrasonic arpeggios.

Alan said it was the first sign Mauyak had shown since her calf died of her once characteristic deep playfulness. A friend of mine snapped a photo at that last moment when Mauyak opened her great mouth to sing. In the photo Mauyak's eye is closed and her rostrum is high under my hand; her expression is engaging and exuberant. In the photo the whale and woman in her yellow rain slicker look locked in an inter-species duet. Between the two there is a bridge, not only of human hand and whale melon-mind, but also of camaraderie and care. Anyone looking at this photo without knowing the whale is mourning a lost calf and the woman a lost mother would believe these two are cele-brating a bond even they cannot understand or name. It doesn't usually happen in captivity, but in the wild, a whale will mother another not her own. It is what happens when a human recognizes kin not her own species.

The woman in her yellow slicker, her silver hair tousled by Northwest wind and drizzle, leans far over the aquarium tank, so far she is almost in the water with the whale, who has also come far out of herself for this moment, far away from her lethargy and grief, from the burden of carrying the unborn and unburied buoy that she knows is not her own. Far out of themselves, they meet at someplace between species in this moment of acceptance and quiet rapture.

Neither whale nor woman suspect what is to come: between Mauyak's first calf's death in 1992 and 1999, she will give birth to three more calves, all of whom will die at birth. Some of the local marine mammal biologists will comment that perhaps the belugas have pur-posely drowned offspring to keep them from a life in captivity, because the tank is already too small. These biologists will say that all across America in other aquarium breeding programs, the story will be the same—a mortality rate of 65 percent among beluga births. By 1999, 11 out of 17 captive calves will die in this country, leading many to wonder about the ethics of such an aggressive captive breeding program among the 33 belugas now in aquariums in the United States.

The belugas are carted around from city to city by plane and truck, causing the whales undue stress and perhaps even sterility. "This transport involves carrying around an animal that weighs thousands of pounds," Toni Frohoff, who has a Ph.D. in marine mammal biology, will tell me. "The possibility for injury is high. You've got physiological stress as well as being subjected to loud noises, uncomfortable temperatures. It's a dangerous business, this beluga breeding. And believe me, it is a business."

Officially echoing Frohoff's dismay, Dr. Naomi Rose of the Humane Society of the United States would in 1999 protest that captive beluga programs are not good for the animals. "They're hauled off in a truck, put into an airplane—all of that is incredibly stressful for them and not in any way natural. Their bodies are not equipped for them to be out of the water for that long." Rose would also point out the dismal statistics accompanying these breeding programs. "Six successful births in thirty years, and most die within minutes of birth or are stillborn. Pregnancies are aborted or they miscarry. This is obviously not normal."

An article in the *Tacoma Tribune* in February 1999 exploring the increasing controversy over captive beluga breeding programs would cite evidence from two Canadian researchers at Ontario Veterinary College. Their 1987 study showed that "when belugas are stressed, thyroid hormones drop. Those hormones regulate metabolism and interact with other endocrine systems to control tissue growth and reproductive functions. Stressful events include capture and handling."

In 1994, after Mauyak had lost two calves at Point Defiance, the zoo closed their breeding program. I believed that Mauyak might be left in peace for a while. But that same year, she and her sweet mate Inuk would be hoisted from their tank in the middle of the night and air-lifted to Chicago's Shedd Aquarium for a more aggressive breeding pro-gram. There Mauyak would quickly became pregnant again and again would lose her baby after long gestation—her fourth calf lost.

If I had known that day in 1992 when I leaned far out across the concrete barrier to rest my hand on Mauyak's forehead what I know today, I would have done everything in my small power to protest the relentless breeding of this beautiful beluga, a mother four times over who still had no calves. I would have visited her more often and told her story more vigorously. But the day that photo was snapped I believed that Mauyak would heal from her loss, that she might be allowed to rest and find solace in her male and female companions, so cloistered together in that small tank.

—

AND WHEN MY mother called to find me floating in my own bathtub I did not tell her that, for a wild beluga, living out her days in captivity would be like me living inside my own bathtub all my life. I never told my own mother about giving a grieving whale my hand and in return feeling both her sadness and my own. I didn't tell my own mother that we also shared an inexplicable joy in our meeting. Nor did I say that I'd discovered that Mauyak had been first captured with two other belugas in Hudson Bay, in Manitoba, Canada—since Mother well knew that a branch of my father's family was once part of the Hudson Bay Company. She certainly wouldn't understand me claiming Mauyak as a distant mammal relative.

But back in 1992, when Mauyak had just lost her very first calf and I was trying to speak my mother's Biblical language to engage her in this whale's story, I wasn't yet having nightmares of belugas dying in captivity. I was still freshly elated from my meeting with Mauyak and the whale's tenderness at taking my hand, the whole world of me, in her great self.

"Mom," I tried to explain, "Do you remember that Jonah and the whale story you used to read us all the time?"

"Oh, yes," her voice was excited. She is always so happy when I remember my Bible stories. "It was always your favorite—that and Noah's ark."

"Well, that mother beluga I met after she lost her baby—she was like Jonah's whale, the whale who took him to the place God wanted him to be all along."

My mother was quiet suddenly, suspicious of where I might be taking her with my story. "What do you mean?" she asked, and there it was, all the distance of different beliefs between us—a whole continent, a lifetime.

I knew better than to push her into territories outside her chosen dogma, so I simply said, "Well, that whale was God's will, wasn't it?"

She hesitated, then tentatively agreed: "Yes."

"All I'm saying is that in the Bible a whale took an unwilling prophet into her belly and kept him safe until he could be delivered up again on dry land. So that whale was like God's way of working in the world, of teaching Jonah . . ."

"Jonah's whale is just a symbol, honey," Mother interrupted, and I could tell she wanted to get off the phone. This is rare; usually I am the one to disconnect. Again I could hear her shaking her head, those eyes bright with bewilderment. "Sometimes I think you believe that God is some kind of whale!"

"Well, Mom," I said, "God does work in mysterious ways . . ."

". . . His wonders to reveal," she finished, delighted that I could remember a Bible verse. "Love you, honey. And God does, too."

Within the next several weeks I received a number of religious tracts and articles from my mother, well underlined with pink highlighter. But I also got a very unusual present, one I proudly set in my study next to another gift my mother has sent me that I love. In her hasty, high-spirited scrawl, Mother wrote, "Found this and thought you might like it back now. Lovingly, Mom." It's the only writing my mother ever kept from my childhood. A creased and worn-out sheet of old Jumbo tablet paper with my almost illegible third-grade cursive corrected by a teacher's red pencil:

January 22, 1959
Revere Beach, Massachusetts
A Description

I am thinking of a horse. I like a horse better than any animal though would like to pick a few other. I like the horse the best. I like the horse because they are a well-natured thing. They also have been used very much in the old days for cabs or work or for driving people somewhere and for just plan feld work or for races and lots of other things. They are good for people and good for you. They will love you if you love them and are willing to do every thing. You must be used to them and not treat them bad. There is lots of bad horses because when they were little they were treated very bad from driving people or from mean men that treat them very very meanly. Now you know why I fell sorry for horses and like them the best.

I keep this little school composition in my study to remind me of where I've come from and where I intend to go in my life with other animals. It's framed and sits atop a bookshelf, right next to the other gift from my mother—a beautiful, small stuffed bear made out of real fur, cut from her own long-loved leopard-skin coat.

And next to that leopard-skin bear is a photo of a woman in a yellow slicker with a beluga named Mauyak. Not a day goes by that I don't gaze up at that photograph of myself with my hand on Mauyak's luminous forehead. Not a day passes that I don't wonder about her life now.

I no longer visit the belugas down at Point Defiance Zoo. They are forlorn strangers who have never known the wild. Born in captivity at Sea World in Texas, these two belugas, Turner and Beethoven, were raised in the San Diego Zoo and are now at Point Defiance. But for how long? And I wonder about Mauyak's existence at the Shedd Aquarium. I imagine her being gazed at through glass walls by throngs of adoring zoo visitors. Do the admirers know that this whale has lost four calves in her short life? Like Smokey Bear who was shunned by a fickle public when he did not breed with Goldie, is Mauyak's future clouded if she is not considered by zoo officials a good breeder?

And what exactly is the difference between a good mother, as Mauyak certainly proved herself to be as she mourned her first calf, as she mothered me, and a good breeder? I wonder where Mauyak will end up next and what her perceptions must be of humans who shunt her around from tank to tank, insistent that she keep producing an offspring.

Is Mauyak still as gentle and open-hearted as she was with me all those years ago after the death of her first little one? Has grief darkened her great spirit? The last I heard of Mauyak and her mate Inuk was that they were scheduled to be moved on to New York City in early 1999. But their trip was aborted after weather and mechanical problems. According to news reports, Mauyak and Inuk waited for six hours at O'Hare airport in Chicago for transport trucks before at last being returned to their tank at Shedd Aquarium. Will they be moved again? Where?

By scanning the Internet for news of Mauyak I discovered that in July 2000 she gave birth to a male calf named Qannik, which means "Snowflake" in Inuit, who is, as of this fall, still surviving. So at long last, at eighteen, Mauyak is a mother. Often I go online to watch live-camera images of Mauyak and her new son in Chicago's Shedd Aquarium. Is she well and the grief of losing so many calves now eased?

One day I hope to visit Mauyak again and to pay my respects. To express my sorrow that her captive life has been further marred by loss and transience, to offer hope that her son will survive alongside her. For this most sweet and sociable of whales, I would wish a better fate, and that the world might one day mother her as tenderly as she did me.

ELEVEN

WOLF SUMMITS

ALASKA, 1993

I N THE EARLY morning darkness of the Alaska land, where winter
daylight waits until nearly noon to show its slight glow, my father
and I arrived at the Fairbanks ice rink to attend the January 1993 Wolf
Summit. We walked a plowed path between six-foot snowbanks and
picketers carrying signs: "Wolf management, not wolf worship"; "Iraq—
Want some wolves?"; "Eco-Nazis go home!!" Word had gone out when
the then-governor of Alaska, Walter Hickel, had first called this so-called
summit that Alaskans who favored aerial wolf killing should show up at
the summit en masse. Among the crowd, but far fewer in number, were
the signs "Don't kill the wolves on my public land," "Respect the wolf!"
and, attached to one sled dog, "The wolf is my sister."

My father and I had shared a ride from the hotel with an Alaska
Board of Game member, a veterinarian who was in favor of wolf control. Amid the yelling crowd, even he seemed awestruck, startled by the
media glare and the Alaskans' feisty resistance to control, wolf or otherwise. "It's a circus," he said, "not a summit."

My father and this man hastened into the summit, but I decided to stay outside a while and listen to the protesters. I was wearing two hats: first I was covering the Wolf Summit as a freelance journalist for the *Seattle Times*; second, and no less important, I was here at my father's persistent invitation. He was officially attending the summit as an impartial observer in his role as executive vice president of the International Association of Fish and Wildlife Agencies—a job he'd taken after retiring as chief of the U.S. Forest Service.

"The only thing I like about retirement is more time with my horses," he'd told me when he first announced his decision to return to work. None of his children had believed he would last long as a retiree. For several months he'd tinkered with his personal computer and consulted on wildlife management and forest issues around the world. But he was not content to sit at home, even though it did mean he could ride and groom and fuss over his two Tennessee Walkers and few cows.

The month before the summit, when I'd read about Governor Hickel's plan to run wolves down and shoot them from airplanes, I'd done some research and written an article against wolf control titled "Wolves, Wild Women and Wild Men." At that time Clarissa Pinkola-Estes's bestseller *Women Who Run with the Wolves* was drawing parallels between wolves and humans.

In my article I'd voiced concern that so many women identified with the wolf in their inner territories but took no action in the real world to help preserve wolves in the wilderness. After all, without the real wolf in our world, it wouldn't matter if we had symbolic wolves running through our dreams.

"Okay, Dad," I told him, "I'll meet you in Alaska. I've always wanted to see the Far North."

"We'll have fun," he said, pleased, "though I doubt we'll see any wolves—just a lot of political sheep dressed up in wolves' clothing."

MY FATHER WAS right. At the summit, many of these wolf-control proponents were dressed head-to-toe in bear, fox, or wolf skins and were passing out fluorescent orange armbands to crowds already clothed in bright orange hunting vests and hats. The crowd was angry, my face chafed and frozen. In my ankle-length down parka I was shivering against the subzero arctic temperature, yet I could almost feel the heat of the angry crowd.

A bearded man wearing an entire wolf skin—its sleek, glossy snout atop his head, its pelt fully embracing his back—singled me out and started lecturing, seemingly from within the animal: "You people from the Lower Forty-Eight just don't understand that we've got plenty of wolves up here. What we don't have is enough caribou. And if we let you goddamn eco-terrorists take over our state, we won't have any game to eat at all!"

"I eat game," I told him, mesmerized by the powerful presence of his wolf-head hat, "sometimes."

"Over here!" a man in buckskin pants and wolf-fur parka commanded me. "Let me tell you the real story of this summit: it's just the governor's shill game. A setup. Wolf traps are already bought. This is just a publicity stunt for media folks like you who believe you have any say in what Alaskans want for Alaska!"

I kept my distance from the angry man, but I felt a nagging despair and suspicion that he was telling the truth. And if this summit was a sham, then why was I here? Following my father's invitation and a moral sense that it was wrong to shoot wolves after our country's history of maligning and murdering them, I had only recently recognized any connection between my work with whales and this new territory of wolves. In the Seattle airport bound for Fairbanks I'd thumbed idly through a book, *People of the Totem: Indians of the Pacific Northwest.* I read that the Nootka Indians on the Pacific coast off Canada, living just north of Washington's Makah tribe, believed that when the orcas went walking on land, they did so as wolves.

So this was the connection, the mythical and historical lead that I was intuitively tracking. As I moved now through the Wolf Summit crowd, I realized with growing uneasiness that I was the only woman among these fur-clad hunters. This was not the moment to remember the chilling statistics: Alaska leads the nation in per capita incidence of forcible rape; a white woman has 1.5 times the chance of being a homicide victim here than elsewhere in the country. For Native Americans, the statistics of murder and rape are even higher.

Clicking off my tape recorder and hiding it in my parka, I tried to make my way through the throngs into the summit, which was already underway. Shivering almost uncontrollably now, I realized I did not want to be here, even at my father's invitation, even to help the wolves. I was freezing and I was scared.

My eyes scanned the angry crowd, looking for my father. But I couldn't find him. Inside the ice rink that served as our auditorium, a thousand hunters in the bleachers booed and hissed at the Defenders of Wildlife speakers, who advocated protecting wild wolves from aerial shooting, trapping, and other forms of wolf control. And even though I was still afraid of the angry hunters, I could also feel my own fear mirrored in these men. Clearly they believed themselves victims, terrorized by outsiders who would change their lives and traditions.

Already the statistics, if not the Board of Game policies, were against them: only 10 percent of the U.S. population were hunters; in an independent poll, 80 percent of Alaskans described themselves as "non-consumptive wildlife supporters." On the issue of aerial shooing, 66 percent of Alaskans were opposed. And yet the Board of Game was overriding this public outcry in its continuing insistence on wolf control. What I was witnessing at this Wolf Summit were vestiges of the nineteenth-century frontier, stuck in time while the rest of the world moved toward more enlightened wildlife conservation. I wasn't surprised to learn that in other states, the agencies that oversee wildlife are called "Fish and Wildlife," whereas in Alaska the Department of "Fish and Game" reigns supreme. Made up mostly of hunters and trapping families, the Board of Game has a history of managing wildlife with a single-minded, pro-hunting bias.

As I circled the cavernous rink with its vast bleachers, I was reminded that this sports arena betrayed the bottom line: participants would not be arguing the well-being of wildlife so much as preserving a blood sport.

A hundred or so of us press and speakers sat at long, folding tables full of thick media kits and programs. As I took my seat I realized with a shiver that in this huge hockey stadium we were sitting directly on the ice. Between my frigid boots and the dense ice was only a thin layer of plastic. I flipped on my tape recorder and tuned in to the procession of summit speakers.

My impressions outside the rink were confirmed inside: about 90 percent of the summit's official attendees were male. Of the thirty or so people who were slated to speak, all but three were male. And support for killing wolves seemed nearly unanimous in this rowdy stadium. Whenever a speaker argued against wolf control, the bleachers thundered with the thick boots of protesters. The atmosphere was indeed like a sports event, and the wolf had few fans.

All day long, biologists and wildlife managers offered evidence, pro and con, on wolf control. Their pointers and slides and graphs on predator-prey relationships never addressed the deepest bond—the intimate territory, psychological, physical, and spiritual, we share with wolves.

When Governor Hickel had first called for this summit, fending off a tourism boycott threatened when the Board of Game approved plans for a wolf-control program, he had made headlines by saying "nature should not be allowed to run wild." The Board of Game had designed a plan to decrease the wolf population with the hope of ensuring an abundance of its prey, caribou and moose—also favorite prey of human hunters. What was causing the biggest outcry was the Board of Game plan authorizing Department of Fish and Game personnel to shoot wolves from helicopters and airplanes. In addition, private citizens with the appropriate licenses would be allowed to track the animals from the air, as long as they landed before shooting them.

Inside that ice rink the rhetoric was low-key, the scientific dialect of population densities and distribution, of "predator pits" and prey collapse, of ungulates (hoofed mammals, such as caribou and moose) and habitat conservation. It was accompanied by the language of the wildlife managers, who spoke of "harvesting the wolves" and "caribou calf crops." In contrast to the drone from the podium, the bleachers were alive and boisterous, with boos and catcalls whenever Defenders of Wildlife or Alaska Wildlife Alliance speakers took their turn to argue that the wolf-control program was not sound science. They asserted that the predator-prey relationship between wolves and moose or caribou is still not understood well enough for our human intervention, and we cannot manage what we do not understand. They also argued that state-supported wolf controls were costly, based on inaccurate and overestimated wolf populations, and defied state, national, and international demands to stop all wolf control and reconsider "nonconsumptive relationships" with other species.

As I listened to the men from the state and federal wildlife agencies, I perceived beneath their language of "control" and "lethal management" and "sustainable yield" a subtext. Since the Middle Ages, our European traditions have trained us to fear the wolf as evil. Our human need to control nature for our own purposes comes from some ancient, at times religious, terror of the "chaotic" and "destructive" animals in the world around us. It's as if some part of our psyche is still entrenched in the worldview that we are tiny humans, victimized by a brutal, uncaring natural environment. We try to control what we believe is out of control—whether it's nature or her wild creatures.

When Renee Askins of the Wolf Fund made a poignant appeal to stop the hunting, she was met with raucous catcalls and hisses. "We have engaged in a holocaust against the wild wolves," Askins said.

"Since Europeans came to this country, almost two million wolves have been killed." The wolf's territory had shrunk from our North American continent to Alaska and just a few other states, Askins noted. "Here in Alaska," she warned, "the wolves are making their last stand."

As Askins concluded her passionate case for wolf reintroduction, it seemed the bleacher crowd might riot. When an Alaska Wildlife Alliance speaker took the podium he was greeted with vigorous hisses and boos. "There's a saying here in Alaska," a Defenders of Wildlife speaker said, " 'What makes the deer so fast? The wolf's tooth.' The proper predator-prey relationship needs the balance of both caribou and wolf. Humans are not the balance. Wolves are." At this the bleachers erupted in shouts and obscenities as the furious chorus drowned out the speakers' words.

I held my tape recorder up high to record the chaos as I glimpsed plainclothes cops taking up their stations by the ice rink's exit. At any moment I expected a gunshot to ring out, and I was ready to duck. A rumbling in the rink rose as again the thunder of winter boots beat against bleachers.

Hunkering down as if expecting a blow, I found myself instinctively reaching into my book bag to touch a familiar talisman that had long protected me: the fierce wolf teeth of my Navajo necklace. I closed my eyes and felt the wolf's sharp fangs in my palm. For just a moment I held the memory of gazing up at the deer who stood guard above my crib, the deer who roamed a forest without wolves. Had they slowed down without wolves, had the very shape of their spines gone slack and slow without the evolutionary fit of wolf teeth?

As I held my wolf necklace under the table, I felt a light hand on my back and whirled around, expecting to face a hostile stranger. Instead, it was a woman I recognized from a state agency. She was dressed demurely in a tailored suit and scarf, perhaps so she would not stand out as an easy target among all the men there. I noted she wore intricate silver whale earrings and I reckoned her age as fifty.

Conspiratorially she whispered to me as she handed me a small packet of clippings, "I saw your orca earrings. I just hope you're sympathetic to the wolf." When I nodded, she continued, "I can't go on record with this because I'd lose my job in wildlife management, but you should really research the link between orcas and wolves. Like humans, wolves and orcas are both top predators, you know. And top predators are indicators of the health of any ecosystem. Look at the dwindling prey populations for all us top predators. Start from the bottom of the food chain and go up."

"Explain it to me, will you?" I asked.

"Well, the orcas' desperate feeding patterns show us that something is really wrong and everything's out of balance from the bottom up in the predator-prey relationship," she said. Then she showed me recent studies that revealed that wolf predation is *not* the determining factor in stabilizing ungulate populations. "We have overfished, overhunted, and overkilled," the state agent whispered. "The scary thing is that we really don't know what we're doing! Now we're trying to fix it by killing the other top predators, like the wolves. What next? Will we start shooting orcas to compete for fish?" She sighed and concluded, "Forget wolf control! How about a little self-control?"

In a flash I saw the native myth of orcas shape-shifting into wolves behind the biology of this woman's words. I saw orcas practically beaching themselves on shores to search for once-plentiful prey; I saw caribou populations dwindling and wolves going hungry. Here was the ancient myth acted out: orcas were walking on land, and they were starving just like wolves.

This was more than a myth. This was disturbing prophecy. Six years after this summit, the orca-wolf connection would no longer be just a hushed-up Alaska story that one woman risked her state job to detail to a reporter. News of the orcas' desperate search for food and the crash of their intricately interconnected food chain, which stretches from mussels and starfish to kelp forest, would make headlines as far away as the

New York Times. In their Science section on January 5, 1999, in an article titled "A Mysterious Tear in the Web of Life," *Times* reporter William K. Stevens explores this deeply disturbing fissure in the ecosystem. First there was the crash in herring and pollack from overfishing and climatic changes, which led to a dive in the population of sea lions and seals, who fed on those fish. The decline in sea lions and seals forced the orcas to seek other prey in strange, shallow waters, where they ended eons of peaceful coexistence with sea otters. The otter population plunged by 90 percent; in some areas, otters simply vanished. Once the sea otters disappeared, the kelp forests could no longer sustain the diverse species dependent on them, because the sea urchins, the usual prey of sea otters, were now so abundant they deforested the kelp. Since kelp forests are the mainstay of marine life, this deforestation affects mussels, fish, ducks, gulls, bald eagles—all the way back up the food chain to sea otters, sea lions, and orcas, already in trouble. Scientists and government biologists have no idea how to repair this terrible tear in the web of marine life.

In the late fall of 1999, Canada was the first nation to do something about the starving orcas by officially declaring their orcas an endangered species. New research has revealed that the orca populations in the far Northwest, off the coasts of Washington and British Columbia, are the most heavily contaminated marine mammals in the world—saturated with toxic PCBs from the waters. Even though these damaging chemicals were banned in Canada and the United States in the 1970s, it will take decades, perhaps even centuries, for the foul effects of these pollutants to disappear—if they ever do. Meanwhile, PCBs are still pouring into the world's waters from industrializing nations.

Northwesterners were stunned to discover in the winter of 2000 that our beloved and much-studied resident orca pods in Washington's Puget Sound had been documented hunting for salmon as far south as Montery Bay in California. Before this unexpected sighting, our orca pods had never been known to travel even as far south as Oregon. But it has turned out just the way the state agency woman predicted at the 1993 Wolf Summit: Chinook salmon populations are plummeting, and the orcas must now live off their own blubber or starve. Subsisting off their own PCB-saturated body fat, the orcas fall prey to disease brought on by these endocrine-disrupting pollutants. Since 1996 the southern orca populations have fallen by 15 percent, a fact so disturbing that some researchers wonder if Puget Sound orcas—proud symbol of the Northwest—will even return to our waters.

At the 1993 Wolf Summit, after the woman from the state agency disappeared, I felt moved by her courage and what would turn out to be a troubling prophecy. I was also heartened by the prospect of the next speakers to take the podium. There were speeches from the National Audubon Society and Greenpeace, as well as Defenders of Wildlife, all of whom passionately pleaded against wolf control, and especially aerial shooting.

As I diligently scribbled notes, I noticed my father had entered and taken up his official seat right behind me. He smiled and stamped his boots on the ice rink, making a mock shiver. I nodded and we exchanged a smile. Listening to the pro-and-con speakers, I'd feel my father watching me with his tireless scrutiny—the way a hunter will sit all day behind a blind waiting for the wild animal to come.

I felt a deep affection for my father at that moment, as well as a sense of shared destiny. We had come full circle since those early days in the forest when he had assured me that there was no more Big Bad Wolf in our wilderness home. One of my friends had told me before I'd left for this summit, "The forest and the wildlife, these are the great loves of yours and your father's life, aren't they? It makes sense you might grow up in his footsteps and help him save wildlife. Just think, in the next generation, our kids might hear wild wolves howling again in the national forests."

My father, my family trees, our shared forest and all its wildlife—this is the family and the collective legacy that I carry and try to reconcile.

That first night of the Wolf Summit, my father asked me to join him with some Board of Game and U.S. Fish and Wildlife Service cronies at a local hangout. "You might get further if you took off your press badge," he whispered as I joined him and his buddies.

Without my press badge, and keeping very quiet as the men talked of "wolf harvests" and fluctuating caribou populations, I realized the men thought of me simply as "Max's daughter," the way his hunting buddies once accepted me on their trips. I was fascinated to hear their sense of authority and control over the natural world. It was like watching these wildlife managers play poker with the fates of other species.

One wildlife manager at our lunch table sipped his beer thoughtfully and when asked what he was mulling over, he shook his head in dismay. "You know," he said, "the way that Wolf Fund gal talks, you'd think she believed wolves had souls or something!"

It took all my will to stay quiet. I wanted to enter the dialogue and say, *Eskimos certainly believed in the souls of animals—and they still hunted them to survive.* The difference was that instead of assuming attitudes of management or control over animals, the Native shamans respectfully asked the *innua*, or animal spirit, to sacrifice its life to feed the village. In return, the villagers, whether they were Pacific coast whalers or wolf, caribou, and moose hunters, gathered in seasonal ceremonies to praise and acknowledge the survival debt that they as humans owed the animals. There was a sacred relationship between humans and animals, predator and prey, a kinship born of interdependence.

In that Fairbanks bar I was quiet, listening to their talk, tracking them. One of the wildlife managers mentioned that this fading New Year's moon, according to the *Old Farmer's Almanac*, was called "Wolf Moon." Then he told a story striking in its difference from the other hunting tales.

"My Grandaddy was a trapper," the man said. "Once he'd found a fierce wolf with his paw clamped shut in the metal teeth of a trap. 'That wolf just stood there looking at me,' my grandaddy said. 'He just kept staring at me and wagging his doggone tail. That wolf wagged his tail like that—until I shot him.' "

Surrounded by these hunters, in an Old West bar full of wood smoke and animal trophies, I was reminded of another frontier, another century. Back when we didn't have environmental wars or wildlife managers. Back when there was only the Way the West Was Won. Back then there were mountains of buffalo piled high across the plains; there were bounty hunters who lived off Indian scalps; there were thousands of ex–Civil War soldiers engaged in Indian wars that decimated a whole nation of Native Americans, scattering the Natives until many faced extinction on tiny reservations where disease and despair set in like slow poison.

One of those Native elders, Chief Dan George, could have been speaking for the wolf when he pleaded, "If you talk to the animals, they will talk to you and you will know each other. If you do not talk to them, you will not know them. And what you do not know, you will fear. What one fears, one destroys."

In that Fairbanks bar, sitting invisible at a round table of hunter-managers, I stared up and saw a gigantic moose head with antlers right above us. On the opposite wall of the tavern were deer heads, and a bearskin stretched out taut with rack after rack of shot glasses. I closed my eyes remembering those first faces I ever loved—my family of elk and deer. And then I knew that I had been born and raised beneath the eyes and skins, not of the guardian deer prey, but of the conquered, the controlled.

AS IT WOULD turn out, the protester outside that ice rink was right. The 1993 Wolf Summit was a cynical shill game by the state of Alaska to distract the public from officials' hidden agenda. Unbeknownst to both the public and the Wolf Planning Team at the summit, personnel of the Alaska Department of Fish and Game had, even before the summit, begun radio-collaring wolves in the Nelchina Basin area, anticipating approval by the Board of Game for wolf-control programs. The radio collars ensured that the wolves could be easily tracked from the air so that entire packs could be effortlessly killed by public gunners. It was also learned that the traps for the wolf-control programs were purchased before the summit, with the same anticipated end: officially continuing the killing of Alaska wolves.

The much-ballyhooed Wolf Summit had accomplished exactly what some suspicious observers believed the Alaska Board of Game had hoped it would do: it merely defused the protests against wolf control and hoodwinked the public into believing there would be an end to aerial shooting. The summer after the Wolf Summit—with the major tourist booking season over and vacationers locked into their Alaska trips—the Board of Game authorized a "ground-based" wolf-control policy, with state wildlife officials setting traps and snares, as well as land-and-shoot "trapping" by private citizens. The difference between the new policy and the old land-and-shoot proposal was largely a matter of semantics, but the effect was the same. As Sandra Arnold of the Alaska Wildlife Alliance wrote, "Anybody with a $15 trapping license may spot wolves, land, walk 300 feet, and shoot wolves (many people hold both a hunting and trapping license)."

With only two U.S. Fish and Wildlife Service enforcement officers patrolling the vast Alaskan interior, the 300-feet rule was difficult to enforce. In fact, a New York Times article in spring 1994 would cite a federal study of wildlife regulation, which found that agents "may catch no more than 2 percent of the violators."

In detailing the case of one of the few wolf hunters actually brought to justice, the Times article showed how brutal aerial hunting could really be. According to the article, Anchorage surgeon Jack Frost, who in 1991 pleaded guilty to hunting wolves from his airplane, envisioned himself as a "mechanical hawk." Frost would "chase his prey to exhaustion, then land the plane and kill the wolves." Federal agents induced the guilty plea, the article said, by confronting Frost with transcripts of radio transmissions from the plane he was piloting. The transcripts quote someone saying, "He wasn't completely dead. . . . We'll go back later. The damn thing jumped up and bit my wing." A federal agent found wolf teeth marks on Frost's airplane wing. "They had chased the hell out of those animals," the agent said.

The ugliness of the wolf-control project, then as now, goes largely undetected by the national public. The Alaska Board of Game has not made it easy for the media to film or photograph the actual kills, and few of the official photos released appear in the news because the images of skinned wolves are too graphic.

At the summit's end an anonymous source handed me a packet of clippings. There were horrific photos of skinned and strangled wolves strung up. One photo of an illegal wolf hunt haunts me still: On a snowy field lay six black creatures splayfooted against one another—an entire wolf family, dead. In ever-tightening circles around this fallen pack are snowmobile tracks. The tracks seem frenzied. I imagined these wolves loping across frozen tundra for hours on end in their graceful nine-mile-per-hour gait, then the whine and roar of the engines as several snowmobiles speed after the wolves. This is not the skillful chase of wolf against caribou, the speed and agility of each animal almost equal, so that the kill comes down to strategy, stamina, and knowing the animals, as my father said. This is overkill.

At the time I was handed these photos and reports snowmobile hunting was controversial in Alaska but not illegal. By the spring after this Wolf Summit, Governor Hickel would sign into law Senate Bill 77, authorizing the Board of Game to designate certain areas for "intensive wildlife management"—i.e., killing the wolves to ensure higher populations of bigger game. Around the same time, the Board of Game would enact a regulation requiring hunters using a snowmobile or any other vehicle to simply turn off their engine before shooting a wolf.

Who knows how many wild wolves have been killed since that 1993 Wolf Summit? Official statistics vary, but they are all in the thousands. What is most variable and unstable is the state's treatment of its wild wolf populations. At a time when most of the West is reintroducing wolves to their former habitats, Alaska continues its Old West war on wolves. In 1999, the Alaska state legislature passed a bill, SB74, subverting a 1996 public-initiative ban on same-day aerial shooting. SB74 is a means to turn the existing ban on shooting wolves from aircraft into a vehicle for actual wolf control, or slaughter. Even a veto of SB74 by the new governor, Tony Knowles, and a 1999 poll showing that 70 percent of Alaskans oppose any attempt to repeal their citizens' initiative ban on airborne wolf control, did not stop the state legislature from again passing SB74. So once again, in the fall of 2000, wolves in Alaska are being set up for another season of aerial shooting.

As a new century begins, Alaska's legislature stands facing firmly backward, to a time when the wild wolf was no more than a competitive predator to be managed, controlled, and killed—all to manipulate higher prey populations for a dwindling but vociferous group of game hunters.

"What Alaska desperately needs is what the rest of the world is already discovering—a true conservation ethic," explains Dr. Vic Van Ballenberghe, a wildlife biologist with the U.S. Forest Service in Anchorage, who has studied wolves since the 1970s. Van Ballenberghe believes that decades of state wolf-control programs have been "poor biology, often poor economics, and almost always poor public relations." He hopes in the twenty-first century for an Alaska that is "more in step with the rest of the world, where presently the dominant theme is to conserve wolves where they occur and restore them in areas where they are gone."

Recently I met my father in the Seattle airport as he was returning to Washington, D.C., after a meeting with Alaskan wildlife officials. Over endless cups of his coffee and my tea, we talked about the continuing wolf slaughter in Alaska.

"Will you finally tell me, Dad," I asked, "what you think about Alaska's land-and-shoot aerial hunting of wolves?"

He sat silent for a long time, sipping his coffee. Outside swirled strong, slanting Seattle rains. At last he said, "You know, honey, I belong to the Boone and Crockett Club. It was started by Teddy Roosevelt and is one of the country's oldest conservation organizations. They have a fair-chase ethic and have been known for expelling or disciplining members who violate that ethic. It clearly states that fair-chase hunters must not use snowmobiles or shoot from vehicles or motorized boats. They must not locate animals from the air, then land and shoot. A hunter also cannot use artificial lights at night to spot animals.

"Hunters are expected to use only their skills and wait to know an animal; then they plan their hunt. We must take a clear shot and minimize suffering. We are also obligated to use all the meat and other parts of the animal." He looked at me intently; his eyes seemed very old. "Now *that's* hunting," he said.

He went on to say that he did believe in some form of wolf control, but he didn't say exactly what form. After a moment, he added, "We could, of course, just wait fifty years for the caribou population to rebound, because nature balances things out over time," he smiled. "Nature is never static; it's always cyclical."

For a long moment he paused, then he handed me a small, unwrapped box. "From Alaska," he said softly, "for the wolves."

Moved by this gift, the first of many wolf talismans he and my mother would send me over the years, I embraced my father. And then he gave me the most important gift, his confidence.

"What is going on in Alaska should not be called a hunt," my father said. "It's wolf control."

"Like pest control," I said flatly. "Like what that Alaskan state senator called wolves: 'rats in a dump.' "

"No, honey," my father said respectfully, "the wolf is a hunter. The wolf is here to stay."

TWELVE

~

THE RETURN

MONTANA, 1995

I N THE COOL dawn light easing across Yellowstone's panoramic Lamar Valley, a few of us witnesses waited quietly, watching hundreds of placid bison, an even larger herd of elk, and above us two full-curled bighorn rams gazing down serenely.

I was here in the early summer at the invitation of off-duty Yellowstone Park ranger and wolf researcher Rick McIntyre, who had recently published my Alaska Wolf Summit essay in his comprehensive history, *The War against the Wolf: America's Campaign to Exterminate the Wolf.*

"This is history in the making," McIntyre had called to say. "Isn't it time you saw your first wild wolf and the first wolves returning to Yellowstone in sixty years?"

And now I was here on a steep hillside peering through a powerful telescope at the lush Lamar Valley below, scanning for wolves.

"What do you think our chances are?" a Colorado man whispered over to McIntyre, who is unofficially called Yellowstone's "wolf interpreter." With his sharp, green eyes, his mane of red hair under a Park

Service hat, his tanned, freckled face and lanky stride, McIntyre has the lean and fiercely loyal manner of many researchers who have devoted their lives to wolves. For McIntyre, it's been twenty years of study, of watching and waiting for the day when he would finally see the wild wolf freed from our history of persecuting these creatures, who in their society and packs so mirror our own families.

Wolves and this historic reintroduction were what our small pack of strangers was all about this early summer morning. The hope of seeing any of the first wild wolves to roam our nation's oldest park in almost a century had roused us at 3:45 A.M. We hightailed up switchbacks to stand so attentively, like a small human herd on this precipitous hillside.

"Well, now," McIntyre smiled, perhaps recognizing the potent mix of wonder and mystery that has compelled his own study of wolves for decades. "Never know with wolves. But last night that guy over there saw all six of them—the whole Crystal Creek pack—take down an elk."

Several of us immediately surrounded this fortunate observer, Joseph Brady from Kalispell, Montana. He was delighted to tell his story, just the way a wolf will share a successful hunt with his own pack.

"It was amazing," Brady said in a low voice, so as not to disturb the nearby abundant wildlife. "All of a sudden the bison herd down there in the valley just parted in the middle and six wolves ran right between them. I couldn't believe I was really seeing wolves hunt together." Brady had glimpsed wolf packs before in Glacier National Park, where wolves have successfully recolonized themselves over the past decade, setting an exemplary record of calm co-existence with ranchers and livestock. But for Brady, witnessing wolves at the grueling work of earning their daily survival was a revelation. "How many people in the whole world ever get to see a wild wolf?" he whispered, awestruck. "It's a sight people in this country haven't seen for generations."

And ever since the wild wolf was systematically all but exterminated in the Lower Forty-Eight states due to tragic official wolf-slaughter politics, even fewer people have ever seen a pack of wolves tracking, affectionately playing, or leaping exuberantly around a vast meadow as if in celebration.

After several years of covering wolf killing in Alaska, I was so happy to be clinging to a chilly hillside for this historic spring in Yellowstone. Standing in the freezing cold of this Yellowstone valley, I longed to see my first wild wolf and personally celebrate this return to co-existence between species. For much of this century, Yellowstone had been incomplete without the balance and beauty of this valuable predator. Now was the healing, the reunion.

"Look, over on the far ridge right behind that cottonwood tree," a woman with binoculars breathed softly, pointing. "A grizzly."

Fifteen sets of telescopes and binoculars swung to the far right, following her lead to watch a powerful grizzly walk with wide, shambling gait across the ridge. Silhouetted against the soft dawn light, the grizzly seemed out for a morning stroll. I couldn't help but be reminded of the spirit of Smokey Bear surviving in this massive, wild grizzly who, like a bear-god, a premier predator, stood up on his hind legs and sniffed the fragrant morning air with confidence and ease.

"Do the grizzlies recognize that the wolves are back?" I asked Ranger McIntyre as he adjusted his telescope for a better view of the great bear.

McIntyre grinned, "There's a kind of professional courtesy between top predators such as wolves and grizzlies, a mutual respect," he commented. "Certainly they are totally aware of each other's presence." He went on to say that it was the ravens who first caught on to what was happening when three packs of wild wolves were released into Yellowstone in March 1995. "The ravens watched the wolves and learned to show up immediately after they made a kill or tore open a carcass," he explained. "The wolves seemed pretty tolerant about letting the ravens share their leftovers. Grizzlies and coyotes have also shared in the wolves hunts. The grizzlies take what they want, the coyotes take what's left. Everybody benefits when the wolves take their place again in the food chain."

A wide cross-section of people was gathered here, from a biologist to Yellowstone campers to ecology students to an elderly tourist. He used his walking stick to trek up to us and ask, "Seen any wolves yet?" We shook our heads, binoculars scanning the wide valley. "Well, maybe we'll be lucky." He took up a position on the hill and exulted, "So far I've seen several grizzlies and cubs, moose galore, two bald eagles, lots of elk, deer, buffalo, and even a kestrel—you know, the smallest falcon in North America." When I commented that the man certainly knew his wildlife and birds, he shook his head. "Yeah, but I never did see a real wild wolf. That's why I drove all the way out here from Florida."

Ranger McIntyre told us that in the animal kingdom, wolves are one of the most efficient species when it comes to keeping their own numbers in check. In a pack normally only the dominant alpha male and female breed and produce offspring; the rest of the pack, made up of yearlings, sub-adults, and nonbreeding adults, male and female alike, acts as hunters and affectionate babysitters for the pack's precious next generation. In fact, Rick told us, the Rose Creek pack released nearby had already suffered a deep loss. The Rose Creek alpha male was shot in late April, just two days before his mate gave birth to their eight pups.

"This alpha male, whom we called Arnold but who was officially known as Alpha No. 10, was really very special," McIntyre said admiringly. "He immediately bonded with an unfamiliar adult female and her yearling daughter in the acclimatization pen. When the biologists opened that pen to set the wolves free, the male left, but the two females were afraid and didn't venture out. Arnold, that alpha male, was so committed to his mate that he patiently waited several days for her. Finally she followed him out and they began exploring the Yellowstone region. A month later, just as she was about to give birth, he went out hunting for her. He never came back."

A Red Lodge, Montana, man, Chad Kirch McKittrick, aged twenty-six, was sitting in his pickup truck with a buddy when he spotted Arnold, the alpha male wolf, from the road. Without hesitation, he shot the wolf, though his buddy protested. Later McKittrick skinned the wolf, cut its head off, and threw the radio collar in the creek. Under the Endangered Species Act, McKittrick faced maximum misdemeanor penalties on two counts of up to six months and up to a $25,000 fine, and one felony count that could bring him up to 1 year and up to a $100,000 fine. A jury convicted McKittrick of a felony in killing Alpha No. 10, and he served six months in jail.

The shooting of Alpha No. 10 was a life-threatening loss for his mate, Alpha No. 9, and their vulnerable pups, whose survival was in jeopardy. So the Yellowstone biologists managed to capture her and the pups, moving them back to the acclimatization pen until they were old enough to venture out again. The Rose Creek pups flourished and would be released later this season. Meanwhile, the alpha female's yearling daughter returned outside the pen, perhaps waiting to be reunited with her pack.

Mike Phillips, a Yellowstone biologist, had just reported a sighting of a second litter of pups from the Soda Butte pack. "We know they're doing well," Phillips said. Rick McIntyre added, "What we're seeing now is not only the reintroduction of the wild wolves into Yellowstone, but the actual birth of a new generation of wolves. These litters may be the first sets of wolf pups to be born in the Yellowstone area in almost six decades."

McIntyre told me about his conversations with John Marshall, the Sicangu Lakota author of the essay "The Wolf: A Native American Symbol." Marshall explained a prophecy his grandfather told him in 1952: the spirits of all the dead wolves are waiting on a far-off mountain to return when the time is right. As McIntyre told this Lakota prophecy I felt the weight and beauty of my wolf necklace in the backpack I wore now for ballast as I balanced on the hillside. It was reverentially wrapped in an elk skin my father had given me and packed along with thermal underwear, a water bottle, trail mix, and the wolf earrings, made of elk antlers, that my father had given me.

Since the Wolf Summit, my father had returned to Alaska many times, now as director of the International Association of Fish and Wildlife Agencies. He'd sent me presents and updates on the wolf-control programs still in effect in Alaska. First there was the music box with a pack of wolves, heads upraised in silent howl as the tinkling song played "Born Free." Then there were the wolf t-shirts, more earrings, an exquisite Hopi wolf kachina doll, a bronze sculpture of a howling wolf pack, and a beautiful wolf fetish necklace that echoed my Navajo necklace.

Without directly acknowledging it, my father and I were at last working together for the wolves. We practiced a new ecology of love toward each other after many years of misunderstanding and, one might even say, mutual "mismanagement" of our relationship. My father had even sent my articles against wolf control to some of his buddies in Alaskan wildlife management agencies. I would find this out only years later, when a Department of Fish and Game manager in Alaska called me up for an unexpected chat when passing through Seattle. He'd said, "Some of us don't always agree with the state. We're as trapped up here as the wolves. Has it never occurred to you that you father might also sometimes be speaking through you?"

As I stood on that historic hillside scanning the verdant valley below for my first glimpse of a wolf in the wild, I wished my father could have been with me. Then this restoration would feel complete. I did not know then that the next five years would bring a growing bond between myself and both my parents as we joined together to support my father's tireless work on a bill, the Conservation and Reinvestment Act (CARA), which would earmark billions of dollars for conservation and wildlife by mandating that the government shift the majority of revenue it receives from fees for offshore oil drilling to support environmental causes. My father refused to retire again until CARA passed; he and I would find true common ground in this conservation law—my father's biggest legacy to the wild and other animals.

I did not know as I perched precariously on that Yellowstone hillside witnessing the restoration of these wild wolves that my own restoration with my parents was also deepening. We were finding our way back to each other, and wildlife was our guide. By the turn of the new century I would find myself meeting them on a New York City street. Watching them unseen as I waited to cross a busy West 57th Street, I saw my parents with a new detachment that was loving, proud, and protective. There they stood waiting for me outside the Russian Tea Room, looking the very definition of "out-of-towners." My father's tie was a brilliant pattern of wild Canadian geese with a Smokey Bear tie tack. Both he and my mother proudly wore buttons of a black-headed loon that declared, "I CARA about Wildlife." I half expected them to be handing out press releases on the conservation legislation to New Yorkers—who, my father said, might care about wildlife because of its "scarcity."

Perhaps it is this scarcity of our endangered wildlife that calls out to us in the howl of the wild wolf now making a brave comeback in the West. On the Yellowstone hillside, someone was saying, "You've heard they're trying to bring the Mexican wolf back to the Southwest?" I felt a bolt of warmth along my spine as if the Navajo medicine necklace I carried there had heard this wolf news from its homeland. This wolf necklace had come a long way from its Arizona desert, empty of wolves, to Alaska where they still killed wolves, to this Yellowstone valley, which once again echoed with the wild howling of *Canis lupus*.

"I'll believe it when I see wolves back in those deserts," the elderly man from Florida said. "Never been very friendly to wolves down' the Southwest. Not wolves, not Indians."

A woman whispered to Ranger McIntyre, "Have you heard the wolves howling yet?"

McIntyre was about to answer when his whole body suddenly stood taut and he adjusted his telescope. "All right!" he said, and a ripple of excitement ran up and down the twenty binoculars raised like tentacles along the line of observers. Turning to our group, he spoke with a soft intensity: "A sighting, down by the river, mile and a half away. Let's go!"

With more grace and quiet then I would have believed possible, we all scrambled for our cars and drove around the bend where the wolves had been sighted. Then we literally ran straight up another hillside, the seven-thousand-foot altitude winding us. I was surprised that the elderly Florida tourist had beat all of us up the cliff. He calmly set up his tripod, tele-scope, then breathed, "There they are, crossed the river. All six of them!"

"The whole darn pack!" someone happily cried out and was hushed by all of us perched like bighorn sheep on the steep side of the moun-tain. Though we were more than a mile away from the wolves they were notoriously reclusive, and even Ranger McIntyre was surprised at our great luck to spot all six of the Crystal Creek pack.

"Who has never seen a wild wolf before?" McIntyre asked with a wide grin. About thirteen out of fifteen hands shot straight up with all the urgency of schoolchildren desperate to be called on by their teacher. He generously offered his spotting scope as observers caught their first glimpse of a wild wolf—not a languid, trapped zoo wolf, not a photo of a dead wolf with its paws clamped in a steel trap, not a fairy tale or National Geographic wolf, but a real wolf going about its daily survival.

All around there were soft exclamations and sighs and even a few glad tears. "I'm so ecstatic that I could just scream," Marlon Husley, a Billings, Montana, man told me.

"Don't scream right now," someone whispered with a grin.

A big man who looked like his job could be anything from lumber-jack to rancher, Husley could barely contain his excitement. "I've been waiting for this day with anticipation ever since they first started talking about the project back in 1988," he laughed. "Oh, man, this is just awe-some! This return of the wolves—it makes me proud."

"You know," Joseph Brady took up again, "I'm just an ordinary guy, but I volunteered to be part of the environmental impact statement for

this reintroduction of the wolf. We read through hundreds of citizens'
letters and most all of them were overwhelmingly in favor of bringing
back the wolf." Statistics bear out Brady's assessment of the public's
interest in seeing wolves restored to our nation's parks and forests.
According to the *Daily Missoulian*, a majority of people polled nation-
wide were in favor of bringing the wolves back to Yellowstone Park.
McIntyre was astonished that so many tourists had been able to see
these Yellowstone wolves firsthand so soon after reintroduction.

"I thought if I had one wolf sighting this whole summer, even if it
was five miles away, I'd be happy," McIntyre told us. "But I'll bet more
than two thousand people have been lucky enough to spot wolves so far
this summer. And these wolves are allowing us to actually witness their
daily life. That's something most wildlife biologists don't even get to see
in decades of study."

"Right," agreed Suzanne Laverty of the Wolf Education and
Research Center in Ketchum, Idaho. "I've been studying wolves for ten
years and I've never seen anything like this!" She was referring to the
way these wild wolves have deigned to show us so much of their pack
behavior and not elude our rapt observation.

When it was my turn to watch the six wolves, I saw them at play. The
four yearlings, all male, were splashing in the river, tails raised up, leaping and chasing each other like rough-and-tumble kids. The alpha male
and female seemed more serious, scouting around until they found a
coyote den, which the male and later other pack members tried to dig
out. I was startled to see several bison slumbering a few hundred feet
away, as if there were no dangerous predator around, and then, in an
amusing role reversal, an elk actually chased a yearling wolf.

Witnessing my first wild wolves, I was surprised that my reaction was
not the tears of several others, men and women alike, near me, nor the
elation of Brady and Husley. I felt the most profound calm, a coming
full circle for a forest child born in a wilderness without wolves. It was
as if the wolves and I had both come home to where we hadn't been for

so long, where we had always belonged. And I was grateful to witness this, not because of history, but because some wilderness in me, in all of us, was reclaimed when the wolf returned to live alongside us again.

Noting the young wolf chased by the elk, McIntyre told us, "Elk, deer, and pronghorns know they can outrun the wolves if necessary. Bison can outfight wolves; bighorn sheep can outclimb them. Wolves have to work really hard for their supper. So often they go hungry."

But they would not go hungry that year. Yellowstone researchers estimated there were about a hundred thousand prey animals in the ecosystem. Out of these there would be enough lame, sick, diseased, and malnourished animals to enable these original wolf packs to find plenty of prey. If Yellowstone's funding continues for this valuable project, fifteen wolves will be released annually in both Yellowstone and in central Idaho over the next few years. The recovery goal for Yellowstone and Idaho is to establish a population with at least ten breeding pairs in each area. For Yellowstone that would result in a total wolf population of around one hundred animals, a level thought to be roughly the same as the original number of wolves in the park before they were killed off.

Since the original thirty-one wolves were reintroduced to Yellowstone in 1995–96, the program has been more successful than anyone's expectations. Breeding within the packs has thrived. Canadian wolves have also migrated into northwestern Montana. As of January 1999 an estimated three hundred wolves populated the recovery area of the Northern Rockies. If this birthrate and low mortality continue, by 2002 the wild wolf in Yellowstone may even be taken off the endangered species list.

The deep resistance of the ranchers to any wolf reintroduction in Yellowstone was somewhat mollified by the astonishingly low predation on livestock and quick action by the Defenders of Wildlife's Wolf Compensation Fund, which promptly reimbursed any ranchers who lost livestock to wolves. Wolves always prefer wildlife to domestic stock, and the prey populations in Yellowstone were so plentiful that in 1995, the year of reintroduction, wolves killed no livestock and only twelve bighorn sheep.

Yellowstone's reintroduction program is being carefully studied by other states and even other countries, such as Scotland and Japan, who want to restore original wolf populations to their regions. In fact, Ranger McIntyre is descended from Scottish tenant farmers forced by land barons to become predator-control agents against wolves in the Highland glen. So for McIntyre the restoration of wolves in this country, as well as in Scotland, has a deep personal meaning.

"It's been a long journey," McIntyre told me, his voice as fiery as his hair. "But we're finally winning the war to save the wolf."

Watching this wild wolf pack prance and trot around the valley, I realized how familiar and yet how startling it was to see real wolves. Years of watching wildlife films had certainly prepared me for the visual displays and even behavior of this wolf pack. What was startling was how primitive and personal it was to be near the actual wolf in the wild. Witnessing documentaries of wild creatures is a one-dimensional, armchair experience. But here we were, perched none too safely on a steep hillside, peering through telescopes that brought the wolf so close that an animal alertness arose in us, as well. There was nothing one-dimensional about this experience: eagles and red-tailed hawks soared overhead, the sweet pungence of wild sage wafted everywhere, the cold chafed our hands and faces, and suddenly we heard the eerie yip and bark of coyotes as they circled around the wolves, defending their own dens.

As I watched the black alpha male wolf fiercely digging out a coyote den, I whispered to McIntyre, "Do you think the wolves know we're here?"

"Sure," McIntyre said, "they can easily see us. They're keeping track of us, too."

At that moment, the alpha male glanced up from his digging and turned to look directly up at the humans on the hillside. It seemed as though he was staring straight at us, as if from only twenty feet away. And many of us were so overwhelmed by his stately presence that we actually teetered unsteadily on the hillside. Someone dropped his binoculars and I slipped to my knees. All the while the alpha wolf stared straight at us, tracking us with his cool assessment.

Then I realized, *We are also being watched.* This is what wild animals do, with every instinct alert. The way I, too, was now watching. This was the startling difference between every image of a wolf I'd seen before; those wolves could not exchange this deep gaze, because they were only on film. Now things were more equal. And there was something else—a subtle acknowledgment between species. This was a two-way exchange in which, though the humans still had the advantage, we were not alone or unseen. We were also no longer lonely for these, our fellow creatures. This unsettling intimacy of equal predators must be what the Native Americans felt: they bestowed the wolf with a close sibling kinship, calling them Brother and Sister Wolf. But they also taught us to keep a respectful distance.

"Wolves look right through you, don't they?" Laverty from Idaho whispered, herself sensing the effect of this wolf's powerful gaze. The female alpha wolf had joined her mate in studying the hillside where we all perched.

This alpha female was also a fierce presence, her yellow eyes studying us with keen intelligence. "She's assessing our danger to her pack," McIntyre explained.

He told us that until very recently wolf researchers had always assumed that only alpha males led the wolf pack. Then something happened that changed the face of wolf research.

"Several years ago," McIntyre related, "the Portland Zoo asked a thirteen-year-old girl volunteer to observe the captive wolves," he said. When she returned with her reports after several weeks, the zoo biologist was enraged. The girl had observed that the alpha female wolf was the leader of the pack. The biologist was just on the verge of dismissing the teenager when he decided to go back and observe with her. "Sure enough," laughed McIntyre, "the alpha female *was* leading her pack."

This simple observation on the part of an untrained young volunteer who turned new eyes, unprejudiced by old theories, on these long-studied but elusive animals is being confirmed in other wild wolf populations. "Maybe it's because there are a few more women in the field," McIntyre speculated. "But whatever the reason, we can no longer look at wolves in the same old way."

McIntyre went on to explain that in the deeply knit social bonds of a wolf pack, the alpha wolf establishes the hierarchy—who will eat first, who will babysit the much-beloved and nurtured pups, who will hunt. The alpha pair allows no other males to breed, subduing rivals with a terrifying growl and feint of fangs, teeth that can easily crush a moose's skull. Yet for all this imperial power, the alpha wolf rarely does any real harm to the pack. Even the lowly omega wolf, scapegoat and eternal supplicant, rarely receives more than a scratch from the alpha male. The alpha wolf is manager of the family and keeper of the pack structure, which gives stability and peace.

Little is known about the ways in which an alpha female leads her pack, since her power has been acknowledged only recently. Most all the field research on wild wolves has been done by men, with the exception of Diane Boyd's two decades of studying wolves in Montana's Glacier National Park. In a recent book, *Following the Pack: The World of Wolf Research*, of the twenty wolf researchers profiled— from "Wolfman" David Mech, the grandfather of wolf research, to Vic Van Ballenberghe, Rolf Peterson, and Mike Phillips—Boyd was the only female researcher.

In an essay titled "Living with Wolves," Boyd has written, "I realized my approach to science and wolves is innately shaped by the fact that I am a woman. Women can offer another perspective." This other perspective is often that of empathy, combined with acute observation. Women endow "hard science" with intuition and compassion.

The traditional scientific model "dominated by men seeking quantitative answers to theoretical questions," as Boyd explains, is now more balanced and completed by the feminine skills of researchers such as her. It is no coincidence that, as more women have entered the male bastion of wolf research, a pack led by an alpha female wolf has been "discovered." One wonders what the future will bring in our bond with wolves, with more research such as Boyd's, who writes, "I have struggled for years with the perceived conflict of objective science vs. advocacy for twenty years. I have concluded that it is OK to have feelings about the animals you study, without risking damage to your scientific credibility. We should not fear admitting these sentiments any more than we should allow them to interfere with our work. Objectivity and passion about study animals are not mutually exclusive; I wouldn't have devoted my life to studying wolves if I didn't love them."

As we perched on that Yellowstone hillside, obviously being scrutinized by an alpha female wolf, I had to laugh with pleasure when McIntyre concluded, "Nope, she's decided that we're not that interesting—or threatening—to the pack. She'll let us be, let us just keep watching." McIntyre grinned. "You don't know how unusual this is for a wild wolf to let humans observe for so many hours at a time. We're really lucky."

"The luckiest folks in the world," the elderly man from Florida nodded, eyes still glued to his telescope. "I've waited my whole lifetime just for this."

As the alpha female engaged with a yearling, licking its face like the fondest of matriarchs, Laverty said, "The schoolkids have it right. They instinctively recognize this power of the wolf." She told me that in her state, schoolchildren painted bright designs on the radio collars attached to the wolves recently reintroduced there.

How did grown-ups forget what children have always known? I wondered. How did it become official policy to slaughter wolves? I remembered my study of the historical record of governmental wolf-control policies in Yellowstone. In the early 1800s an estimated 35,000 wolves were living in Yellowstone. In the Yellowstone of the early 1900s, the U.S. Army and bounty hunters conducted official wolf-killing campaigns. By the mid-1930s, the last wolf pack was killed. In Montana alone, bounties were paid over a span of forty years on 80,000 wolves.

Knowing the protective devotion of wolf packs to their pups, the park rangers—at the time a virtual paramilitary organization—would chain a wolf pup to a tree, howling piteously. When the adult wolves rushed to rescue their pup, the park officials clubbed the wolves to death. Another favorite wolf-control tactic was to locate a den while the adult pack was off hunting. Dragging the pups out of their earthen womb, the park officials killed them with wooden clubs. This wholesale extermination of wolves in the West was so successful that today only 2,200 wolves survive in the Lower Forty-Eight states, mostly in Minnesota and Yellowstone. In Ranger McIntyre's most recent book, he definitively documents this calculated campaign to eliminate all wolves—still being officially waged in Alaska.

Next to me on the hillside, watching the Yellowstone wolves, Penny Preston, a Cherokee and television reporter from Colorado Springs, was spending her vacation watching wolves. She told of growing up in the South and reckoning with the wrongs of racism. "You know," she said with a sigh, "even though I was part Indian, I was also a racist; it was in my family to be so. Just sitting around the kitchen talking bad about blacks, and pretty soon it was all blown out of proportion like they were evil or something. When the federal government brought down those troops to integrate us, my family raised Cain, just like the ranchers around here are doing against the wolves. But you know what? We were wrong down South. We had to learn to change and accept the truth."

"Listen," Ranger McIntyre said sotto voce, so as not to disturb the resting wolves. "For nearly sixty years there has been an unnatural silence in Yellowstone, the absence of a sound that would have been heard here every day and night for thousands of years. This year, 1995, is the year that long, unnatural silence is broken. The other morning, we heard them, two of the packs howling back and forth to one another across the valley—like singing to their own kind."

Like music. As I stood there among my own kind I realized that it had been a long time since I'd felt so much pride and pleasure in my own species. And I wondered if perhaps the return of the wild wolves would teach us more about being loyal, generous, and self-regulating, and most of all, about belonging—to a place, to a pack.

As I watched the wolves run along the riverbed and one by one at last disappear into the high, cooler woods, I held an image of their rightful return, their natural native land, their future generations here for our children to witness and to again hear their call. I also held in my heart an image that signals a profound change in us, a maturity and respect for other animals, which is a kind of spiritual practice exemplified in my long-ago favorite Bible story of Noah's ark. This image was an official photograph of a U.S. Fish and Wildlife Service agent facing the camera with his bearded, proud smile. He is holding aloft a black-eyed wolf cub, three weeks old and weighing only five pounds, so tiny the newborn fits in the man's hands. The man carries this cub as if it were the most precious offspring on earth, as if the agent is a new father. And the wolf cub stares out with his intense direct gaze, already fierce and aware that he belongs here with us.

If this were 1906, that government official would not be tenderly holding the wolf cub, he would be clubbing him to death. But in 1995, the official was protecting this tiny newborn. It was the father of this cub, the much-respected Alpha No. 10, who was shot to death the same day his mate, Alpha No. 9, gave birth to the first litter of pups born in Yellowstone in more than half a century. This cub's father was murdered by an Old West mentality, but the New West is beginning to nurture a new generation of the wild wolf. The future for these Yellowstone wolves is still clouded with legal challenges and a lawsuit by the Farm Bureau to stop wolf reintroduction. In the winter of 1997, a judge upheld the lawsuit and ordered that the Yellowstone wolves be removed—in other words, exterminated. This ruling was appealed by Defenders of Wildlife. In January 2000, a federal appeals court judge in Denver, Colorado, made a landmark victory for wolf restoration by overturning the Farm Bureau judgment. For now, the wolves can stay. But in a troubling move the U.S. Fish and Wildlife Service proposed in July 2000 to reduce federal protection of wolves, delisting them from "endangered" to "threatened" throughout most of the Lower Forty-Eight states. Many wolf advocates fear this may drastically set back wolf recovery and wolf reintroduction plans in Washington's Olympic National Park and other areas.

But back in 1995, that first spring of the wolves' return to Yellowstone, all we knew of the wolves' uncertain future was that we were witnessing one of the greatest moments in conservation history—a long-overdue apology and reunion with Brother and Sister Wolf.

As a parting gesture at the end of my Yellowstone visit, Ranger McIntyre showed me a lustrous and awe-inspiring wolf skin from a wolf who had died naturally in the wild. McIntyre often offers it to schoolchildren in his educational talks about wolf reintroduction all over the world.

"Children always want to touch the wolf skin and feel this rich, winter fur. It's like something of the wolf is still here and can reach out to touch the children in return. They are not afraid of this pelt, they instinctively want to be a part of it, to have it become a part of them. Who knows how old this bond is between us and the wolf?" McIntyre smiled. "But the children's response to this wolf skin shows us that it's a natural human instinct for us to recognize and feel deeply drawn to the wolf."

I held the pelt respectfully in both hands. In the twilight it seemed to shimmer a luminous silver-gray, with deep brown patterns around its ears and tail. The wolf skin was heavy to hold, as if it still possessed some spiritual weight that lent its dense fur a gravity all its own. Like my wolf necklace, this lavish pelt also had an inner warmth and presence that spoke its own authority. All but overwhelmed by the power of this wolf skin, I handed it back to McIntyre.

He shook his head and commanded me, "Here, this is how it should be worn, if you want to respect the spirit of this wolf." Then he lifted the pelt from my hands and in one quick movement draped the wolf's head over mine, the wolf's long skin down my back. "You'll never forget how this feels," he said solemnly. "Biologists and other scientists don't talk much about spiritual matters. But the wolf is a most spiritual creature and you've earned this moment."

I stood in the falling light with the massive head of a wolf atop my skull, with one of his elegant, slender legs across my breast, thick fur embracing me from my shoulders to my knees. It was as if an otherworldly or distinctly different energy surrounded me, an electricity running from head to foot. Galvanized to the ground, I let the wolf skin's primal strength run through my body. Closing my eyes, I saw flickering images: snowdrifts and the long, efficient stride of the wolf, paws splayed like snowshoes, breath hot and visible in the cold, fur so warm that snow melted along its lengths. Inside this wolf skin I felt profoundly protected, even though this wolf had not been able to outrun death.

When I opened my eyes it was as if I sensed the world around me with a double vision—my own and the wild wolf's. The embracing circle of dark summer woods was my home as it once had been in my first forest; my ears were pricked and alert, like the fur-lined ears of the head atop my own. And the luxurious smells of summer flooded my senses with sudden scents: mountain lupine, spicy sage, delicate lavender, Indian paintbrush, and Rocky Mountain purple delphinium swaying in the evening wind. This world was a paradise, not yet lost, even though this wolf's life was lost.

Sometimes what is lost is restored. It's cyclical, my father had said. That moment of return for the Yellowstone wolves was also a return for the forest child in me who had wandered so far all these years, so far I had forgotten that I was still seeking the sanctuary, my native forest. As I stroked the wolf skin still draping me, I felt again the reverence for fur that as a baby I'd known touching my father's deer trophies. But unlike the short, sleek deerskin, this wolf's fur was thick and soft and long. One could get lost, and found, in it.

As I stroked the wolf skin I was also suddenly aware of the sweater I wore; it was a present my parents had sent from their trip to an international wildlife conference in New Zealand. Woven of raw sheep's wool with brown and white patterns of leaping deer and their dainty tracks, it had kept me warm in the arctic blasts of the 1993 Alaska Wolf Summit. It struck me now, several years later, that the wolf skin, wool sweater, and deer tracks encircling me not in wariness, but in warmth, were a balance of predator and prey. We all belonged together. *What makes the deer so fast?* I repeated softly, like a mantra or a prayer. *The wolf's tooth.*

And then I said a private prayer, embraced by that wolf skin—a hope that the wolves are also fast as they begin to come back to the Lower Forty-Eight, as they try to outrun the airplanes, snares, and bullets in Alaska, the legalities and politics in Yellowstone. I said a silent prayer for all the wolves who are returning to our lonely woods, who are still giving birth in Yellowstone, slowly restoring themselves to Minnesota, Washington's Cascades, New Mexico, Arizona, and Montana's Glacier National Park. My prayer to bring back the wolf was also a yearning to restore some part of my own kind who have been too long separated from their forests, their kinship with other animals—too long lonely, like lost souls seeking their bodies.

This wolf skin was supposedly dead, inanimate, but like those wolf teeth adorning my necklace, it felt very alive to me, shimmering with a spiritual presence and palpable power. Was there ever simple death for this wolf, or for any of us, I wondered. This wolf felt truly like the most supernatural of all creatures, able to hunt and slip between the worlds of skin, of dream, of afterlife. Inside the skin of this wild wolf, I knew again that primitive conviction of my childhood bond with those deer guardians: some of an animal's spirit stays forever with its skin, and teeth, and bones. Skin does walk between worlds.

THIRTEEN

⁓

WOLVES IN OUR BACKYARD

E YE TO EYE with a wolf. So close that all I saw was an amber glow and then the sunlit warmth of black fur against my forehead as the wolf lapped my face, all the while holding my gaze with those pale-fire, reflective eyes that are luminous even in the dark. Warm breath as the wolf sniffed my hair, then again licked my face with a quick, accepting tongue.

I had come to the spring 1997 Wolf Summit in Olympic National Park, sponsored by Defenders of Wildlife and U.S. Representative Norm Dicks of Washington state, expecting to hear more from humans than wolves about the wolf reintroduction program proposed for the Northwest. What I had not expected was the powerful impact of meeting wolves face to face—or nose to sensitive snout—for the first time in my life.

As this wolf held my gaze, his eyes only inches away from mine, I was startled by the sheer intelligence blazing there in those brilliant yellow irises. Here was a very astute creature who scrutinized me with all his considerable senses: a nose one hundred times more sensitive than my own, that can track prey from a mile and a half away; radar-like ears that recognize sounds several miles away; sharp eyes that can scan hillsides from a half-mile away; a delicate tongue that can taste fear in prey; a pace swift and strong; and a sixth sense honed from an evolution that includes being driven to near extinction.

All my work with wolves had not prepared me for this fierce inti-macy with a creature so majestic and intense. If Yellowstone had been a return for the wolves and myself to a native forest, this close encounter with a wolf was like restoring some wildness that was long ago lost in myself. Everyone else around echoed this as the wolf fixed each alert person with those glowing eyes. With his huge paws, his imperial and long-legged stance, his direct stare, we knew we were in the presence of a powerful peer. This black wolf allowed no "good dog" pat on the head, interpreting that as a sign of dominance. Instead he responded only to an open palm, like a show of goodwill, an offering.

This young male, Merlin, was a two-year-old ambassador from the Colorado haven Mission Wolf. Along with his elder alpha female Sila, he was on an educational tour to teach us the real story of wolves. Sila was shy and wary of this crowd and hesitated on the outside of our human circle. And before Merlin bounded into our midst, Mission Wolf Director Kent Weber had schooled us in proper wolf etiquette. "Wolves, like humans, engage in a lot of eye contact to figure out if an expression says 'threat' or 'play,' " he taught us. "So when you meet the eyes of these wolves, keep an open attitude."

Sitting cross-legged in a quiet semicircle awaiting the wolf's gaze and physical scrutiny, many of us leaned forward, hoping to catch the wolf's bright, amber eye. There were one hundred humans and only two wolves, but still there was a tremor through the crowd, as if we were outnumbered. Around the circle the regal black wolf explored, a lick to the face here, a sniff of the open hand there. The wolf was care-ful and curious.

"You ask people about wolves and still to this day they believe in the

Big Bad Wolf," Weber explained to us. "But most of what we believe about wolves is a myth and has nothing to do with the real animal."

Education, not fear, he said, was the key to restoring the ancient co-existence that our species once shared with the wild wolf. He told us about taking these ambassador wolves to visit nursing homes, school-children, and congressional leaders in our nation's capital. Kent explained that as people met and studied the real wolves, not the fairy tale, they developed a respect for wild wolves and favored reintroduc-ing packs to their proper habitat. "After all," Weber said, "if an ecosys-tem can support wolves, it will likely sustain all other life forms as well. Wolves restored as top predators are a sign of a healthy ecosystem."

Our early human ancestors learned how to hunt, to form strong fam-ily packs, and to survive by studying wolves, he said. Once, when our lives depended on the predator-prey balance, we included wolves in our spiritual ceremonies. I remembered reading that among Northwest tribes such as the Makah and the Nootka, wolves were some of the strongest spiritual guides, revered as hunters and for their mystical powers. On our lush Olympic Peninsula wolves were plentiful until early settlers and fed-eral or state agencies began a systematic extermination policy in 1890, until there were no wolves left in Olympic National Park by the 1930s.

So here we were at the Wolf Summit sixty-some years later, and a wolf—not wild, but certainly not less than wild—was here on the Olympic Peninsula in our midst. Before the wolf bounded into our cir-cle, I had been astonished to find myself somewhat afraid. Why? I won-dered as we awaited the wolf. I knew the facts: Not one single human being in North America's history has ever been killed by a healthy wolf in the wild. The wolf is shy and reclusive. Wolves do not seek out peo-ple; people seek out wolves. Since 1995, in Yellowstone, thousands of visitors a year have witnessed wolves in the wild, watching them as I did that first spring of reintroduction from the hillsides of the Lamar Valley through telescopes and binoculars. Few if any people have met the elu-sive wolves face to face.

Perhaps the rarity of this close contact with wolves was why I found myself still afraid that day when Merlin bounded into our human circle. Around me an anticipatory murmur and palpable, primitive fear ran through the crowd. There was that thrilling electricity of all our senses heightened, as if our ancient, reptilian brains were still encoded with this memory of wolf: powerful, mysterious, and most of all, untamed.

I realized at that moment, before the black wolf made his long-legged leap toward me, that I was afraid of the unknown. I didn't know the real wolf, didn't know how to behave. Though I'd read much about wolves and their true nature, I'd never come upon a wolf in the woods or experienced the real animal so close without a cage or binoculars. And there was still a scary story sunk deep in my childhood memories.

Now here was a real wolf, pacing around our crowd with those astonishing amber eyes, pricked ears, and paws the size of a man's fist. Though he was taking the Mission Wolf co-director Tracy Brooks for a walk at the end of his strong leash, I still expected to feel terror as the black wolf approached me, nose raised to take my scent. But instead I felt something else: a rush of gladness when I first met the wolf's gaze. Steady, clear, and open—this was the wolf's expression. Dignified and curious, playful and penetrating, those eyes held mine for what seemed minutes before the sniff and his tongue and fur covered my entire face.

"You've so lucky," a large man next to me sighed as the wolf lingered a moment more to gaze at me and then moved along our circle. "Passed me right by."

"Sorry," I said. Who could explain why Merlin engaged with some of us and, after a quick sniff, dismissed others. I shrugged, "Maybe next time."

"If there is a next time," the man said morosely. "You really think the locals here will let wild wolves come practically into their own backyards?"

"We're thinking about our livestock," one of these locals reminded us. Although the wolf was a distance from us, she still kept her eyes on him. Her expression showed that she was as mesmerized by the wolf as she was apprehensive. "We're the ones who'll have to make the sacrifice for this wolf recovery," she said.

A Defenders of Wildlife representative sitting right behind us on the picnic table leaned forward and assured her, "Ma'am, we have a special fund for reimbursing ranchers for any loss of livestock, if the wolves wander outside the park. It's worked really well in Yellowstone so far. Wolves prefer wild prey and they have so much that livestock predation is minimal—an average of only three cattle and two sheep per year. All the ranchers have been compensated."

"Reimbursed at market prices," someone else said. "That's not much of a sacrifice, when we can get the wild wolf back here where he belongs. Besides, it's really the wolves who have sacrificed the most, don't you think?"

All this talk of sacrifice troubled me, throwing me back to the Southern Baptist dictums of my childhood, linking sacrifice with the divine. I remembered clearly the day my Montana Sunday school teacher all but destroyed my bright and only forest faith when she told us the story of Noah's ark all the way to the end. It was all about sacrifice.

"'To make a sacrifice means 'to make sacred,' " our teacher told us, reading from the spiritual journal in which she recorded her daily notes, what she called her "personal journey with God."

We seven-year-olds were just learning to read real books, so we were all very impressed with her journal because it was covered in sleek, tanned deerskin from a doe shot by her husband. The only other book we'd ever seen embraced in precious animal skin was a leather-bound King James Holy Bible.

"Now, what was the very first thing that Noah did when he left that old, waterlogged ark and walked out upon God's beautiful, new land?"

"Pray?" a smart boy who also answered all the questions in our small mountain school volunteered.

"Ah, but this was a special prayer," the teacher smiled. "Listen," she commanded, and took up her other leather-bound book. " 'And Noah built an altar unto the Lord; and took of every clean beast, and of every clean fowl, and offered burnt offerings on the altar. And the Lord smelled a sweet savor.' "

In my rural Montana mountain community, whose people were raised on wild game, such a story of animal sacrifice, of a God who "smelled a sweet savor" at the scent of animal offerings on the altar, was not disconcerting to the other seven-year-olds in my class. After all, many of our hunting congregations barbecued elk or venison steaks as easily as a suburbanite might grill up hamburgers at a church picnic.

But I was horrified, the only one in class to interrupt the teacher with an outcry. "Noah *killed* one of each of the animals he was supposed to save?" I asked, voice trembling.

My sense of Noah's betrayal toward the animals was deepened by my earlier belief in his heroism. Noah was not like my grandfather—a farmer who survived by slaughtering his own barnyard animals. He was supposed to be a saviour of all the animals. Didn't a saviour protect others from death, even if one had to die oneself?

"Yes," my teacher said, rather impatiently. The lesson was finished for the day and she wanted to step outside the garage church and smoke a cigarette before the long-winded sermon. "In those days the people offered animal sacrifices to the Lord. Don't you remember the story of Abraham and Isaac and how the Lord asked Abraham to sacrifice his beloved son, but at the last minute the Lord sent a ram instead?"

It did not help me at all that the teacher referred me for clarification of Noah's sacrifice of ark animals to another Bible story. Abraham and Isaac had already broken my heart and left me suspicious of all parents. Abraham's willingness to sacrifice his own son was one of the reasons I had turned away from the Bible stories and hidden during the sermons in Mrs. Ashworth's bear coat. In my illustrated Bible I had often pondered the painting of Abraham with his arm raised up, holding a vicious knife. Under him lay his precious son, whom he was willing to slay at God's command.

What did this mean, I often wondered, that parents could kill their children by divine commandment? And why should we honor our parents if they could sacrifice us to a God who showed his love for the world by sending his Son to be killed? It was a dangerous world, I had concluded, and parents were no protection.

"You see," our teacher concluded, "Jesus's sacrifice gave all of us sinners a chance to be restored to sacredness if we accept His redemption."

"I'd rather be a sinner and escape with my skin than be sacred and get killed," one of the boys whispered.

My teacher threw up her hands. "Don't think about it too much, will you? It was just the thing to do in those days, animal offerings to God. Like a scapegoat, those animals took on our blame, like Jesus Christ took our sins on His poor head. I mean, at least Christians were better off than those pagans who burned each other up on false altars! We're lucky the Lord God accepted animal sacrifices in our place."

It was as if the world stood still at her words. Here at last was a big truth: the animals were not only dying for me so that I would not starve; they were also dying for me so that God the Father wouldn't kill me. He would take a ram instead. Animals were being sacrificed to make my soul sacred to God. But what about the animals, my seven-year-old heart cried out, though I kept silent. Why didn't this sacrifice make the animals sacred, too?

I was sitting on a metal folding chair in a garage with guns and trophy animals in the back storeroom. It was the winter of 1957 in Montana, and many wore fur or tanned hides. At most meals my family ate the wild deer or elk my father shot for us. I understood hunger and survival by sacrificing animals. "But why kill those animals in Noah's ark?" I made my feeble protest. My legs, dangling from the metal chair, were trembling and I felt my teeth chitter together as if it were bitter cold. "After forty days and nights, those ark animals were like Noah's own family!" I was on the verge of tears.

With a sigh, my teacher sat back down with me and dismissed the other kids, who ran outside into the bright snowdrifts to play. "Whenever I'm in doubt," she began, "I turn to the scripture for comfort. Here, let's read on." My teacher licked her index finger and turned the delicate parchment pages of her Bible. Her Bible bore my teacher's very own name embossed in gold on the cover.

"Okay," I leaned near her as she read the words.

" 'And the fear of you and the dread of you shall be upon every beast of the earth, and upon every fowl of the air, upon all that moveth upon the earth, and upon all the fishes of the sea. . . .' " She skipped down, looking for a verse that might explain it better to me. "Oh, here," she said with satisfaction. " 'Every moving thing that liveth shall be meat for you.' "

"But God wasn't eating all those animals Noah sacrificed," I made my child's argument to the teacher. "God doesn't have a body or ever get hungry—except for people's souls. So why burn up animals just so he can smell them? Everything in the animal goes to waste and no one eats the meat. My father says that's wrong."

With a worried shake of her head my teacher closed her Bible on Genesis and Noah's ark. She turned to me and managed a weary smile. "Many things we don't understand, dear," she said. "Like figuring out that saving and sacrificing can be the same thing: like God saved us by sacrificing his only son, like Abraham slayed a little ram instead of his son, like Noah giving back to God some of the very animals he saved. It's even beyond me, sometimes."

I sighed and accepted her brief embrace before she grabbed her parka and headed for the smoker's circle. If it was beyond my teacher's mind, then how could I ever understand it all?

⸺

I STILL DO not understand, at the age of fifty, the Biblical practice of animal sacrifice, or the divinity that shows His highest love by offering his only Son up to be killed. And in this sacrifice, how exactly is the world made more sacred? But more and more I understand the consequences of this religious tradition's underpinnings as it affects our spiritual tenets and our bond with other animals. Christians have, for the most part, abandoned the ritual of animal sacrifice. But the mindset lingers. Often, and quite unconsciously, we still act out of this spiritual tradition when we regard other animals. Animals are to be sacrificed for our human survival, both body and soul. This seems our right, given us by the Lord in his covenant with Noah.

I am still uneasy with these Christian stories of violence and destruction made into holy acts. Such deification of sacrifice makes it that much easier to sacrifice other people, species, and an entire earth. And I wonder, if we had another story, one based not on sacrifice but on *reciprocity*, could we endure the extinction of so many other species? Would it be so easy to make the ultimate sacrifice to this concept of a consuming God—the destruction of our planet? As I sat cross-legged at the Olympic Wolf Summit in 1997, watching a wild wolf move among the crowd like an animal ambassador, a foreign dignitary, blessing some and seriously eyeing others, I wondered if there could be a new story of Noah's ark for a new century.

"We have an opportunity to correct a historic mistake," Representative Dicks said now. He told us that the total cost to taxpayers of all previous wolf reintroduction has only been a nickel per person—a small price to pay for helping to rebalance an entire ecosystem.

A *small price to pay*, I repeated to myself, as I watched Merlin coming full circle back in our direction. No real sacrifice at all. No worlds destroyed, no animal burnt on any religious or political altar. Just a reciprocal act—all beings back where they belonged, together to balance a new world, a new millennium.

As Merlin approached us again, the hopeful man next to me leaned forward, palms humbly outstretched. The wolf paused before him, sniffing.

"Meet the wolf's eyes," Weber advised the man, "not as an aggressor, but as an equal."

The man steadied his gaze and Merlin faced him, those amber eyes assessing. And then with slow grace, the wolf took the man's entire face in with his strong tongue. Grinning ear to ear, the man rocked back on his knees and whispered, "I feel as great as the first time a girl said 'yes' when I invited her to dance." He paused. "I guess this *is* a dance."

His relief and rejoicing reminded me of a story, "First People," retold by my friend, the Chickasaw writer, Linda Hogan:

In a Tewa narrative, people and animals lived together beneath a lake in darkness. The first Mothers—powerful women—sent one man to find the way to the surface world, the one we now inhabit. When he reached this world he saw the wolves, mountain lions, and coyotes. On seeing him, they ran to him and wounded him, then told him, "We are your friends" and healed him, showing him special abilities they possessed, their abilities to harm and their equal abilities to heal. When the Tewa man returned to the Mothers he said to them, "We have been accepted."

Again I leaned forward, palms up, accepting and accepted. But this time Merlin passed me by with a friendly sniff and a glance. "He doesn't need to greet you again," Weber called out. "He remembers you."

"And I'll always remember him," I smiled.

Then I turned to the ranch woman to see what Merlin might do. Her fear and distrust were palpable; even I could almost smell their stringent scent.

The black wolf calmly gazed at the ranch woman, neither coming forward nor retreating. He sniffed the air as if she were far away. Merlin kept his respectful distance. What he did next surprised us all, even Weber, his human companion. Suddenly stretching and arching his long back, the wolf sat down next to the ranch woman's outstretched legs. There was nothing domesticated about him as Merlin yawned to reveal startlingly white fangs. Then his huge jaw clamped shut, he shook his massive black head, and with great poise he lay on his side only inches from the ranch woman's boot.

They remained like that in a motionless dance of opposites, as Dicks finished his speech, eloquently endorsing further study of wolf reintroduction. We all, especially the ranch woman, kept our eyes riveted on the supine wolf. Was he dozing, daydreaming of arctic woods and bounding through deep drifts with those snowshoe-sized, splayed paws? His legs trembled now and his paws shook as if racing through sleep.

"Well, Merlin will be wanting to take a real run now," Weber said and called over to the wolf where he slept near the ranch woman.

Merlin sleepily roused himself, but made no move to get up. He stretched, let out a soft growl, then turned over on his back to look directly upside down at the ranch woman. Lying so near her, he was no threat, and the ranch woman could at last meet Merlin's eyes without fear.

"He's . . . he's really something," she said slowly. "He does have a way of getting right up into your heart, doesn't he?"

At that moment, witnessing this ranch woman and the wolf sharing the same territory, I realized that the first work of restoration is not a political or even an ecological process. Before we can truly share our land and our backyards with the wolves, we must again open our hearts and our souls to them, like this ranch woman who in sitting down quietly with the wolf replayed the Noah's ark tale of the lion lying down with the lamb—when all animals are restored to a new land.

"Time to go, Merlin!" Weber was calling the wolf back. Then he grinned and shrugged, "Merlin, like the magician he was named after, makes his own time."

The wolf still lay, splay-footed, near the ranch woman. We all watched now, and time slowed way down. Our circle seemed ancient and as if we had nowhere else to go, nothing else to do but watch this ranch woman and this wolf.

At last she reached out a tentative, open palm. Only then did Merlin leap up with unexpected energy and sniff her hand, her shoulder, and at last, as she bowed her head, her hair. But he didn't lick her. Instead the wolf looked directly into her eyes, inches away from her face. Then he simply leaned his black, soft forehead against hers.

It was the briefest of touches, before Merlin bounded back to Weber. But it seemed like those two minds, once opposites, rested together a long time — longer than our history, our generations of fear.

As we sat there, the alpha female, Sila, at last joined Merlin in our circle. Our crowd literally fell back with a murmur of amazement. With her luminous white coat and dark eyes, her energy was utterly different from young Merlin's. Whereas Merlin was inquisitive, Sila's energy was at once aloof and completely assured. I have never witnessed such self-possession in a canine, as Sila leapt toward Merlin. In a moment, the young black wolf was on his back, legs akimbo, paws upward in submission. With her huge jaw, Sila held Merlin's entire snout in her vise; calmly she shook him once or twice with a fond but firm hold and then let go.

"Your majesty!" Weber threw his own hands up, but was completely serious in his tone. "That's what both Merlin and I are smart enough to say to Sila with our body language."

Sila allowed him to offer her his hand. She sniffed once, then turned her profound attention to the crowd. Sila, at seven, is the mature female of the pack at Mission Wolf. She was born in a Colorado roadside zoo and sold for $400, misrepresented as a wolf-dog to avoid legal battles. Even at three weeks, Sila was headstrong and independent, leaping up onto the supper table to share food.

"Merlin and Sila are, sadly, captive for life," Weber told us. "They will never be returned to the wild because people have wrong-headedly bought them as pups and tried to raise them as dogs. A wolf will never be domesticated!"

He went on to tell us that in the Lower Forty-Eight states there are about 3,000 wolves in the wild, but more than 250,000 captive wolves and wolf-dog hybrids living in cages. "Most of these captive animals will die within three years," Weber said, "because of irresponsible human ownership." Weber can no longer take in captive or hybrid wolves at his refuge. "It just breaks my heart," he said. "Once a wolf pup bonds to a family it can seldom transfer that loyalty to another family."

Then he told the story of a man who kept his wolf pup on a chain, trying to domesticate him with daily tranquilizers and beatings. The wolf pup paced itself almost to death. Finally the owner abandoned the pup to Mission Wolf. Two months later, the owner visited the refuge.

"What do you think that wolf did when he saw this man who had enslaved him?" Weber asked. "He greeted his former owner with complete devotion, just like Merlin did me. It was as if the wolf was crying out 'Father!' Even after all the man's beatings. Then, for weeks after the owner left again, the wolf paced and howled, as if he'd lost his best friend."

Such devotion, even in the face of human cruelty, tells us something about this other animal our species has so long maligned. It also tells us about the wolf's capacity for loyalty and relationship. The wild wolf is not fighting back; it is simply returning, shyly and even in the face of our fears and resistance. The wild wolf is coming home to its native lands.

As Weber accompanied Sila and Merlin outside our circle, we all rose to follow the wolves to the edge of a lake, where Weber ran with them. Pacing each other, around and around they ran together, like the same pack. At last they slowed down and returned to the rest of us.

"There is no more Big Bad Wolf." Weber and Merlin collapsed in a heap together on the summer grass. Sila took up a more dignified posture, settling in the ground. The man was streaming sweat; the wolves barely seemed winded. Sila ignored us, but Merlin fixed us all with a familiar gaze. Turning back to Weber, Merlin lay both his huge paws on the man's shoulders. Kent exchanged a faint smile with the ranch woman, who nodded back slightly. "Never was."

And watching the human and wolf pack resting together, I smiled, remembering another childhood story told me back in 1993 at the Alaska Wolf Summit. This story might well replace the Little Red Riding Hood myth. It seemed century ago when a native of Alaksa, Julia Barnes, told me her true wolf tale.

Julia was raised as a child in the Alaskan bush, and often she heard wild wolves howling outside her isolated cabin home. The sound was familiar and comforting to her, a communal lullaby that assured her that another animal was awake and watchful in the night, so she could sleep. Only once in her life did she ever see an actual wolf in the wild.

One day she was walking home from elementary school when suddenly there on the dirt path stood a wolf, eyeing her with a keen scrutiny and curiosity. Neither she nor the wolf made a move; for the longest time they just held their intense gaze. She was surprised to realize she was not at all afraid of this wolf. She was simply grateful for the company.

The wolf accompanied her, keeping a respectful distance, pacing itself to her short-legged walk for the several miles to her home. To this day, Barnes said, she remembers that wolf walk. After that, she never felt alone or unseen in the forest—she remembered that a wild wolf was once her companion.

Barnes finished her story: "Whenever I lose my way, that's what I remember. A wild wolf once walked me all the way home."

PART THREE

THE WORLD AS
AN ARK

*The future survival of humankind depends upon
return to a right relationship to nature. The
need is both inner and outer. In this endeavor,
the animal soul is our most dependable guide. If
we befriend the animals, they can lead us, show
us what we need to know.*

—Ladson Hinton,
"Return to the Animal Soul"

FOURTEEN

SPIN OF THE DOLPHIN

V ERY EARLY, IN the vog—that volcanic mist off Hawaii's Big Island where Pele births new land in brilliant, bright-red lava flows—we quietly slipped our three kayaks into warm, turquoise waters. The bay itself seemed to be breathing slightly sulfurous inspirations and sweet, drifting exhalations. This graceful curve of protected bay is one of the world's rare reef waters where spinner dolphins swim close to shore. Here they rest in small groups during the long tropical days before joining up with larger, superpods to fish in the Pacific's deep coral canyons. Here, too, the spinners breed, birth, and nurture their next generation, in a watery nursery.

I was in Hawaii on the fifteenth anniversary of Earth Day, on assignment for the *Seattle Times* to study and celebrate one of the most vital whale nurseries. Here in warm, winter Hawaiian waters, humpback whales breed and give birth from January through mid-April before their long migration back up to their summer feeding grounds in Alaska. All week these island nurseries echoed with sonorous bass and subsonic singing that we could hear through hydrophones. From our fishing shack on this quiet lagoon we watched the stunning breach and embrace of these gracious sea giants, who rose like skyscrapers from the waves, their graceful pectoral flippers flung wide as wings, giving them the nickname "angels of the sea."

On this Easter week whale-watching in the Hawaiian islands, I was excited about encountering humpbacks. As a friend, the Cuban author Flor Fernandez Barrios, and I paddled with our kayak guide at six A.M., we scanned the smooth, bright waters, searching for that mystical spume of air and mist that is a great whale's breath in open seas.

Speaking in a whisper so as not to disturb the nursery lagoon, our guide, Don, told us that he'd given up a successful business in Southern California to come to the islands as an acoustics amateur and research the songs of the humpback whale. "So complicated," he said, "their songs. They are always changing, reinventing the notes." Then he whistled with a sense of wonder. "When humpbacks off Hawaii change the patterns of their songs, other humpbacks as far away as the Azores will make the same exact adaptations. It's a musical puzzle far beyond anything a human Mozart might have invented."

Above us the emerald-green cliffs gleamed through marine mists as we slipped farther into warm waters. Don continued his soft rhapsody on the humpbacks' vocalizations. "Once about fifteen years ago, on my first visit here," he began, "I was very deep down diving, listening. Then suddenly this huge humpback is right before me, his song blasts into my whole body and echoes off every bone inside me, singing down to my marrow, changing my heartbeat. Whoa," he said and shook his head. "That first humpback song is still vibrating inside me.

"No one knows why humpbacks sing," Don continued. His paddle made hardly a ripple in the calm sea. "But theirs is a true song, with ordered, repetitive sequences, like birdsong. Most scientists say that only the males sing and it's probably a courtship ritual, a love song. But I swear I've heard females sing as well, especially with calves in tow. Each individual humpback has its own personal signature, which other humpbacks recognize. And these low-frequency songs carry so much information—we just don't know what it is."

Don paused, resting the paddle on his kayak as he let the slight current steer and slide us near shore. He grinned. His sun-darkened, weathered face showed a mature man who has made discoveries here not only about other species, but about himself as well. "I've just come off a two-week silent retreat at an isolated Zen center on Kauai," he confided almost shyly to us. "What I mean by silence is no human sounds, just dropping my hydrophone into the sea and listening to humpbacks singing. It is the most restful thing you can imagine to listen to nothing human, just birds, whales, waterfall, waves, and once, a rainstorm that was more lyrical than Debussy." He sighed and again we took up our quiet kayaking, our paddles making perfect figure eights, the symbol of infinity.

I wondered about Don's life, how his fortune had not brought him any happiness tantamount to that of listening to a humpback's song. Money, prestige, status, he told us, it all paled next to a life devoted to this kind of vital connection with something greater than himself. "Cetaceans are our true elders," Don concluded. "They've had sixty million more years of evolution. What would happen if more humans really *listened* to their elders?"

I remembered a quote from a children's book written by Katy Payne, who with her husband Roger was the first to document the songs of the humpback whales. "I try to help people understand what the world is losing," Payne wrote. "It is losing deep voices—and some of the richest sounds that have ever been heard are in the songs of whales." Later Payne made another startling discovery: that elephants have their own subsonic language, lower than human hearing. This language, which rumbled across miles of open savanna, told other herds exactly when a female began her twenty-four hours of estrus, where to find watering holes, and most of all how much distance to keep between herds so there would be enough vegetation for all to survive.

When I'd first heard the humpbacks singing, through hydrophones on a research vessel earlier this Easter week, I'd also marveled at the complexity of their songs. I couldn't identify a single repeated refrain in the subsonic singing. Humpbacks sing with their snouts pointing straight down at the ocean floor, which was why some aboriginal tribes and native Hawaiians believe that the humpbacks are literally tuning the magnetic or *lei* lines of the earth. If the humpbacks ever stop their singing, these indigenous myths teach, the world will literally spin off its axis, because there is no great song or soul to balance it.

The humpback researchers had been particularly excited by a rare display. Right near our boat two humpbacks had slowly risen out of the ocean together, belly to belly, their massive bodies poised in midair, gleaming flippers flung out as they fell backwards in a synchronized splash that rocked our research vessel like a toy. The humpback pair performed this gravity-defying duet fourteen times in twenty minutes. No one on our boat had ever witnessed such behavior in decades of observation.

"It's courtship display," one researcher said.

"No, they're two escort males fighting over a female," someone else theorized. But no other whale was in sight.

"Maybe they're just . . . playing?" a third researcher grinned and shrugged.

Now, in the early morning mists of this dolphin sanctuary, as we stroked our slender kayaks into the bay, deftly dipping our paddles into the water, the sun rose above the vog and the whole world woke up. I could understand why this warm bay, calm and spacious, was nursery to large pods of spinner dolphins.

"I think of spinners like little sprites, or sea fairies." We could hear Don's smile in his voice. "You know, like those benevolent, loving spirits on Prospero's island in *The Tempest*," he laughed. "My girlfriend teaches literature here on the island. She's also a master canoe racer. Anyway, that's what spinners remind her of when they dance and pirouette to get a better look at us humans with kayaks for bodies."

As we slipped quietly through the azure waters, it did feel like my body was sleek, with its long tail of fiberglass, as we glided through the waves like mer-people, our arms stroking in steady motion with long paddles. Complete silence, except for the gentle wake of saltwater behind our kayaks.

After another half-hour of paddling, Don said in an almost whisper, "I don't tell most people this, but what I'm hoping to do just once before I die is to be able to sing my own remedial human version of just one complete humpback song—that is, one season's song. I could never learn more than one because it's just too difficult for the human brain. Listen, this is what I've memorized so far this season." He stopped paddling and took a deep breath, then sang out a tremulous, bass line of groans, eeeesss, and oooooos, so low his voice creaked with the weight of the borrowed song. Ululating, elegiac, and otherworldly, his song rose up over the waves. Descending low and then moaning high, his imitation of humpback song was so beautiful, I wondered if indeed we had entered into an enchanted world, much like Prospero's lost island paradise.

And suddenly, as he sang what sounded like a walking bass without a melody, there was a quickening around us in the water and in his kayak's gentle wake leapt three shining dolphins. They spun together wildly in midair and then splashed so close our boats bobbed in the wake of their tiny tail flukes.

"Spinners!" I heard Don sing out in a fond falsetto.

But as I spun around myself to better see their nearby acrobatics, my world turned sideways, then upside down. With a loud splash I capsized and came up sputtering, laughing. Treading water warm as blood, I tried to climb back inside my tilting kayak, but Don stopped me.

"As long as you're underwater," he grinned, "why not listen?"

Underwater I heard that familiar click, bleep, and Geiger-counter ratchet of dolphins' sonar as they scanned me. Their sonar is so sensitive that dolphins can hear a teaspoonful of water poured into an oceanarium pool. The sound pictures of their echolocation, like an advanced version of our ultrasound, let them see the tumult of my stomach gases, my heartbeat, and the pulse of my nervous system. We listened, one to another, and in that underwater reverie I felt the deep privacy and nurturance of this nursery, where another species births its new generations.

Here was a song different from the one I knew well after my many years with the bottlenose dolphins at the Key Largo research center. These were the same ultrasonic chirps and whistled ricochets of dolphin talk, but here also was intensity and vibrancy that even my half-trained ear could discern. Whereas in my swims with the semicaptive dolphins I'd heard gentle crackles and creaks, curious whistles and bleeps, these wild spinner dolphins had such a variety of voices and tones. It was like the difference between listening to one small group of singers and hearing an entire chorus of hallelujahs and hellos. The exuberance and freedom in these signature whistles announced to the entire world their presence. And all the world was listening—from the static noise of brine shrimp to the crackle of living coral reefs, from the pop of phosphorescent fish to the pulse of the salt-laden, buoyant sea itself.

One of my marine mammal biologist friends had told me his computer had tracked captive dolphins carrying on seven simultaneous conversations. Often I'd heard a syncopated and harmonious dialogue in the Keys, but here in the open ocean that flowed into a nursery lagoon, I heard a multitude of dolphin voices. Their Ping-Pong bounce of sound inside my body lit up my nervous system like a pinball machine with all the whistles and bells clanging at once. My ears, my chest, my belly, and an electric zinging down to my feet barely contained all the spinners' sounds—from the probing sonar of their echolocation to the chatter of their underwater voices. There must have been hundreds of dolphins in that lagoon, judging from the symphony of their vocalizations. Even my skin vibrated as if in harmony with their complicated, curious chorus.

When at last I surfaced for a deep breath, Don called out, "Not a bad way to go if you were drowning, eh? But of course, the spinners would never let you drown; they'd even save you from a shark, though their beaks are not meant for ramming like the bottlenose's. They're so fragile, like a hummingbird's beak. Still, they'd give up their lives to save you—like their own young."

Back under the waves, I opened my eyes as well as my ears and saw dozens of silver bodies and luminous white bellies gleaming as they swam in formation below my floating body. Without a snorkel mask I could make out only the blur of pearl-gray and white spinners whose snouts, or rostrums, gently bumped my belly, my knees, my toes as if listening to make sure I was not unconscious or taking water into my lungs. They listened carefully, echolocating each lobe of my air-filled lungs. Once satisfied that I was not dying but breathing and perhaps an interesting float toy, they began to play.

I turned on my back to better see two spinners leap over my chest, pirouette in midair in a dazzling display ten feet above me, and then perform a perfect corkscrew splash at each of my outflung arms. No one really knows why spinner dolphins engage in such mesmerizing and gravity-defying acrobatics. Scientists have their theories. The "grandfather" of all spinner dolphin research was the late Dr. Kenneth S. Norris. His thirty-year study of spinners illumined what cetologists had previously dismissed as a "wastebasket" genus (*Stenella*) because so little was known about spinners. It was Norris who theorized that spinners twirl and leap like figure skaters in a "flickering blur of flukes" for other reasons than simply "evident *joie de vivre*" But what purpose does this behavior, which requires such high energy and skills, serve?

Norris discovered over his decades of study that the spinning and extraordinary leaps always matched the energy level of the pod. If the spinners were "sleeping" in their rest coves—the male coalition guarding their calves and females as they all swam slowly in sync near the white, sandy sea bottom—there was very little aerial activity. But at night when the spinner dolphins swam far out to their feeding grounds in the shark and human-patrolled open ocean, their acrobatics greatly increase to what Norris called "broad jumps, nose-outs, salmon leaping, and tail slaps." One dolphin was recorded repeating fourteen spins in a row as it neared the bow of their research boat. Perhaps the dolphins were spinning to shake off parasitic remora fish, or to get an aerial view of their own pod, Norris theorized.

After much observation, he noticed that a spinner would announce each athletic leap by diving down and "barking" as it rocked back and forth; then with a mighty thrust of its muscular tail, the spinner shot straight up through the water, performed its glorious spin, then landed with a *smack* from its fast-revolving tail fluke, or its dorsal or pectoral fin against the waves. Norris concluded that these percussive smacks and trail of bubbles from the rotations are actually an acoustic signal to the other spinners to locate the dolphin's position, as well as the boundaries of the pod. Norris's theory still stands: that the spinner dolphins spin to give their pod-mates "crucial geometric organizers of the traveling society."

Another playful reminder comes from Bernd Wursig, one of Norris's early associates and another leading authority on dolphins. Wursig, with his research associate and wife Melang, notes that "Dolphins seem to be performing, and it is difficult to imagine that they do so for any reason other than 'pure joy.' "

As I floated now face down in that warm Hawaiian bay, several spinners cruised alongside me, their bright brown eyes, rimmed in black masks, holding mine. And in those eyes I saw a wildness and otherness I had not seen in the captive dolphins I'd encountered. Though those spinners were curious, they were also very distinct and separate from me. They eyed me without any need or desperation, without any request. They were sovereign here and though every day there were perils from sharks and boat traffic, from pollution and intruders like me, this was *their* element. And I must behave like a good guest.

We were surrounded by spinners now, perhaps a hundred of them. So many wild dolphins accompanying our three fragile kayaks were like a great gift after my years of encountering only captive dolphins. As they leapt and cruised alongside us I remembered my last swim with "the girls" at the Dolphin Plus Research Center. Surrounded by this superpod of spinners, I wished I had telepathic skills to send these exhilarating images back to the first dolphins who had ever shared their world with me. And I held in my mind the image of one particular dolphin I'd recently encountered at Sugarloaf Dolphin Sanctuary in the Keys. There I'd attended the first international meeting of a group calling themselves Dolphin Gadfly—a working coalition of one hundred dolphin activists, researchers, and advocates from around the world, all devoted to rehabilitating captive dolphins back into the wild.

The one particular dolphin in my mind was a U.S. Navy dolphin named Luther. Captured by the military and conscripted into such unnatural services as wearing harnesses to carry bombs, using his sophisticated sonar to detect underwater military targets, and other assorted warfare duties, Luther looked like a veteran hero. Luther's face was etched in long scars, as if he'd been slashed in sword fights or duels. Though his natural dolphin smile promised playfulness, Luther's manner was skittish, as if his spirit had been shattered or he suffered from battle fatigue. Whenever any human came near, he hung back in fear. But once he trusted, he was as devoted as any domesticated dog. This loyalty was a problem in rehabilitating Luther back into the wild, where he would need to steer clear of humans, boats, and any interspecies interaction to assure his safety.

Luther, Buck, and Jake—"the soldier boys," we called them—had been released from their military duty after the tireless crusading of Dr. Naomi Rose of the Humane Society of the United States had persuaded the military that these dolphins did not belong in military research. The Navy was already discovering that dolphins made very bad soldiers: they preferred to play with, rather than attack, designated enemies. Luther's real-life story had been told in such popular novels and films as *Day of the Dolphin*, but few people knew the plight of the Navy dolphins after their usefulness was over, their time served. Like so many other captive dolphins, they could not easily be retired or returned to the wild; they had to be retrained to fish for themselves and survive all the rigors of the open ocean.

I had sat cross-legged on a Florida Keys dock and observed several rehab trainers who once worked in aquariums or military programs but were now passionately committed to restoring these creatures to the oceans from which they had been traumatically captured. It was Luther who most moved me.

His battered face and often bewildered eyes told me that he was now an in-between creature, caught between captivity and the open sea that beckoned just beyond his saltwater lagoon with its small underwater fencing. At any moment he could leap free, but he and the others were not psychologically or physically ready to return.

"Prisoners of our wars, that's how I think of these guys," one of the rehab volunteers told me.

Across the dock from the Navy dolphins were Molly, Bogie, and Bacall, three other captive dolphins being rehabilitated. These females were being kept separate from the Navy dolphins because any pregnancy might compromise their safe return as well as complicate the labrynthian governmental red tape snarling release plans.

There were already several successful precedents for the return of captive dolphins to the wild, most notably in the work of Dr. John Lilly, famous dolphin researcher, who had returned his research subjects Joe and Rosie to the wild after studying them for years. And marine mammal biologist Randy Wells had successfully released captive dolphins back into their native Florida waters. Then there was the lively case history of captive-born Bahama Mama, who startled the world by defying the scientific skeptics and escaping her captivity in a storm. Bahama

Mama was spotted many years later happily adapted and accepted by a pod of dolphins in the wild.

As I floated on my back in the Hawaiian spinner dolphin sanctuary, I happily watched dozens of dolphins leap near me, their silver bodies sharply outlined against the bright green lava cliffs of the Big Island.

"Look out to sea!" Don's melodic voice called me from my floating reverie. As I lolled over to tread water and gaze far out beyond the bay into the open ocean, I saw what I'd only before imagined or read about. A hundred dolphins flying just above the waves, their pectoral fins and tail flukes skipping across water, whipping up tiny whitecaps in their wake.

"Crossover!" I spun around in the bay, exhilarated.

I'd waited almost two decades to witness this astonishing display of wild dolphins traveling so swiftly, with such splendid aerodynamic skill it's as if the element of air carries them along in its own warm slipstream. What must it feel like to be one of those hundred dolphins speeding in perfect sync with one another, the water, and the buoyant air? I could only imagine the joy and pleasure of such symmetry and superpod communion. And I was grateful at last to see the power and grace of crossover behavior for myself. I tried to memorize the image of so many dolphins sailing between sky and sea. And to this day, whenever I am feeling lost or low, I close my eyes and see them: the flying, free dolphins traveling toward wide open sea.

As I clambered back atop my kayak, a spinner's wake actually helped nudge me up from below the waves, and this thrust gave me the strength to pull myself completely into the sea kayak. Steadying myself with my long paddle, I smiled as the spinners stayed alongside our boats, gliding to include us in their formation.

Back in my kayak I had an even better view of a hundred spinners cavorting and porpoising through the waves. The dark blue water of open sea shone white from their splashes. I imagined that in a far-off

Florida dolphin research center, Luther, Buck, Jake, Molly, Bogie, and Bacall, as well as the girls of Dolphins Plus in Key Largo, were all feeling my telepathic transmission: pictures of these, their wild cousins, who would travel many miles today without knowing fences.

Resting more peacefully in the warm bay, a dozen or so spinners spun cartwheels near our kayaks and cruised by, turning their eyes to take us in individually. Don whistled softly, "This is the closest I've ever seen these spinners come to people." For almost an hour, the spinners courteously accompanied us through the bay, their dorsal fins only ten feet behind my kayak, their affection and company their own choice. At last, as the spinners veered off in sync to feed and rest nearer to shore, my friend Flor laughed, "Next lifetime, that's how I'm coming back—as a dolphin or a humpback."

"If you're so lucky," Don grinned. "If you're a saint, maybe you'll come back as a spinner. But if you're a Buddha, only then can you come back as a great whale."

As we paddled, Don again took up a refrain from the complicated humpback song—eerie, sonorous notes echoing off the green, misting cliffs. And I joined in with my higher, hopefully ultrasonic dolphin harmonies. As we paddled into the morning and far out to sea, I knew this was an island I would return to again and again, a sanctuary not only for cetaceans but also for myself.

Over the next five years I did return again and again to the little fishing cottage on the dolphin sanctuary, and I actually recognized some of the same spinners from previous seasons. On these visits, it seemed that my friends and I did nothing but float with the dolphins, day after long, tropical day. Early mornings, when the returning spinners were still high-spirited from night feeding far out at sea, we'd swim into the bay and bob about from dawn until 10 A.M., when the spinners sought sleep and retreat. Those hallucinatory dawns are forever a part of my memory and dreams: watery visions of snorkeling among schools of convict and yellow tangs, silvery blue Picasso triggerfish, rainbow-

colored Hawaiian blue parrotfish, and my favorite, the shy but dangerous moray eel, whose open mouth looks as if it has spent a lifetime
gnashing its spikey teeth.

Careful not to touch or swim too close to the living reef, I've found
myself surfacing for breath in tandem with a green sea turtle who gazed
at me curiously before we both dove down to glide through scarlet and
green colonies of brain and cauliflower coral. This sanctuary's fine,
sandy bottom is a brilliant white with ridges and ripples like dunes
blown into patterns, not by wind, but by the rhythmic pulse of the sea.
In these gentle, morning waves, the dolphins rest—a hundred strong.
They are safe here from the sharks, whose dark bodies would cast warning shadows against the shallow sand. They are also safe from the huge
purse seine fishing nets that since the 1980s have drowned hundreds of
thousands of dolphins every year—a number that has dropped considerably since the recent dolphin-safe monitoring efforts. But thousands
of dolphins, especially the delicate spinners, still die each year, and
proposed U.S. legislation may soon undermine the dolphin-safe labeling laws for tuna and return us to a world of dolphin slaughter.

For years, whenever I visited this dolphin sanctuary, there were very
few people. It was possible to be a lone human in this fertile, resting cove
teeming with marine life. Floating thirty feet above so many dolphins it
was impossible to count or even take them in. In what we call sleep, the
dolphins skim the sandy bottom in perfect patterns—protective males
along the outside, nursing mothers and calves in the center, juveniles
and aunts well-known for their babysitting skill in smaller groups of twos
and threes. The pops and ratcheting sounds of their echolocation, their
high-frequency whistles and click trains give the water world a percussive
and comforting reassurance. All is well, it seems.

But on my most recent visit to this Hawaiian dolphin sanctuary, in
the early spring of 2000, I was shocked to discover that the once-quiet
bay had been discovered after being listed in a tourist guidebook. We
counted the daily human toll on the dolphins: at least four zodiacs full

of snorkelers, twenty kayakers, and twenty to fifty swimmers per day. And most of this human intrusion took place during the hours from mid-morning to afternoon, when the dolphins most need refuge and rest.

Most of the people did not mean to be invasive. They simply wanted "the dolphin experience" and had not educated themselves enough to know the animal's needs, habitat, and behavior. We watched one man dive-bomb a pair of spinners just as they were swimming in a lovely belly-to-belly ballet. He had no idea they were mating.

"How would you like me to crash through your bedroom ceiling when you were making love?" one of the people I was swimming with demanded of the intruder.

"I had no idea," the man sincerely apologized. He was with a large group of people who had been promised by their tour leader, a self-pro-claimed "dolphin-communicator," that the dolphins had healing pow-ers. Her pamphlets also proclaimed that the dolphins were divine messengers and perhaps even extraterrestrials. Many of this group were gravely ill and barely able to stay afloat without hanging onto Styrofoam boards or kayaks; they had paid up to five hundred dollars per day for three hours with the spinner dolphins, even though this was a federally protected reserve open to all. Yet for all their travel and expense, no one had given this group any instructions in the most basic marine mammal biology or the proper etiquette when near a wild animal.

"Don't touch, don't dive too near, stay quiet so they can rest, and just observe without attracting any attention," my British Columbian friend Darryl and his wife Sylvia politely taught several people in this group.

Apparently these common-sense rules were the exact opposite of what this group had been told. "I thought we were supposed to whistle, spin around, dive down into the dolphins, and get them to play with us!" a woman from Australia said, confused. "If the spinners don't like what we're doing, can't they just leave?"

The woman had no idea that this bay was a retreat for the spinner dolphins and that they were here to rest, give birth, mate, and nurse their young. She did not realize that if the spinners were harassed into leaving the sanctuary they would face predators and rough waters just when they were the weariest and most vulnerable. When we told her all this, she was chagrined and stopped her shrill whistling and diving into the resting pond. Instead, she floated with us quietly at the surface, simply observing.

Others, however, were not so respectful. One woman repeatedly chased the dolphins in her kayak and made a great belly flop into the bay, scattering a resting pod into disarray. When one of my friends courteously asked her not to keep disturbing the dolphins, she shrugged, "Well, I've already got *my healing,* anyway," she said. "I'm ready to go back to shore."

As my devotion to this spinner dolphin sanctuary grows, so does my concern. Worried that these human intruders might disturb the spinners, I have spent more time in land-based observation of the spinners, documenting an independent research team that is now studying the bay to gauge the effect of boat traffic and swimmers on the spinner dolphins.

One of the naturalists in this land-based study conducted by the Ocean Mammal Institute, Leigh Calvez, has studied dolphins and whales here and around the world for more than ten years. She published her conclusions after two seasons of studying this spinner nursery. "Boat traffic and too much intense human interaction are interfering with these dolphins and their rest cycles. When the spinners come into the bay, weary from their open-ocean fishing and traveling, they need quiet time. It would be like a human coming home from a grueling eight-hour-a-day job and being greeted by a parade of boats and people throwing a big party. Too much interaction in any species is stressful, and we need to respect the dolphins' privacy."

Much of the research done by Calvez, and Dr. Marcia Greene has focused on protecting marine mammals in Hawaii. It was their data and scientific observation that helped stop motorboat traffic noise and parasailing during the winter calving season in the Hawaiian islands.

Their research and a concerned community would eventually lead to an official study of this bay in 1999 as a possible-swimmers only area — so the dolphins could truly escape people and rest in their sanctuary.

⌐

IN 1996, WHEN I returned to this dolphin sanctuary with my co-editors Linda Hogan and Deena Metzger for a book titled *Intimate Nature: The Bond between Women and Animals,* I was just beginning to understand my own journey from writer to activist. Deep in the open ocean, Linda and I were drifting along one early morning in our sturdy two-person sea kayak. We had learned that spinners preferred quiet between ten A.M. and one P.M., so we respectfully ventured through their bay at six A.M., when most of the dolphins were out sea-fishing. It was March, mid-calving season for humpbacks; every day from our sprawling veranda we'd watch humpbacks breaching.

"No one has ever witnessed a humpback birth," I echoed stories I'd heard from my marine mammal scientist friends. "It's the Holy Grail of humpback researchers."

"Maybe we'll be lucky," Linda smiled.

In our kayak we were silent, scanning the azure horizon for any sign of humpbacks or spinners. So far out from land we were not afraid, even though we probably should have been, since sharks patrol the Hawaiian Islands. When we did talk it was usually about the many stories by women around the world we were reading for our anthology. All of us had been struck by the differences between the way women in the field relate to their study of animal behavior and the previous, male-dominated research, in which animals were given numbers, not names. Jane Goodall used names in her pioneering work with chimpanzees. Two other primate researchers, Dian Fossey with mountain gorillas and Birute Galdikas with orangutans, with Goodall made up the

"Trimates" chosen by renowned paleoanthropologist Louis Leakey. He believed women were better observers than men and that these three women had not been exposed to the bias of too much academic training before they entered the field.

Birute Galdikas often tells the story of her first interview with Leakey after she had requested he send her to Borneo to study the elusive, solitary orangutans. Leakey's test was to ask her to observe a deck of cards. "Which are dark cards?" he asked. When she studied the cards, she noticed instead that there was the slightest suggestion of a bend in certain cards. She told Leakey, "I don't know which are dark, but some of the cards are bent." This skillful observation, showing that Galdikas was insightful enough to note something other than what she had been directed to see, delighted Leakey and showed him that here was his third primate researcher.

Goodall, Fossey, and Galdikas would all be criticized by the academic worlds, even when they went on to dramatically revolutionize the world of primate research with new discoveries. Goodall found that chimpanzees use tools, Fossey showed that gorillas are peaceable, and Galdikas discovered that orangutans are at once solitary and fierce nurturers of their young. Some scientists damned the Trimates for their intimate involvement with the species they studied. And in Fossey's case, when poachers murdered her for her efforts to save mountain gorillas from their guns, some critics sniped at her as if she had brought on her own death by being so connected to her fellow primates.

But it was these women, as well as others living in the field such as Katy Payne and Cynthia Moss with elephants, Alexandra Morton with orcas, and Denise Herzing with spotted dolphins, who most inspired my own burgeoning work with and study of wild animals. Galdikas had given a ringing answer to her critics. In the mid-1990s, her beloved orangutans were running screaming out of Borneo forests set aflame by developers whose short sight would destroy entire rain forests for cattle-raising and timber. Galdikas said, "If we're studying a species in the wild, and that species is on the verge of extinction, then I don't understand how any-body can say it's more important to study that species rather than to save it." Such heroism, even when her own life has been threatened for her activism, has earned Galdikas the nickname "the third angel."

And when Goodall crusades for the cause of laboratory chim-panzees, she rises above the pettiness of her hard-science critics and inspires multitudes to consider empathy an appropriate relationship to other animals. "Humans are a species capable of compassion," she writes, "and we should develop a heightened moral responsibility for beings who are so like ourselves."

With such inspiration as Goodall and the other scientists, I too knew that I was crossing the line from observer to participant, from journalist to advocate. Though I hadn't quite made that choice consciously. But that day, floating in the sea kayak, I felt a stirring in my heart and a deep gratitude for all that animals had given me. I wanted to give back some part of the pleasure the animals had offered me. By helping to save other animals, I was also saving myself.

With all this in mind, that day Linda Hogan and I floated out to sea, I asked her, "How did you come to the animals? I mean, over and above what you inherited from your own traditional Chickasaw culture?"

"They just come to me," she answered with her usual directness. "The animals come to everybody, not just Native Americans. All of us. But not everybody listens or sees what the animals are offering."

As we rocked on gentle swells, surrounded by an ocean warm and spacious, I pondered my recent years and how the animals had come to me not only in daily life and dreams, but also in a sense of moral obli-gation. All my life animals had surrounded me—from forest birthplace to ocean shores, from desert to New York City, and now in my chosen watery Seattle world. I had always been guided and defined by animal presence: from Smokey Bear to that snake who encircled my tiny two-year-old chest, from wild wolves and grizzlies to domesticated horses, cats, and dogs, and finally to the choosing of one species, cetaceans, to which to devote a lifetime apprenticeship of study, encounters, and relationships. Animals had inspired my life's work and my sense of the sacred. But there was something more than celebration and encounter with another species that seemed required of me.

As we floated out to sea, I realized that in the past several years I had grown from an advocate to an activist, without quite acknowledging it. Since the early 1990s, when I'd found myself in Alaska at the Wolf Summit, or the years I'd been involved with rehabilitating captive dolphins and protesting the Sea World captivity of orcas, I'd been acting more as an advocate than a journalist. Now, bobbing about in the wild ocean with spinner dolphins racing past us back to the sanctuary of their calm bay, I lay on the hull of the boat and smiled up at the tropical sky. There was no going back to days of observation without activism or conservation, I knew. But times like this of simple rest in sync with the spinner pod were a respite from the fray of advocacy.

As if sensing my meditative mood, Linda paddled for us both in a leisurely way as we lazed about on the waves. The sea was so still, even this far from shore, that it was like a saltwater siesta. We didn't make a sound, just a whoosh against the waves as we wafted, watching, eyes on the moving horizon. With my back leaning against the fiberglass kayak I felt just the smallest vibration along my spine. Before I could sit up, Linda was raising the paddle high above her head and whispering, "What is that sound? I can feel it in my legs more than I can hear it. It's like . . . like thunder, but soft."

Or audible heat lightning, I thought, and the lines of one of my favorite George Herbert poems, "God's Grandeur," echoed in my mind:

It will shimmer out.
Shining like shook foil.

There was such a shining and shimmering now in the sea as the humpback's song rose up from fathoms deep and vibrated along our kayak,

our limbs, swirling deep into our bellies and racing up spines like electricity. So alive, this song, and resonant, and we were just little tuning
forks struck to vibrate alongside this exact and grand chord. From
beneath us, as the song surfaced, we listened to sonorous, bass rum-
blings, eerie French horn and elephantine trumpeting, then a series of
otherworldly chirps and mewling like small, lost kittens. It was mournful and triumphant, this song, moving and mesmerizing.

We assumed the male escort humpback was deep beneath us in the
ocean, so we were not prepared for a quivering in the waves around us.
Not ten feet from the kayak, a sudden upsurge of sea, and a dark, behemoth body thrust up and up—almost two stories she seemed—as the
female humpback breached before us. Powerful geysers of saltwater
splashed upwards with her leap and her flippers flapped warm air with
the thwacking sound of her gigantic water wings. We rocked in two-
story-high waves, our stomachs full of flutters as when an elevator
drops. Amazed at the gliding rise of this humpback, we stared, open-
mouthed, at her high ridge of spine and fin curving into the deep and
slow-motion grace of tail flukes. Her massive flukes, the most powerful
muscle of any animal on earth, seemed to walk on water as she leaned
on the air and crashed into a mighty back dive. She dove beneath us
where the male was still singing and for an eternal moment we, too,
were part of that ancient love song. At last, like a wave goodbye, the
humpback surfaced again, just the dark mountain ridge of her sloped
back, then her black and white, notched tail flukes lifted, poised to
gleam in the sunlight, slapping water as she dove.

Linda and I confess to this day that neither of us has been quite the
same since that intimate encounter with the humpback in our tiny
kayak. With one flick of her immense tail, she could have sunk us. But
her breach was perfectly coordinated, so careful of our little boat, as if
this great being had a consciousness that was far beyond anything we
could fathom. Several hours after that encounter at sea, we saw from

shore in the same place a humpback with a newborn calf. We realized that although we had not witnessed the birth of a humpback calf, we had been afloat in the ballet of the birth labor and the escort's singing. No wonder we both felt changed forever. No wonder we vowed each in our own way to keep working for the whales of the world.

O N OLOWALU POINT, a gentle, green bluff high on the
island of Maui, a scientific plainchant of humpback whale
researchers rises like a lilting call and response. I had returned to
Hawaii in 1998 to profile the Ocean Mammal Institute's lone, land-
based independent research team.

"Blow at 180!" cries a young woman, scanning the panoramic sea
below. Ten sets of powerful binoculars swing left to fix on the misting
plume of breath puffing up from the turquoise waters as a great humpback mother surfaces.

Suddenly there are whales everywhere, at least five pods, surfacing
to breathe within 30 seconds of each other. Are any of these humpbacks the same mother I encountered in my kayak three years ago? I
wonder how she and her calf have fared through their several migra-
tions. I steady and fix my binoculars on a raised tail fluke, studying the
patterns of white and black, the slight notch out of the tip. My heart
rate increases.

"Peduncle arch! Pec slap!" another researcher shouts as a humpback's pectoral fin, gigantic even from this height, slowly rises out of the bright water.

"Fluke up!" a young woman calls as a whale tail shoots straight up, lingers in midair, then disappears. This fluke signals a long dive that may last up to 15 minutes. The calves, however, can hold their breath for only about five minutes, so these island waters, with their shallow and warm protection, are perfect for newborns.

"Slip under!" A researcher spies a whale's signature arch of its humped back before its deep descent.

These ten researchers, with more than twenty-three years of whale observation experience between them, all take a moment themselves to breathe, drink quick sips of water, and smear on more sunscreen against the glaring, midday sun. Several glance over a precisely plotted graph that shows a grid of red and blue triangles and squiggles.

"You see," explains Dr. Marsha Green, the psychobiology professor and scientist who is overseeing a study of boat noise and traffic on these humpbacks, "we chart the exact position of the whales and the boats. Then we watch all the behaviors around these boats, such as the whales' speed of travel, their time underwater, their aerial behaviors, as well as when the whales change directions."

This land-based research is unique in that most previous studies have been done from the water, with a perspective limited to what can be seen from sea level. Perched high above the Pacific Ocean, these researchers can truly study the big picture, watching up to ten pods at a time, documenting the activity of both whales and boats.

"We're whale-sitting," someone says, then raises his binoculars. "Double breach! Look at that, will you! Never seen that before." Everyone scrambles to get a look and there is much good-natured laughter.

"Is that our pod?"

"Yes, that's *our* pod," another calls back like a proud parent.

"Check out that red boat at 186," a researcher warns. "It's way too close, don't you think?"

There is an ironclad marine rule here in this whale nursery that no boat can come within a hundred yards of these humpbacks. Among most whale-watching boats there is a protective manner toward these whales, even as thousands of island visitors each year are brought here to watch the humpbacks' aquatic dance.

Dr. Green worries about the effects of too much boat activity here. Five boats used in the study range from large whale-watching boats with two 200-horsepower engines as loud as 120 decibels down to a sailboat and a zodiac. The type of boat and loudness of engine causes dramatic changes in the whales' behavior.

Green found that whales swim more than three times faster (13.98 miles per hour) around big boats with 120-decibel engines than around the sailboat under motor, with which they dove deeper and swam more peacefully (3.96 mph). Her concern about the effect of boat noise and traffic in the Hawaiian humpback nurseries was intensified to alarm a month after this research study on Maui when she learned of the U.S. Navy's plans to target singing humpback whales in the middle of their calving season off the Big Island. The reason given for their sonar tests was to research new sonar for use against enemy submarines.

Moving her Ocean Mammal Institute's research team to the Big Island, Green hoped to provide baseline data and the only independent monitoring of these sonar tests outside the Navy itself. As one well-respected marine mammal scientist put it, "The sad fact is that much of marine mammal research today is funded by the U.S. Navy. This is a clear conflict of interest—like setting the hawks to guard the hen house. Without independent research, the data can be contaminated by a military or warfare agenda."

When the Navy's low-frequency active sonar (LFAS) tests began in March 1998, Green's research team was there to document any change in behavior. And her dramatic data caused her to file a lawsuit in federal court on behalf of the humpbacks to stop the targeting of singing humpbacks. Her suit was soon joined by four other lawsuits on behalf of environmental groups and native Hawaiians to stop the testing. These suits were unsuccessful.

"I couldn't just stand by and not voice my concern," Green told me on her field cell phone, crackling with static and her outrage. I was back on the mainland writing an article on the Navy's sonar and her research during this testing period. She cited studies showing that whales avoid sounds higher than 120 decibels—60 decibels lower than the 180-decibel Navy sonar tests. "The problem is," Green continued, "it's impossible to really document long-term effects on the whales' hearing, communication, and reproduction rates—the most important issue for a species that is already struggling to survive."

"Humans wouldn't let these loud sounds into their own nurseries," she said sadly. "Why would anyone allow war games in a whale nursery? The Cold War is over in our terrestrial world, but in the oceans it's just beginning. The really frightening thing is that the sonar the Navy plans to use—up to 235 decibels—in oceans around the world produces a pressure wave that is 100 billion times more powerful than a loud motorboat engine. This level of pressure can deafen and kill not just whales, but other marine life." She paused, then concluded, "And a deaf whale is a dead whale."

I held the phone and all I could think about was my last trip to Hawaii: kayaking, floating in the embrace of a humpback's singing— how my bones had echoed with those elegant and low vibrations. It was almost unbearable to listen as Green continued her explanation of what was happening in these same waters that I'd come to believe were, if not holy, then another home for me, as well as the whales. Like the professor she is, Green lectured me on sound and its acoustic powers, to heal and to harm.

Both humans and whales are vulnerable not only to the loudness of any sound, but also to its energy, pressure, and vibration, she said. In humans, sounds above 155 decibels inflict immediate ear damage; sounds above 170 decibels cause generalized tissue damage. Underwater at a certain proximity, the low-frequency sonar can rupture human or whale tissue and cause internal bleeding. The Navy usually issues divers' alerts before their sound tests to protect human life. But what about the whales?

A storm of foreign scientists broke forth on the Internet and in scientific papers decrying the Navy LFAS testing. In the March 1998 issue of the prestigious magazine *Science*, zoologist Alexandros Frantzis of the University of Athens linked mass strandings of Cuvier's beaked whales to military LFAS tests along the Kyparissiakos Gulf in 1996. Canadian marine mammal expert Dr. Lindy Weilgart of Dalhousie University has studied whale communication for seventeen years. Weilgart asked a Hawaiian federal judge in her testimony against LFAS, "At what point are all scientists and policymakers going to be convinced of the harmful effects of LFAS? And will there still be marine life alive in our seas when this point is reached?" In an October 1999 article published in the *Christian Science Monitor*, Weilgart went on to state, "Use of LFAS could well alter hearing ability in whales and other marine animals over a 15-mile radius, and could cause profound behavioral disturbance over an area bigger than Texas." Weilgart joins many other marine mammal scientists internationally in demanding that the Navy halt its LFAS program. "I cannot imagine why we would subject marine inhabitants, the majority of which are highly sensitive to sound, to yet another source of pollution."

During the Navy's sound tests, Dr. Green's Ocean Mammal Institute research team documented an unusual sight: an abandoned humpback calf who for five hours breached in a panicked search for its mother, who was assumed to have died. "In all my years of studying Hawaiian humpbacks, neither I nor anyone I know has ever seen an abandoned cetacean calf," Green told me. "Yet this season during the testing, there were three abandoned—one humpback, one dolphin, one melon-headed whale—all within the LFAS testing area. This is the most damning evidence there is that these sonar tests are damaging and disorienting to cetaceans."

As I interviewed others on Green's research team, I felt a rising despair. Her longtime assistant, naturalist Leigh Calvez, documented a March morning during the most intense 1998 LFAS tests off the Big Island. The concerned team was watching from the hillside over several hours as a distraught, orphaned humpback calf searched for his mother. "The bond between calves and mothers is very strong in the first year of the calf's life, with moms fighting fiercely to protect their calves from harm," Calvez told me. "Physical contact is crucial. A humpback mother often hovers just below the surface, supporting her resting calf across her nose, or hangs motionless about twenty feet down with her baby tucked under her chin between her fifteen-foot-long pectoral flippers. It is unusual for a calf to wander even four body lengths, or 180 feet, from a mother."

And yet there was this orphaned humpback calf searching frantically for his mother. It seemed to give evidence of earlier warnings from Weilgart, among others, that "unnatural acoustical disturbances to which these animals are not adapted could interfere with the crucial mother-calf bond."

In the first four hours of documenting this abandoned calf's plight, Calvez and her team recorded a total of 230 breaches by the little calf—almost one frantic breach per minute. After five hours of observation, they had also noted 671 pectoral slaps, sure signs that this baby was in trouble and on the edge of exhaustion. "As we left," Calvez said in a low, sorrowful voice, "that weary calf was drifting so close to shore that it was slapping its flippers in the breaking surf near sharp, lava rocks just below our observation station." Later that night, someone else saw the calf, still alone as darkness fell. At this point the calf had been without its mother for at least seven hours from the research team's initial sighting. "We never saw the calf again," Calvez said sadly.

"Shark-bait," someone less scientific said, as I related the research teams' documentation of the abandoned calf, as well as other evidence of the abandoned humpback and melon-headed whale calves. "That's what the Navy sonar has left the next generation of whales."

On March 30, 1998, the Navy did halt testing in Hawaii, but not in response to international outrage. The reason for stopping was simple: the whales had abandoned the testing area a month earlier than usual. The vanishing whales were no surprise to Green and her team. It reminded them of similar sonar tests off California, in which Navy scientists themselves documented that gray whales changed migration routes to avoid the low-frequency sounds and that blue whales had decreased their vocalizations essential to finding mates by 50 percent.

"War games in whale nurseries," Green repeated sadly. "And whales disoriented and fleeing from their own ancient migration paths. This is what the future is all about if the Navy sonar continues. Scientists won't stop it. It will have to be the peoples of the world and especially U.S. citizens whose tax dollars are being used to support this dangerous sonar." She concluded, "It's really a matter of educating ourselves and our young people to understand that the fate of the great whales is really our own fate, because what happens in these humpback nurseries shows the health of our oceans. And the way the oceans go, we go."

This was the International Year of the Oceans and yet this 1998 season in the Hawaiian islands would be remembered as one of the most hazardous to marine mammals, as well as to those trying to protest the LFAS sonar test. Several protesters who dived into the water when they knew the Navy was conducting its playback sound tests on singing humpbacks were injured. One of them, Chris Reid, a naturalist from Kona who has observed spinner dolphins for the past eight years, witnessed a pod of spinners "dangerously close to the shoreline, clustering in a tight, defensive posture on the surface and exhibiting constant and excessive vocalization." Reid was in the water with the spinners during this sighting and heard the sonar, although the Navy ship was not in sight. Reid described her rather heroic efforts to join with the spinners during the sound blasts as simple empathy: "Because of the erratic behavior of the dolphins, I felt compelled to dive down and experience what they were experiencing." Reid described the sonar as "a very unusual sound, with a piercing quality and no harmonic. I felt as though the sound were penetrating my entire being."

When she left the water after experiencing the sonar tests alongside the spinners, Reid was taken to the emergency room, complaining of intense nausea and disorientation. The examining doctor, Barbara Schmid, noted Reid's symptoms: "She could barely talk, had difficulties in expressing and finding words, expressed dizziness and confusion. My diagnosis with this healthy person would be normal post-traumatic reaction—but what was the trauma? The only possibility would be the LFAS testing to which she was exposed." Reid would suffer symptoms of this sonar testing for almost a month, including sleep disruption, inability to concentrate, loss of short-term memory, and depression. According to Calvez's article, "By the Time We Have Proof," published in Britain's *Ecologist* and *Ocean Realm*, Reid was exposed to 125 decibels, which the Navy compared with the song of a humpback whale at 400 meters. But Reid adamantly disagrees, saying, "It's like comparing apples and oranges. The quality of the sound was entirely different."

The Hawaii legislature, the local press, and other Hawaiian activists all vehemently protested the Navy's sonar tests. Members of Congress Patsy Mink and Lynn Woolsey wrote to the National Marine Fisheries Service, which originally gave permits to the Navy for its sonar research, "The National Humpback Whale sanctuary was created to provide a refuge for these whales. These booms violate the very concept of a sanctuary." But while the Hawaiian islands were roiling in anger and outrage over their whale nursery turned into a military war game, the mainland press was eerily quiet. Except for my long article in the *Seattle Times*, brief reports in the *Los Angeles Times* and the *Christian Science Monitor*, and a small piece in the *Washington Post*, media coverage was not as widespread in the mainland press as it was on-line and internationally. When a science writer for ABC News Online contacted me about the sonar tests and I gave her all my sources, she wrote an article only to have her ABC News editor tell her, "We have to kill this piece for now. The Navy called and asked that we not run any negative press until the environmental impact statement [EIS] next year in 1999."

In fact, in February 2000, I did get a call from ABC News, at last researching the Navy sonar, but after the EIS was released. "It is much more difficult to stop something once the EIS is filed," commented Green. By now hers and others lawsuits to stop the Navy's sonar and protect marine mammals had been joined by an expanded protest and investigative outcry. CNN did an extensive three-part on-line report on the sonar, titled "Is Spreading Sonar Smart Science or Overkill." The CNN online series also asked, "Does the Navy need LFAS? Not everyone agrees that there is such a need or that LFAS is the way to go. A contractor warned in a trade magazine that active sonar would reveal its source, drawing enemy fire."

The Natural Resources Defense Council has called for a ban on the sonar, labeling LFAS "acoustic harassment" that is "already taking a toll on marine life." And slowly other commentaries raised moral and scientific questions, calling for more research and scrutiny of this new sonar before the Navy finally deploys it.

The EIS itself was highly controversial. Dr. Green dismissed the EIS as "a sham. It is inconclusive and misleading." Noting that the official tests were carried out over a matter of weeks on only four species of whales, Green asks, "Why did the Navy not test at the highest limits (up to 235 decibels)? Their EIS gives the public *no idea* what might really happen in our oceans if the Navy uses this sonar at its highest intensity."

In their EIS, the Navy admits their "research did not use the full source level of LFAS." Joe Johnson, the LFAS program manager, stated that the Hawaii tests were not deployed at full capacity "because we were too close to shore. There's an issue of diver safety." If there were people in the water and the LFAS were tested at 215 decibals, would they be harmed? he was asked. If those divers were at a certain depth and very close to the refracted sound beam, Johnson conceded, "it's probably not going to be any good for them."

The sonar proved not to be any good for whales six months later, in mid-March of 2000, when sixteen cetaceans of various species beached off the islands of the Bahamas while the Navy was testing its LFAS at still-undisclosed decibel levels. Mass stranding of multiple species is very rare. A renowned marine mammal specialist, Ken Balcomb, the director of the Center for Whale Research in Friday Harbor, Washington, happened to be in the Bahamas at the time. He and Dr. Darlene Ketten of Harvard Medical School were on the scene to conduct necropsies on the sadly stranded whales. In meticulous dissections of the dead whales, they found evidence of blood in the eyes, blood in the brains, and lesions from imploded and exploded lungs in the beaked whales that had beached themselves. It was not a pretty picture and spoke tragically to an inquiry by the National Marine Fisheries Service (NMFS), which had officially issued the Navy permits for their sonar testing in Hawaii and California.

After the Bahamas stranding, the U.S. press ran poignant photos of children in the surf trying to save the dying whales, which included a minke, an Atlantic spotted dolphin, and Cuvier's and Blainville's beaked whales. At last LFAS's was a mainstream controversy; *60 Minutes*, *Dateline NBC*, and NBC's Miami station developed stories for widespread distribution. A story that had for several years been censored or buried because it happened far away in the Hawaiian islands, in the Mediterranean, or off the West Coast suddenly became a hot topic on television and in newspapers in the United States, as it had been internationally and on the Internet.

The country's largest animal conservation organization, the Humane Society of the United States, and the National Resource Defense Council wrote strong letters to the Navy and the NMFS to protest the sonar tests and demanded that the tests be stopped because they were in direct violation of the Marine Mammal Protection and the Endangered Species acts. The Navy dismissed these protests. After less than thirty days of their own investigation, the Navy announced that the mass stranding off the Bahamas was a "coincidence." And it continued with its plans in May 2000 to test the sonar off the coasts of New Jersey and Greece—in the very waters that had seen the mass stranding in 1998 of Cuvier's beaked whales.

At last the Navy's arrogant disregard for its own government's Endangered Species Act, as well as its denial of growing concern among international scientists, drew fire from the NMFS, which finally seemed to be standing up to the military by writing it a warning letter. Patricia Kurkul of the NMFS criticized the Navy for not allowing adequate time for the agency to review the Navy's renewed proposal for continued testing of the sonar. In May 2000, when the Navy was preparing to conduct more tests—at levels as high as 210 decibels—off New Jersey, the Natural Resources Defense Council and the Humane Society sued to block the tests. The environmental groups worried that the sonar would devastate already endangered squid and other marine life. Quietly, the Navy dropped its plans for New Jersey. But it continued its LFAS tests in the Mediterranean and pushed ahead for more LFAS tests in the Azores in the late summer of 2000.

How can the Navy always know where a whale pod or people might be in the open ocean? Whereas humans can always leave the water, whales and other marine life cannot. The sea is their whole world. And it is our life-support system as well, providing us with food, medicine, transportation, and climate control. We are more threatened by our planet's environmental degradation than by phantom enemy submarines. Do we really need this new sonar detection when, as Senator Russell D. Feingold told Congress in 1999, "the submarine capabilities of our potential adversaries have noticeably deteriorated or remain far behind those of our Navy"? And in light of the recent sinking of a Russian sub, the *Kursk*, in the Barents Sea, which showed the world just how unequal the Russian Navy is to continuing Cold War capabilities, why is the United States rushing to develop a sonar that may well prove more dangerous to our environment than our national security?

As this story plays out into the next century and the Navy spends $350 million to continue developing its new acoustic defense system and ships for deployment into the world's oceans, the international outcry is increasing. Changing their earlier argument that the United States needs LFAS for self-defense, the Navy's Web site now claims that LFAS is necessary to protect against a future in which other nations might "disrupt peace and stability by interrupting transportation and commerce, thus impacting world economy."

It will probably not be the scientists who police the military or protect other species. As Calvez ends her article, "The military used to protect people. Now it protects commerce. My years as a scientist have led me to wonder if the threat from our enemies is as real as the threat we pose to ourselves and other creatures with whom we share the planet in our race to defend ourselves." Green is more blunt: "Scientists can be bought on either side, that's why independent research is so crucial to the whales' well-being." And Katy Payne, in her new book *Distant Thunder: In the Company of Elephants,* offers this harrowing look at science and its ethical limits: "Since science is without morals, it offers itself as a sanctuary from the dangers of emotional commitment."

And yet emotional commitment is what my own and others' bonds are all about in our lives with animals. More than any other event, this LFAS story taught me that true change and concern for other species would not come first from the mainstream scientists (and often Defense Department–funded experts) who study animals. True reciprocity and respect for other animals would come most from ordinary people. I have found that in advocating for animals, one doesn't need a Ph.D. or a scientific grant. All that is needed is an open heart, observation skills, and a willingness to get actively involved.

In South America it is said that when one is born, an animal is born alongside, whether we recognize that animal or not as a kindred spirit. And when we die, the myth goes, that same animal goes with us to accompany and guide us into the other worlds. When we discover the species with whom we are aligned at birth or whom we come to recognize in life, it is simply a matter of apprenticing oneself to education and study and lifelong conservation.

On my last trip to Maui for a Whales Alive conference I watched as a respected humpback researcher showed a video with never-before-seen footage of humpback interaction. The researcher's vessel had come upon a lifeless, floating male humpback. No one knew the cause of death, but as the divers entered the water to observe and document the whale, they were surprised to see another male humpback move toward the corpse. In a series of startling maneuvers, the living humpback lifted the limp body of the other again and again to the surface, the way a mother will nudge her calf to take its first breath. After what struck the researchers as a ritualistic repetition of this breathing attempt, the huge male humpback floated motionless beneath the dead one. Slowly he rose up, his expansive pectoral flippers wrapping around the other humpback. In this graceful elegy, the living humpback floated for five hours, fully embracing his dead kin.

"Some people at first thought it might be sexual behavior," the scientist said, rather doubtfully. "Or some sort of display of dominance." The scientist cleared his throat as if to make a radically bold statement: "But after a time it became clear that this was, well, what we might call *caretaking* behavior." He paused, as if he had taken the greatest risk of his career, then his voice rose out over the darkened room where some, no matter how scientific their bent, quietly wept. "That's why I've named this video 'No Greater Love.'"

"No greater love"—there, he had said it and in public. No greater love than to lay down one's life for a friend. It is something that Birute Galdikas understands every day as she works to save orangutans orphaned by forest fires on Borneo; it is something Jane Goodall understands whenever she braves a visit to a medical laboratory and looks into the eyes of a chimpanzee victim of countless experiments. It is what Dian Fossey embraced that led to her own murder. And it is what Katy Payne means when she pleads, "I dream that a day will come when people will value wild animals not for money but for who they are and what we can learn from then. If we learn to listen as often and as well as elephants do, it is possible that listening will keep the world safe."

There is no greater love than to recognize love between species and within other species quite distinct from our own. This is what I've learned as well in my life with animals, and this is what leads me deeper into a bond that, like that humpback's embrace, lifts me again and again to the surface.

SIXTEEN

LONE, SOCIABLE

ONE LEARNS NOT to ask for directions along the winding, waterfront back roads of Nova Scotia's eastern shore.

"Looking to find that wild beluga baby, you?" A laconic fisherman overheard us trying to chat with the waitress about Guysborough Harbour, without directly asking her the way to get there.

"Yes, we've been lost most of the day," I admitted hesitantly. By now I was leery that this local would again give us inscrutable directions — past the white church, down the alley lane, look for the ferry dock (where we waited hours, only to discover that no ferry had run there for two years).

"Never one of us lost as much as that little whale, our Wilma," the man shook his head and took his last sip of black coffee at the counter.

His tone was sad, but not sympathetic. As with most of the clannish local people we'd met in our travels through the fishing villages that dot this picturesque but depressed marine drive, the man seemed suspicious of outsiders. There was an edge of blame that blanketed locals' faces just as surely as their famous twilight fogs. Something was amiss here: The once-great spruce forests lay in haphazard heaps awaiting logging trucks, the only traffic we saw along the coastal roads; the island's lobster and other fishing industries—cod and salmon—had collapsed from overfishing and governmental mismanagement. In fact, the headlines of the daily newspaper the fisherman tossed aside as he stood to leave the café cried out: "No Easy Sell on Fish Aid."

As we respectfully stood aside to let the fisherman take his leave, he paused a moment as if to truly take us in. What did he see? Several women in rain slickers and waterproof caps, though the mid-June sunshine was brilliant. Perhaps it was our sensible boating gear that softened his sharp features, wrinkled from years of salt spray and weather. Or perhaps it was our hopefulness when he had so little hope left. "Don't matter that you're lost, ladies. Wilma, she'll find you." He almost smiled and pushed back his hat by way of saying goodbye. "She found us."

And so began one of the most heartwarming encounters I would ever experience with another species—a story that would turn out to be a surprising success—here in one of the most unlikely places for any kind of success. Wilma was the nickname the locals gave what scientists call a lone, sociable beluga calf. No one knows what happened to Wilma's mother. In the past, fishermen from the St. Lawrence region had sometimes mistakenly blamed migrating belugas, *other* outsiders, for competing over dwindling fishing stocks. In the 1920s, the only known beluga in Chedebucto Bay was perceived as a possible threat to fishing stocks and was shot. Some in the village now claimed that Wilma had lost her mother to an angry fisherman's bullet, or that the mother was caught up accidentally and drowned in the baitfish nets. Whatever happened to Wilma's mother, her young calf had been as loyal and fiercely persistent as any Nova Scotian. The two-year-old calf had simply stayed put in Guysborough Harbour, claimed the fertile waters as her home, and since 1993 had refused to leave. In 1998, the 3.5-meter Wilma was estimated to be eight years old. Adult belugas can weigh up to 2,000 pounds and reach an average length of 15 feet (or 4.5 meters.) After several years, a sign appeared on a rocky shore near the chilly waters of one of Wilma's favorite playgrounds: "Caution. Whale Habitat. Reduce Speed." And in the tiny town of Guysborough another sign showed up at the restaurant: "Home of Wilma the Whale."

Even islanders had come to admire Wilma's year-round loyalty. She was no Come-from-Away—or CFA, as the Nova Scotians called outsiders. After six years of residence in the rough waters of Chedabucto Bay, Wilma was one of them. Perhaps it was her own instinctive need for community that made the young white whale swim in circles around the harbor, recognizing and approaching certain friendly boats by the distinctive sounds of their motors. Wilma claimed several buoys in the bay, especially a tall red-and-white metal one that clanged and bobbed about reliably. She seemed to relate to this particular buoy as "home." The buoy offered Wilma the sense of belonging, personal space, and identity that other belugas might have given her. These "inanimate companions" were steady objects with whom she had forged a trust and dependence. So when, unknowingly, humans tried to come between Wilma and her special buoys, she often showed signs of stress and agitation, much like the separation anxiety a young child experiences when his or her parents disappear for any length of time.

Belugas are among the most sociable and playful of all whales. Rarely is a beluga ever seen alone, as their smaller dolphin cousins sometimes are. Recently scientists have begun to study the phenomenon of lone, sociable dolphins, which some researchers term "ambassador dolphins." One theory is that perhaps a lone, sociable dolphin has some physical disability that might prohibit its keeping up with the fast-traveling pod. One lone, sociable dolphin who died and was necropsied revealed only half a lung. So perhaps the dolphins who leave their pods and seek interaction with humans are simply adapting to a physical limitation within their own species. Yet still they seek company. And after all, humans *are* other mammals, distant cousins in the same family.

Until Wilma, only a handful of lone beluga whales had been sighted in the world. In 1980, one solitary beluga was seen off Long Island, New York; in 1985, another was identified off New Haven, Connecticut; a third solitary, sociable beluga was observed in 1998 off eastern Quebec, near Labrador. All of these lone belugas were female. Belugas are actually dolphins (*Delphinapterus leucas*) from the family *Monodontidae*. Their intense social bonds and extraordinary vocalizations—high-pitched trills, whistles, squeaks, and exultant "singing"— gave them the nickname "sea canaries." From my years visiting Mauyak in the Point Defiance Zoo, I had grown very fond of the vocalizations of the captive belugas. And I was looking forward to encountering my first wild beluga. In my musings during our long, wandering trek to find her in Guysborough Harbour, I had wondered about this poignant coincidence: Mauyak in captivity had lost four calves; Wilma in the wild had lost a mother.

I was here with my marine mammal biologist friend Dr. Toni Frohoff, an authority in human-cetacean interaction, both in the wild and in captive situations. Toni was research director for the Whale Stewardship Project, under the expert direction of marine mammal researcher and advocate Cathy Kinsman. Toni was leading a behavioral study of Wilma, which included local interns, for the Stewardship Project. Toni, who lives on Bainbridge Island in Washington, and Cathy, who lives in Toronto, Ontario, had invited me to come meet Wilma and tell her story from a conservation perspective.

When we at last found the village of Guysborough, we did not find Wilma. Instead we found a simmering controversy among villagers. Many were afraid that the Whale Stewardship Project was here to capture and move Wilma away from the village. Guysborough did not want to lose their beloved beluga nor the modest eco-tourism industry she had spawned in their depressed village. While Guysborough had flourished in the 1800s and early 1900s as a center for nearby logging, gold-mining, and fishing industries, its fortunes had dwindled along with the trees, the minerals, and the fish. In this last decade of the twentieth century, Guysborough was no longer a center, but a remote village whose young people anticipated leaving home to make their livelihoods elsewhere as Come-from-Aways.

"We've been working with everyone here to reassure them all that the Project has no intention of moving Wilma away," Cathy told us as we gathered at a village restaurant sporting handpainted signs proclaiming "Meet Wilma" and selling small stuffed-animal belugas. "We just want to make sure Wilma survives."

I noted that, as we had often been the only car on the marine drive, we were now the only clients in this restaurant. There was perhaps another connection here between a lone, sociable beluga and this village—both whale and villagers had lost the large and vital society of their peers, both survived on what little attention and affection seemed to come their way, and both faced uncertain, perilous futures.

Fate had not been kind to Guysborough, which, as the fisherman had said, had lost so much. And the loss of a mother and an entire pod left Wilma with a loneliness that must have been unendurable to one of her sociable kind. No wonder she approached boats seeking affection by knocking her luminous head or melon against outboard motors, sometimes unhinging them until they sank to the sea bottom.

"She's a wild animal," Cathy explained, "but Wilma is also a part of everyday life in this village. Children play with her after school. A couple of fishermen tolerate her, but I know of several who are actually quite fond of her and are careful with their engines and gear when she's nearby. There is an old couple here that likes to listen to Wilma in the harbour at night. They told me she makes 'snoring' noises . . . that they're happy just knowing she's out there, like their own 'watch dog.' "

Cathy and Toni went on to discuss that night's important town meeting, when they would try to ease the tension and rampant rumors about the Whale Stewardship Project's "stealing" Wilma away and ask the villagers to help design a program to protect their motherless whale. In the last week there had been a flurry of letters to the editor, commenting on the supposed "tug of war" between the government and Guysborough over Wilma's care.

One letter with the headline "Wilma the whale needs no do-gooders" accused the nonprofit Stewardship Project of being "self-serving wannabe-next-to-Jacques-Cousteau types" who would invade Guysborough and declare plans for a "Free Wilma" campaign. Cathy had worked previously in a Return to the Wild animal-welfare group based in Toronto. Many villagers greeted her Whale Stewardship Project as made up of "meddling Come-From-Aways." In a conclusion that echoed the self-reliant credo and suspicions of many villagers, the letter writer declared, "Let God, not man, give her the instinct to leave when she's ready. Wilma is free; she belongs to no one, answers to no one, makes her own rules. She chooses to stay in a harbor which has the open doorway to the ocean that will take her anywhere in this world."

"I would be the first to defend Wilma's choice for freedom in the wild," Cathy Kinsman sighed as she read over the piles of letters to the editor anticipating the expected ruckus at this evening's town meeting. "Would she be better off with her beluga family, even though their home waters are so polluted? Belugas *should* be with belugas. But Wilma is nearing sexual maturity and there's no mate for her. If she goes searching for family or mate, I fear for her alone in the open ocean."

DNA tests had determined that Wilma was from the highly endangered beluga population of about 800 in the St. Lawrence River, near Saguenay, Quebec. Perhaps her mother had wandered south to Nova Scotia in 1993 and the two had become separated in the ice-dotted waters. It is very rare for belugas in the St. Lawrence estuary to stray more than a hundred miles from their native waters, even though those waters are now some of the most toxic in the world. Most belugas spend their summers feeding in the coldest waters of the northern hemisphere, above the Arctic Circle, near Norway, Alaska, Russia, Canada, and Greenland. From July through September, when the massive ice floes crack and break up, belugas thrive in these frigid arctic waters teeming with fish such as halibut, cod, and capelin. When the ice pack freezes again, the belugas migrate south at speeds of up to 2 miles an hour and sometimes they travel more than a thousand miles in their complex migration. Deep-diving belugas are one of the few cetacean species that can move freely between salt and fresh water, sometimes even purposely entering waters so shallow that they strand until the next tide. While a beluga is beached and waiting for the next tide, its eye will flow with a protective mucous that looks eerily like tears. This moist stream prevents drying from exposure to air and sun.

No one knows why animals migrate, why these belugas don't simply stay in the warmer waters year round and instead venture so far north through dangerous ice. But scientists theorize that their migration might be about more than finding food. Intensely social, belugas have been observed gathering in "superpods"—and not to mate, because that probably happens before the summer ice breaks up. Could it be that belugas are gathering simply to meet and socialize? Belugas also undergo a molting, when their luminous white skin sloughs off in huge patches, giving them a mottled look. In the tiny town of Churchill, in Manitoba, every July the town braces not only for a beluga southern migration, but also for eco-tourists. Hundreds of people come to observe the mighty phenomenon of up to two thousand beluga flowing through the Churchill River. Belugas seem so plentiful that some townspeople tease that one can jump and cross the river on the gleaming backs of the thousand-strong belugas.

There are estimates of 100,000 to 200,000 belugas in the wild, but when compared to human populations, this worldwide population would equal only one medium-sized city. For centuries, beluga were hunted by native tribes of the far north, as well as Russian, Japanese, and early Yankee whalers. Belugas were slaughtered for their oil and skin, which was used in shoelaces. Some native tribes, such as the Alaskan Inuit, decided in 1999 to stop their hunting of beluga because the populations are very endangered.

Aside from overhunting, belugas face other threats. The St. Lawrence belugas were initially devastated in the early part of the last century when the government put a bounty on the whales, who were erroneously believed to be devouring dwindling cod stocks. The military bombing and wholesale slaughter of these belugas so severely compromised their health that their populations have struggled to recover. Industrial pollution of the St. Lawrence Seaway has so devastated belugas in the estuary that their numbers are dwindling pitifully. In his elegiac book *Beluga: A Farewell to Whales*, Pierre Beland writes, "I can no longer bear to brood over belugas. . . . I have reached the conclusion that they are doomed in the world we humans are building." In Quebec, authorities have labeled these living beluga whales as "toxic waste." Dead belugas must be carefully buried as hazardous waste. Heavy metals, PCBs, and other pollutants have been discharged into the St. Lawrence River for decades from factories run by General Motors, Reynolds Metal, and ALCOA. In belugas, these PCBs cause bladder cancer, herpes-like viral dermatitis, gastric ulcers, tumors, and a shocking 50 percent infant mortality rate. Newborn beluga calves suckle polluted milk, which in turn causes toxic shock. And belugas are simply the "canaries in the coal mine," for human populations are now also experiencing high cancer rates and death from our polluted waters.

Up north, in Baffin Island's arctic waters where belugas summer, Inuit women can no longer nurse their babies because PCBs are contaminating their breast milk. And following the seaway south to New York, the Mohawks of the Akwasasnee Nation are working to try to clean up the St. Lawrence River, whose fish are so toxic that pregnant women and children cannot eat them. New York has issued a statewide advisory not to eat too many fish because of dioxin contamination. Belugas are indicator species of the health of our waters, and as such, their failing health foreshadows our own fate.

Perhaps this slow but growing recognition of our shared destiny with other mammals was what made Wilma, the orphaned beluga, seem not like a stranger, but part of the human family. For almost a decade in Nova Scotia and in her own affectionate way, Wilma had become something of a celebrity. Jim Johnson, a professional diver and underwater photographer, first befriended the lone beluga calf. A chance photograph by Johnson's friend Roger McFarlane out on Chedabucto Bay had captured an interspecies friendship that, in turn, drew worldwide attention. McFarlane's Siberian husky, Rocky, had been so delighted when the lonely beluga calf approached their boat that the dog leapt into the water. Wilma and Rocky nuzzled one another. In true husky style, Rocky howled and Wilma vocalized her high-pitched songs. Their interspecies love affair attracted the media. From the Discovery Channel to Canadian Broadcasting, from Halifax to Tokyo, photos of Wilma and Rocky in their affectionate play spawned a wave of tourists to the tiny village. Visitors from as far away as Australia, China, Japan, and Europe sought out the lone, sociable beluga—as if responding to her own need for affection. Wilma may not have had a mother, but she had a village—and the whole world.

But along with this affection came danger. Though well meaning, locals whose boat propellers were not housed in a protective cover ran many of the tourist boats. In the company of humans from 1993 to 1997, Wilma suffered at least sixteen different injuries from boat propellers and other mechanical devices. Two-dozen scars laced her body from these impacts. One of these wounds, near Wilma's right eye, was rumored to be from someone having simply taken a gaff to her, not long after she arrived in Guysborough. Another ominous wound ran alongside her flank. It took more than a year for this wound to heal. The poor calf looked like a war veteran, and prospects for her survival were compromised by the demands of a curious but uneducated public.

Still, Wilma's chances for survival were better in Guysborough's Chedabucto Bay than they would be if she were returned to her home waters—that is, if the villagers and the Whole Stewardship Project could find a way to work together, with Wilma as their common concern. Added to the villagers' distrust of outsiders, especially government "meddling," was the fact that a local man, John Morgan, had quickly recognized Wilma's financial value because of her attachment to boat motors. Using this knowledge, Morgan gained a measure of control over Wilma and lured the vulnerable beluga to the stern of his boat for paying tourists. Morgan even guaranteed interaction with Wilma to his customers while at the same time manipulating and enticing Wilma away from other local recreational and tour operators who had come to encounter her. With certain sarcasm, villagers often referred to Wilma as "John's whale."

On the other hand was Jim Johnson, who had formed a more protective and emotional bond with Wilma. While hosting many media encounters with Wilma, Johnson also worked to protect her from exploitation. Johnson, like many other villagers, resented the high speeds and dangerous boat operations around Wilma, which centered on financial gain, not conservation. Before the Whale Stewardship Project arrived, this controversy swirling around Wilma had villagers choosing sides between John Morgan and Jim Johnson. There were many under-breath mutterings and cliques struggling over to whom Wilma really "belonged."

In my two decades of work with cetaceans I have seen this fierce and protective possessiveness crop up among the most detached scientists. I have even felt it myself, as if I were the only one who could understand the dolphins' needs or how best to protect them. The irony is that such passion sometimes misses the point: what is best for whales or dolphins is usually quite distinct from our own human needs.

Guysborough needed Wilma to revitalize its sad economy. Its residents also identified with her being so badly abandoned, her loss of all that might nurture and safeguard her future. The village was as much a motherless child as was Wilma. And now, in the minds of some villagers, here was an organization coming to take away what little they had left.

On the other hand, the village had no idea of how best to care for their lone, sociable beluga, who as she approached sexual maturity was often mischievous and unpredictable. A local newspaper, the *Chronicle-Herald*, noted that "some townsfolk see Wilma as both child and plaything," a pet and a companion. This notion implied ownership, yet Wilma was very much a wild animal. She foraged for all her own food, sometimes disappeared into the open sea for several days, and any encounter with this beluga was mostly on Wilma's terms. Fisherman complained that they couldn't leave the harbour without attracting Wilma's almost obsessive preoccupation with their outboard motors. Perhaps because the motors were more acoustically stimulating than human voices, their whine and underwater whirling more like beluga vocalizations, Wilma sought their comfort, much as an unweaned infant will bury its head in any human's breast. But the very propellers Wilma so poignantly sought out could kill her.

As if to emphasize her very wildness, Wilma had disappeared for almost a week before this very important town meeting of the Whale Stewardship Project with the Guysborough villagers. Rumors flew: Wilma was dead, killed out of some wrongheaded vendetta against government interference; Wilma was lured away to keep her "safe" from the eco-terrorists who wanted to "free" her when she was already free; Wilma was entangled in a fishing net and her fate would never be known; Wilma was stranded out North in a very low tide. Frantically, local boats and Whale Stewardship local volunteers searched the waters of Chedebucto Bay for their beluga.

The town meeting was held at the Guysborough Fire Department, and the whole village turned out. Elders and children, fishermen and local officials all took their rickety wooden seats, expectantly waiting for the Whale Stewardship Project to plead its case. Toni Frohoff began with an informative look at the natural history of belugas, particularly the interaction between cetaceans and humans. "You know, it's a sad thing," Toni told the crowd in her quiet, thoughtful manner, "but so many lone, sociable dolphins in befriending humans actually make themselves more vulnerable to harm. Sometimes if a whole village befriends them, they then expect the same kindness from all humans." Toni sighed, studying the room sympathetically. "But it only takes one ignorant person to destroy and undo all that interspecies bonding. People have killed so many sociable dolphins. They've been shot at, speared, cut, and even had beer poured down their blowholes. It's really impossible for dolphins to know which people are safe to trust."

Eager to assure the Whale Stewardship Project that their village could be trusted, the crowd passionately peppered Toni with questions: Why did Wilma like outboard motors? What to do when she approached dinghies, demanding affection? How long did belugas live in the wild? How long would Wilma live and would she leave their village looking for a mate?

The expected ruckus and tension never materialized. Townspeople spoke passionately about their hope to take care of "our whale." One very elderly woman dressed in a sensible slicker and a wool hat seemed to speak for the whole village: "Wilma came to us," she said firmly. "She chose Guysborough for her own and she's our responsibility, eh? When I hear her just abreathing in the harbour at night, my husband and I know the world's a better place—because she's here. So," the old woman finished with a nod, "just tell us what she needs."

Cathy outlined the Whale Stewardship Project's guidelines: Slow down in the harbour, no swimming with the whale, and protect Wilma's habitat from irresponsible boat traffic or newcomers who don't know the rules. Again she personally assured them that the Whale

Stewardship Project was in Guysborough simply to observe and safeguard Wilma, never to take her away.

"We want to build a respectful kinship with Wilma," Cathy told the crowd, who murmured in agreement. "If there's one thing I've learned it's that whales have created amazing marine mammal societies in the sea. So, when we approach them, I think if we ask ourselves, 'What benefit am I bringing to their lives?', then we won't be likely to exploit them, poison their environment, or cause them any harm. Instead, we'll experience their world and work to protect a quality of life that is their right . . . ," she smiled and was met with a sea of upturned, open faces, ". . . and our privilege to enjoy together."

The day after this unexpectedly successful and amiable town meeting, and as if sensing it might be safe to come home after the parents had stopped their arguing, Wilma returned to Guysborough Harbour. The word went out at dawn that Wilma was back. Within an hour the Whale Stewardship Project boat and a smaller boat I hired, skippered by Lloyd Dort, a local fisherman, took us out to greet Wilma and assess her well-being. But by the time we were on the water that warm June morning, Wilma had again disappeared. Several Stewardship volunteers, village youth hired as interns for the summer, scanned the waters with binoculars. They seemed as concerned as if searching for their own lost sibling.

As our boats slowly circled the huge harbor, there was a sudden, happy shout. A village fisherman almost capsized his own boat as he jumped up and down, waving his hands about. "Wilma, you!" he called out to us. "She's over there by her buoy!"

At last, exact directions from a Nova Scotian! We sailed toward shore, and Lloyd cut our engines to a low throb—the underwater noise that seems always to attract and comfort young Wilma, as if she is hearing herself called home. The Whale Stewardship Project's boat with its training interns cut their motors and anchored to better observe from a quiet distance. Since touch and hearing are her most primary senses, the soft bumping of a wooden fishing boat against Wilma's back and the acoustic whine of an outboard engine are the main ways in which she connects with humans. In logging their many hours of observation, the Whale Stewardship Project volunteers had discovered an important anomaly in Wilma's behavior: She rarely vocalized underwater. This behavior differed drastically from other of her "sea canary" beluga-kind, who are considered the most highly vocal of all small whales. But Wilma had never been taught her own native language, so had to content herself with instinctive echolocation skills and mimicking the human or non-human sounds in her environment. Wilma was known for her mimicry of human voices, especially high-pitched children's cries; she also did a realistic imitation of the treble whine of engines. But mostly, when not engaging with humans, buoys, or motorboats, she was eerily quiet.

Approaching shore, one of the interns pointed to a luminous white body facing and floating near a rubber orange buoy. Everyone shifted to one side of the boat, but no one called out or tried to engage Wilma. She was obviously resting with one of her inanimate companions. The Whale Stewardship Project had made a commitment to simply observe Wilma and not seek interaction. "We've learned so much just by letting Wilma be and studying her behavior," Cathy said in her lilting, quiet voice. Again I was reminded that she is a musician and singer herself, a woman whose ear is always tuned and sensitive to the sound around her—just as Wilma was tuned to everyone in her domain. "It's in times like these we can really come closer to knowing her. And seeing her alone, we're reminded that here is a very social animal with no one to socialize with. Her family members back in the St. Lawrence are constantly chattering and playing, rubbing up against each other. It's exciting to watch mums with their babies exploring together." Cathy fell silent, watching Wilma along with the rest of us.

We rocked near Wilma, our low-throated engine sound perhaps a lullaby as Wilma rested. Interns took copious notes on her exact location, on the new gash near her tail, on her slow exhalations of misting air through her lovely blowhole. This morning there were no Jet Skis or speedboats buzzing by to disturb this floating reverie, no tourist swimmers demanding Wilma's attention and disturbing her sense of safety or territory. There was only our little fishing boat, the warming sun, and a beluga drifting alongside her orange buoy-companion.

As I rested my eyes on Wilma I remembered another brave and beautiful beluga I'd met a decade ago, held captive in a zoo, captured more by her grief and loss than by anything human. Then, too, Mauyak had rested her bright white head near an orange rubber buoy—except that buoy had been a substitute for her lost calf. Now Wilma's companion buoy was a surrogate mother. How moving and eerie to see this same vision: White whale and orange buoy in a floating dance of longing and belonging. The mammalian instinct for touch and attachment that was echoed here touched me. For isn't this what we mammal humans also long for—to be a part of some family greater than just ourselves, to know our own kind as we struggle to understand ourselves, to rest with another in an unbroken bond?

"She trusts us, don't you know?" Our boatman Lloyd spoke in almost a whisper. His grizzled, sun-darkened face was so wide open and proud. "That's why she always comes back here . . . home to the village."

As if she had somehow overhead him, Wilma lifted her head, dove and swam toward us. There was a thrill in the air that even these young interns, who were in training to observe Wilma with the practiced detachment of budding scientists, couldn't contain. Just under the waves, Wilma's body showed refracted shadows and sunlight shimmering and rippling along her skin. And this skin was a veritable map of human encounters: nicks and gashes, a notch to her lip, a deep grooved scar along her side, countless blade marks in the white blubber as if she had been caught in the middle of a swordfight and barely escaped with her life. I gasped when I saw the array of old wounds, as well as a fresh, bleeding gash perilously near her black, unblinking eye. As Wilma glided nearer, Cathy whispered to her interns, "When Wilma approaches us like this in such a trusting manner," she said, "we really have a responsibility to look out for her. You know, her survival, her health, and her wellbeing are very dependent upon how we treat her."

Toni Frohoff and I sat on the bow of the boat, taking notes as Wilma cruised right alongside, after first checking out Lloyd's lulling engine. So as not to harm Wilma with any more propeller cuts, a protective cover safely contained his outboard motor. "This kind of propeller box should be mandatory for every boat in the harbor," Toni said softly, smiling as Wilma came alongside.

As a scientist, Toni had to content herself with no physical interaction with Wilma. Her mission, like Cathy's, was to promote peaceful coexistence between humans and wildlife. And that mission was most often fulfilled by respectfully observing.

Sitting back on the bow, Toni kept her eyes fixed fondly on Wilma as she and her interns took notes on her behavior. Wilma was, true to her habit, bumping her bright head against our propeller case, and Lloyd cut the engine to let her rub her back on the boat's bottom. "The hardest thing here," Toni reflected, "is to keep reminding the villagers that Wilma is a wild animal. She is in danger of being injured. But as she matures, she can perhaps injure others. Especially if people don't respect Wilma's territory and her 'things,' and if they insist on swimming with her. This is what has happened with almost every other sociable dolphin studied. Not only did people need to help protect the dolphin, but they also need to protect themselves—mostly from human expectations that Wilma be some cute, cuddly pet. She is, and I hope always remains, free and her own unique self. Wilma has her own life to lead. We just want to make sure she *has* a life."

A rowboat lazily drifted into the harbour nearby us. It was Dave Lang, a villager whose children for years have spent their afternoons in this same dinghy, playing with Wilma. Recognizing Lloyd's boat,

Wilma darted away from us and began swimming in affectionate circles around Dave.

"You," he called out to Wilma with a familiar delight. "You again!"

Wilma raised herself out of the water with a thrust of her powerful tail flukes and knocked his oars almost out of his hands. Then she slowly spun his boat around, careful not to capsize him. It seemed a well-known game, one his children had perhaps taught Wilma. Or she had taught them. Dave laughed and let himself be pushed around like a float toy. Then he called out to us, "Anyone want a lift?"

At that moment I was very glad not to be a scientist and bound by my role to stay detached from such a sociable beluga. Wilma was so obviously seeking interaction and she had obviously finished her rest to pursue Dave's rowboat and play. Belugas, like most dolphins, spend three-quarters of their lives at play. These big-brained mammals, like humans, are endlessly inventive and imaginative. Why not let her have her way with me?

I almost levitated from the fishing rig down to the rowboat. Low in the water, I settled into the splintered wooden seats with a delight that still makes me smile. No sooner had I taken my station than Wilma lifted up out of the water to fix me with her bright, black eye. Her regard was at once curious and intimate. I was struck by how young she seemed, how much less aloof and even more playful she was than any other whale I had encountered, either in the wild or in captive settings. Perhaps along with her mimicry of human voices, Wilma had somehow learned something about eye contact that made her seem more human. In every other whale eye with which I've had the privilege to exchange long glances, I've recognized an "otherness" and even benign aloofness. But not so with Wilma. Her expression was childlike and subtly fixed, exactly like the long gazes a human infant will focus on a parent, as if imprinting everything about that person—face, smell, texture of skin, and sound of beloved voice.

In Wilma's gaze was all the loneliness and need, the dependence and pleasure of any human child. With a start, I realized that what I recognized most in Wilma's expression was a searching and intense vulnerability. She was lost and she was found. She was alone of her kind, yet surrounded by well-meaning people. She had the plaintive, engaging look of a child awaiting adoption. And this village had the earnest and doting attitude of adoptive parents who have to go through more scrutiny, more training, and more education than many birth parents. This was a new kind of family model—an interspecies kinship, new and fragile, awkward and inexperienced. But here was a model for what the future might be, between species that increasingly must meet. And Cathy was right—education was the key.

Wilma gave me quite an education in wild beluga behavior. After deciding I was an acceptable human to include in her play, she sought my hands by literally lifting herself up from the water. Much like a cat will insist on being petted, Wilma used her head to lift my hand up from the boat. Then she bobbed there beside me, as my palm rested on her luminous melon. How familiar this sleek, white head felt to my open hand, as years ago another beluga had forever imprinted me. As Mauyak's had, Wilma's melon throbbed and changed shapes beneath my hand as she vocalized a high-pitched squeak-whistle from her blowhole. I sang back with my own signature whistle.

What a long journey to another country to find this little wild beluga, I thought, remembering Mauyak's sleek snout, the way she had trusted and taken me in. Here was a motherless whale seeking intimacy and physical contact, just as once a mother had mourned her orphaned calf with me. I wondered, could I be a kind of human conduit between mother and beluga calf? Could Mauyak somehow have acoustically imprinted my own hand so that now I could pass on that mothering to this orphaned wild beluga? Some of my more far-sighted marine mammal scientist friends have theorized that dolphins do create acoustic images that are somehow attached to objects in the sea, such as brain coral or reefs. Just because humans can't yet "acoustically see" these hypothesized sound-holograms made by cetaceans doesn't mean they don't exist. For years scientists mistakenly believed that elephants had no language, because their subsonic communications are too low for human hearing.

Perhaps it was wishful thinking, but I hope that day in Nova Scotia I was able to pass along to this young orphaned beluga whale some of the pleasure and mother-child bonding that Mauyak once gave me. Our long gaze, with my hand open upon her resting melon, was a gift exchange between species. Wilma's sleek head pulsed with chirps and whistles that echoed in my palm and sent tingling sensations up my arms as she sounded me. I wondered about Wilma's long separation from other belugas, about her exile here among other mammals. Did she seek to find herself in the Other, the way I had in my own early years imprinted on animals as my extended family?

Some animals, like some people, find it is their fate to exist between the worlds and perhaps become bridges so that others may cross over. Wilma was a bridge to bring people to understand the perils and pleasures of beluga life in the wild. She was also an adopted daughter who had found in these many mothers and fathers and siblings a way to survive her long loneliness.

As Wilma sank a little then slid alongside the dinghy, I was shocked to see how deeply etched was the scar along her side. I traced its jagged groove and marveled that she had survived.

Wilma rose up once more to meet my eye. I smiled and said, "Yes, I see you, little lovely. Live long."

As if satisfied, Wilma suddenly turned her tail flukes and dove down for a long time. After five minutes, when she surfaced again, I had given up my place in the rowboat to Terry, another local woman who was studying Wilma and never interacted with her. But just for today, she would allow herself to be closer in the water to Wilma, yet would still make no physical contact. Wilma had another idea: completely unexpectedly, Wilma shot straight up out of the water as Terry leaned over the bow. What happened next I would always remember: Orphaned whale half out of the water and fully embraced in the arms of a young woman. Someone snapped a photo to preserve that moment: a dark-headed woman in an orange life vest leaning over the bow of a boat, both hands atop Wilma's bright head as she kisses her scarred snout. The upturning of the natural beluga smile seems more than simply her nature; it seems a wider smile as Wilma's eyes half-close in pleasure and—what can we call it but an interspecies love between human mother and beluga child?

When we adopt other species and love them as our own, this is the best of all possible worlds. This is embracing more than our own kind and assuring that more than we alone survive. For if humans only survive without the company of other animals, then we will be more alone than any of our ancestors could ever have imagined. To one day find ourselves on this ocean planet alone with only our own kind would be perhaps the beginning of the end of our species.

As we took our slow leave of Wilma that morning, the bay was still and calm. Wilma could again rest with her buoy companion. "We want her to stay on here with us," Lloyd said quietly as we all kept turning back to Wilma, keeping her in our sight as if she were now our own marker, a living beluga buoy with whom we might better navigate our human world.

As it turned out, Wilma did not stay her whole life in Guysborough. That summer of 1998 the Whale Stewardship Project and the villagers gave Wilma their best guardianship and care. And in February 1999, the last reliable sighting of Wilma was out in the middle of Chedabucto Bay by an airline pilot. In their search to find Wilma, the Whale Stewardship Project heard of sightings as far north as Sydney Harbour, and that next June, three belugas were seen off Auld's Cove near Cape Breton. Was this Wilma reunited with other belugas? One of the most exciting sightings was of a white whale, which some hoped might be Wilma, swimming alongside a black pilot whale in Isaac's

Harbour in early May west of Chedabucto Bay. Once before Wilma had ventured off in the company of pilot whales, but then she returned to the village bay. Had Wilma at sexual maturity found a mate in another species of whale? If she and the black pilot whale mated, their offspring would be sterile, but at long last Wilma would know mothering—her own.

As the Whale Stewardship Project searched for Wilma throughout the summer of 1999, they instead found another lone, sociable beluga in Middle Arm, Newfoundland. This juvenile male, like Wilma, had been seeking the society of humans. He was given the name Kuus (pronounced "Koo-oos"), and from June until September he stayed in Green Bay, Newfoundland. His presence made researchers ask whether there were more solitary belugas than previously expected. Why were these lone belugas seeking human society?

Unlike Wilma, Kuus rarely initiated physical contact, except sometimes with boaters who dangled their hands in the frigid waters. Then, as if to participate in the give and take of play, Kuus would engage with humans when they were holding such objects as underwater cameras, seaweed, and feathers. But mostly Kuus was attracted to boats. Also unlike Wilma, Kuus was as highly vocal as most other belugas. Because the Whale Stewardship Project was able to begin monitoring Kuus early on in his residency alongside the communities of Middle Arm and King's Point, there was no tug-of-war between humans who might be emotionally or financially invested in the lone, sociable beluga. Again, as in Guysborough, the beluga's safety was everyone's primary concern and his stay in the harbour was notable for its lack of injury. Kuus suffered only one minor propeller wound, two small notches on his dorsal fin.

With Kuus, villagers respected the Whale Stewardship Program's guidelines of slow boating, no wakes within 100 meters of the whale, and no feeding of the beluga. Whenever strangers entered the harbor and violated any of the safeguarding guidelines, villagers promptly educated the newcomers as to the proper etiquette for being with Kuus. In a way it was like watching a successful exercise in cross-cultural etiquette between whale and humans passed along and established as a conservation tradition, a new ethic.

Such interspecies trust and stewardship hold out real hope for a future in which humans and wild animals will meet more often than ever before. Recently I found Cathy Kinsman on the road in Canada doing more of her remarkable Whale Stewardship Project work. A video she had made of Wilma and the village that adopted her was a big success in Canada, especially among schoolchildren—the next generation of stewards.

In fact, a summer after Kuus appeared in Middle Arm, the village found itself led by an eleven-year-old boy, Timmy Tilley, in organizing an Ocean Net clean-up. The children worried that any other visiting whales might choke and die on the beach garbage. So they collected more than twenty bags of debris, including glass, plastic, wood, two dead crows, and even a dead fox. Timmy Tilley, who wants to be a marine biologist when he grows up, had been fascinated by the Whale Stewardship Project's previous summer's study of Kuus. Personally, the boy renamed Kuus, calling him "Angel," because "he was like a little angel, so sweet and quiet." Timmy and his Ocean Net volunteers still have their garbage bags with a picture of a whale on the side, for future clean-ups and in the hope that another lone, sociable beluga or any other whales might again choose to visit their village.

"There is a world of whales just like Wilma," Cathy told me recently over a cell phone crackling with static. She seemed happy and fulfilled in her work, which was gaining widespread acceptance. "They are all worthy of our protection and respect." She paused and I could almost hear her smile over the phone. "Wilma taught us so much," she said in her musical, soft voice, "not only about whales, but also about ourselves."

She went on to give me an update on Guysborough and a newly formed Waterfront Society, which is hoping to commission a monument of Wilma. A national call has gone out to artisans to sculpt the life-sized, beloved beluga. They have also invited the Whale Stewardship Project back to help develop archival and educational materials about Wilma and beluga whales—all to celebrate and honor the beluga calf who for seven years was part of their extended family.

I wonder now about Wilma's life. Is she still swimming in what are often perilous waters for belugas? Does she have a calf, a mate, a family of her own now? Did she ever return to find her own pod in the polluted Gulf of St. Lawrence, where both whales and people struggle now to survive against toxins they have unknowingly taken deep into their own bodies? Will Wilma, like some migrating seals, return to her human village, perhaps with her own calf in tow? Even now the search for Wilma continues. The Whale Stewardship Project has posted Wilma's photo up and down the eastern shore. Now all the villages keep an eye out for her. A last propeller wound to Wilma's face, permanently notching her mouth did heal; but ironically, this scar is what will make her very easy to identify.

Whatever Wilma's fate, this we do know: For six years she belonged to a little village that came to love and protect her as its own. A village and a stewardship program that took the time and hard work to learn how best to care for a wild, orphaned beluga. Together, what that village and those stewards brought to Wilma's life was educated devotion and respect. And what Wilma brought to Guysborough, to all of us who had the great good fortune to meet her, was nothing less than the curiosity, the courtesy, and the companionship of an ambassador from another world. Who knows if Wilma would have survived without the village and the Whale Stewardship Project? Both nurtured her as any good foster parents, so Wilma could at last venture out into the world. Wilma's story shows us that humans are perhaps at long last learning what we teach our own children—to share, to share with an open heart.

SEVENTEEN

SILKIE

SINCE THE FUNERAL on shore and at sea, the silkies have swum into my dreams, the seals into my days. Before that bright September morning when the harbor seal floated onto my backyard beach, I'd not noticed that many seals in Puget Sound. I'd seen the odd seal or otter, the languid sea lion flapping his four flippers above the waves and barking like my morning alarm clock every spring. But in my decades of living here with the sound as my intimate, daily companion, I'd never witnessed a seal so close to shore, and I sensed something was wrong.

Grabbing a rope from my inflatable kayak, I ran down to the beach. Washing up amid the tangle of driftwood and seaweed was a sleek harbor seal, face down in the cold sound, her fore flippers outstretched like little lifeless wings. As I waded into the churning surf, I called up to my neighbors, whose window was open. Lisa and Victor, newlyweds, keep their windows open year round to better hear these wild waves.

"Oh, no," Lisa called back. "What now? I'm afraid to look!"

"Come down!" I yelled to Lisa. "I don't know what to do except try to figure out how this seal died."

In moments Lisa was by my side, her face full of sorrow as we each took a pair of flippers and hauled the harbor seal ashore. We both knelt in the warm sand to study the delicate corpse. "Couldn't be dead long," I said, noticing the blood flowing from her small snout, which was adorned with dainty, feminine whiskers. On each side of her head were pinprick ear holes, and her wide, dark eyes still held an expression of amazement.

"She's so . . . she's so beautiful," Lisa breathed, gently stroking the seal's side as if to comfort both the seal and herself.

I, too, ran my hands along the silver skin, her short fur ruffled against my fingertips. For the first time I understood the possessive instinct of our seagoing ancestors to strip seals of their skins to grace our own bodies. So luxurious and fine was this pearlized gray seal pelt that for a split second I could imagine it embracing my skin like a radiant, warm, underwater cloak—and me moving inside the graceful, undulating dance of a living seal as she stroked through the waves.

This seal was graceful, though she lay still on the shore. A long, knotted rope of her intestines stretched out from her side like a bowline, an incandescent cord that looked eerily umbilical. Except this cord coiled out not from her naval, but from a bullet hole.

As we mournfully rolled the seal over onto her back, we saw the exit wound like a black bull's-eye in her belly, and there beside this wound were two more bullet holes. I gazed across the sound at the silhouettes of almost a hundred fishing boats.

"They shot her," Lisa said in a voice of quiet fury. "As if this little seal could really compete for salmon with all of them."

I looked at that crowded flotilla of salmon fishermen, arrayed like greed on the horizon.

"Who do we call?" Lisa wondered. "After all, this is a drive-by shooting!"

While I stayed with the seal, Lisa called all the agencies until she found someone who would help. Special Agent Gordon, of the National

Oceanic and Atmospheric Administration, sadly advised, "There's nothing to be done. Those boats out there—I know most all the fishermen have guns. But we can't board them without a strong suspicion of who did it, and they won't report each other just for shooting a seal." Gordon sighed, "I see it every day. All you can do now is send that seal back into the sound. Just let her go home."

As Lisa reported the officer's advice, she stared bleakly down at the seal between us and shook her head. Lisa chafed at our helplessness. "Nothing more we can do," she murmured. But neither of us made a move. It was as if we were spellbound by the sight of so lovely a creature who, even in death, revealed to us such mysterious beauty.

I crushed some wild roses between my fingers, sprinkling red petals on the seal's side. The sweet scent rose up like natural incense over the body. "It wasn't always like this between us and the seals," I said.

Many of the traditional Northwest Coastal Native myths speak of a sacred treaty between sea and land dwellers, the balance between us and our marine mammal cousins. In these stories, we have always taken the skin of other creatures to survive, to see the world more clearly, to fall in love, and to find reunion with our nonhuman kin. As I stroked that seal's rich, furred skin, I felt a child's sense of wonder and awe to be allowed near such an extraordinary creature. So little is known about the seal's life at sea. What we know, the stories we tell, all center mostly on their shore life.

Seals have not fully made the transition back to the ocean womb. They are an in-between species, longing for the sea but returning to land to breed and give birth—and sometimes to die. Unlike other marine mammals who have fully adapted back to the sea, seals are still intimately connected to land. In this way, they are more like us.

"Shall we say prayers for her?" I asked my friend as we both knelt there on our beloved beach by this lost seal. "Should we have a funeral?"

We gathered seaweed and pretty shells, bright stones and fragrant lavender blossoms. We lay the seaweed over the ragged bullet holes and the shells were strewn in a circular pattern across her round belly. We slipped purple lavender between her claws and we didn't cover her eyes because they were so dark and soulful—seeming to take everything in, now that her spirit had slipped out of her skin.

Or had it? I sensed as we performed our funeral chores that like those long-ago deer trophies guarding my crib, some part of this lovely animal's spirit was also still attached to its skin. When we wear the skin of another species, we accept, however unconsciously, the primitive's belief that we become this animal—that the power and perspective of the animal then belongs to us. Even if it is just an echo of the animal's essence, we can borrow its vision and perhaps see the world whole again.

Maybe that is why many of our first sea stories center on the myth of stealing the splendid skin of a seal-woman so that she might stay with us on shore. These "silkie" or "selchie" stories are so abundant that they rival their companion myths of mermaids and mermen. Humans often fall in love with other than our own kind—and this love between species is both a passionate bond and a deep reunion.

There are several common themes in silkie myths. First, there is the seal-people's celebration on shore, in which they slip out of their gray skins and dance and make love all night in their beautiful human bodies. This land-lust and lovemaking may have its basis in scientific fact, because seals do molt their elegant skins on shore. And they've adapted a delayed implantation strategy that enables seals to both give birth and mate again in one trip to land—kind of like a full-circle shore leave. Harbor seals will molt their skin, called the lanugo, while still in their mother's womb. But most other seals come ashore to molt and slough off their silver fur onto the rocks.

Imagine our island ancestors walking the beach and stumbling on such a delicate shedding of sealskin. Stories, like the animals' spirits, must also have attached to those molted skins and given rise to the silkie legends. But even though we fall in love with the seal-people, we can't hold onto them for long. That is another theme that runs through all the silkie stories: a fisherman discovers the onshore revelry of the seal-folk and stealthily steals the skin of the most beautiful silkie woman. She must marry him, for without her skin, her magic and undersea skills are gone and she is mere mortal, mere wife.

My favorite of the silkie legends is "Seal-People," as told by Otta F. Swire in *The Highlands and Their Legends* and reprinted in the anthology *Silkie*, by Dorothy Griffin. I often reread Swire's story, set amid Scottish islands. It tells of three brothers fishing off rocks in Loch Duich who spy the gray, luminous seal-changelings gathered to dance and celebrate. The brothers seize sealskins from three weeping silkie maidens, promising them silk dresses, feather beds, and many children.

But the youngest brother is quiet, eyeing his silkie bride. At last the youngest brother reaches into his peat sack and offers his bride the only wedding gift for which her soul longs—her sealskin. After that offering, the silkie girl comes to her human lover every ninth night of her own free will, and great is their happiness. But for the other brothers, who have stolen both sealskin and freedom from their wives, the story is not so happy. Inevitably, one of the half-seal children finds his mother's skin and the second swims away forever; the third silkie-wife is burned alive when her husband tries to keep her on shore forever by tossing her sealskin into the flames.

I remembered this tale of devotion between seal-people and our kind when I knelt by the slain seal that September morning, my gloved hand resting on her elegant silver skin. I found myself saying a prayer for this sister mammal, recognizing her humanness under the skin as she might the silkie within me—the soul that is always longing to return to the sea. And I murmured a prayer also for the seal-people who are now so unprotected, who face an uncertain future. Somehow seals have devolved from beloved, luminous changelings to "nuisance animals," scapegoats for our overfishing.

I doubted that our small ritual, this seal funeral on our beach, would make much difference as more seals are slaughtered each day in all the world's oceans. But we could not deny this one seal her rightful burial at sea.

Our prayers said to silkie and seal and sea, Lisa and I proceeded to tie a slipknot around one small fore flipper. I brought down my orange and purple inflatable kayak and attached the line to my boat.

"Don't go out too far," Lisa cautioned as I slipped into Puget Sound with my slim kayak and stately seal in tow. "Can't lose you, too."

Carefully I paddled through rough waves, making straight toward Blake Island, an ancient stand of untouched, tall trees. A calm halo surrounds this island refuge, birthplace of Suquamish peacemaker and visionary Chief Seattle. It was this eloquent eulogist who taught, "Our dead never forget the beautiful world that gave them being . . . and ever yearn in tender, fond affection over the lonely-hearted living, and often return to visit, guide, console, and comfort them."

Towing that seal by my side, where she floated easily, buoyant again, I did feel like the lonely-hearted living as I paddled away from shore. The seal seemed to swim there alongside me, her great dark eyes wide open. What did she see now? I wondered. What worlds did this changeling creature wander in her own afterlife? As I carried this seal alongside my slender boat I said prayers not only for all the sea creatures who share this sound with me, but also for my own dead—those I have long lost and still love. Sailing in my little kayak and clinging to another dead animal killed by my own kind, I despaired.

Unlike Noah, my ark was only a tiny sliver of rubber kayak. I really could carry with me so little—a single soul, a small seal.

My eyes blurred as I glanced toward shore to see Lisa waving and shouting out across the waves. "Come back!" she called. Her voice carried clearly over the wide water between us.

I was farther away than I realized and the paddle back would be difficult against the tide. Still I could not let go my dead, this seal floating alongside me. As I gazed at her dark eyes, I remember how once as a newborn I had looked deep into other animal eyes and still seen a soul shining there. And since then, how many other animals' eyes have I looked into, as if searching for my own soul?

It occurred to me then, midwater, too far out from shore, that I had never given those guardian deer—the first animal companions who accompanied me into this world as I rocked in my wooden cradle of an ark—a proper funeral. I had eaten of them, grown strong with their spirit and flesh in my own muscle and blood and bones. But I had never laid them to rest with the elegy, honor, and thanks they deserved. I had never buried them, never said grace to them. Murmuring softly to myself, I prayed that this seal burial would be for all animals.

In my own soul, I took them all back into the ark—the deer, the beluga born but unbreathing, this small harbor seal. And then I spoke out loud the names of my own dead friends. With each knot I untied of my bowline, I said a name, animal or human. And with each unclenching of the rope, the seal's fore flippers trembled in the waves.

When I got to Jo's name, I hesitated and could not include her in my litany. The old anger toward her devastating act of suicide rose up in me like bitter bile. Jo did not belong here in this ritual for an animal slain. Jo had killed herself; there was nothing sacred about her deadly self-sacrifice. Like so many of my species, Jo had harmed others as well as herself.

As I floated mid-sound with that slain seal, I could not say Jo's name. Nor could I take her into my imagined ark with all my other human and animal family. Her self-destruction was to me a terrible mirror of all that humans have destroyed. When Jo killed herself, she ended her whole world, just as that Old Testament God had judged his own creation so flawed that he chose to destroy the Earth—except for Noah's righteous family and the animals he saved. I could not take Jo into my own ark because she was not among the righteous; she was everything I despaired of in my own self-destructive species. Better to keep people like her out, I reasoned.

Far out to sea now, I drifted with the dead seal in tow. But I felt that I was more deeply adrift in my heart than in that fragile kayak. It was supposed to be a simple funeral, but it had turned into a tumultuous struggle within myself. Wanting to let the seal go, longing to let Jo go as well, after all these eighteen years, I still couldn't release them.

Looking to the seal alongside me as if for some help, I gazed into those huge, dark eyes, beautiful and fathomless, as open and unplumbed as any abyss or mystery. Then I was rocking as much as falling right into those eyes that were alien and yet eerily human. After a long time of staring into those eyes, I somehow settled. And I knew something I had never fathomed before. We kill ourselves when we kill animals. When Jo killed herself, she also destroyed a human animal— one she did not recognize as worthy of survival. We are all a little like Jo, who believed in her own extinction, taking the act into her own hand. She believed she acted alone; she did not know how many others she took down with her. And most of all, she did not understand what the seals know: that she could change her own skin, without dying.

Floating on the waves I began to weep a flood of tears that only the seal saw. And I realized that in refusing to take Jo into my own little ark, I was judging her as violently as that Old Testament God who had once flooded the world. But how could I judge her when she had judged herself so ruthlessly? How could I *not* invite her into the ark?

All of us, animal and human, are adrift here, awaiting the ebb of that first, angry flood. We await a new, life-loving world that can be made new again only from this one.

Someone far away on my beach was waving to me as I drifted farther away. How long would it take me to paddle back? I wondered. Did I have the strength? Then I remembered reading the news report of an Irish woman who was swept away while swimming for help after she, her boyfriend, and her six-year-old son were stranded on sand dunes while watching seals. High tide had separated them from the mainland and she, being the strongest swimmer, decided to go for help. She swam valiantly, but the waves got the better of her, and in despair she stopped, exhausted. All she could do was tread water and cry out. But she was drifting dangerously far from shore. Suddenly she found herself surrounded by half a dozen gray seals, so near she could touch their sleek, warm-blooded bodies. Encircling her, they stopped her drift toward certain death. Easing her back toward the beach, the seals stood by her, until at last her cries for help were heard.

Only after remembering this true story could I stop my own drift with the dead seal. Floating aloft on these waves, I was suddenly aware that beneath these waves swam all sorts of life, all moving to the rhythm of the sea. As if sensing the pulse and purpose of so much life around me, I studied the waves, moving with them. I realized that all I had to do was wait a little longer for the tide to turn and then let it carry me back toward my own beach. As I waited, watching the water for the darkening swells that signal the evening tide, I no longer felt alone or adrift. The water held me up, the sea was alive with life — life I loved.

A long whitecap rippling in the west and the waves turned over, obeying gravity, the pull of a much greater force. My rubber kayak spun in a slow circle and then slowly rocked, at last facing homeward. Only then could I loosen my hold on the seal and let her go back to the sea. I did not have to carry her to land. She was already home, this lovely seal, this little silkie in her shining skin. I was too far out at sea. People were gathered on the beach, calling my name.

I could hardly hear them, but their hands waved me in like sails. As I paddled, the seal drifted near me a few more minutes, then fell behind as I took stronger strokes, shivering now as the evening mists moved in.

Above me, seagulls cried as I paddled, pacing myself for the long trip. With every dip and stroke of my paddle, I told myself, *This is my small ark.* I could carry just one animal and myself at a time. But there were other people, each building other arks. Perhaps even the whole world was an ark. And other animals who love life may help stop our lonely drift toward death.

Since that simple funeral, they always come now, the seals. Some of my scientist friends say that once a seal hauls up on a beach, even in death, that expanse of sand becomes a haven of sorts, a refuge. Somehow the seals mark that land as home. Every time I see a harbor seal on my backyard beach, I remember that first seal's burial at sea, and all I buried with her. Some grace is given back to me, some sweet and enduring embrace, like a second skin.

EIGHTEEN

⁓

ANIMAL MUNDI

SEATTLE, 1999

ONE WINTER NIGHT the Northwest was struck by a wild storm blowing down from Alaska. Along the coast and the sound, storm warnings alerted all of us who dwell in this almost amphibious place between solid land and sea to brace ourselves. One-hundred-year-old trees were ripped up and gusts lifted a neighbor's roof off like a doll's house, hurling it into splinters littering the street.

Above the high-tide poundings of Puget Sound, my little waterfront studio apartment rocked all night, creaking on its old driftwood foundations like a Yankee clipper. I expected to be shipwrecked by morning, so I slept wearing my black watchman's knit cap, goose down vest, wool mittens without fingers, and two Siamese cats draped across my body.

All night the wind battered our beach with eighty-mile-per-hour gusts, but by dawn the storm had moved through. In its fierce wake was left a lovely morning illumined by rare winter sunlight. As I studied the beach, noting new driftwood, a chaos of kelp and seaweed strewn over backyard barbecue and lawn chairs, I also was surprised by movement: a small harbor seal lay on its side between two huge driftwood logs.

The juvenile seal was all but hidden from the street above by the vast stump of an ancient tree whose striated trunk lay flat like dark feathers of a huge, wooden wing. This driftwood wing seemed protective of the half-grown seal. My protective instincts were also aroused. I knew that in spring mother seals park their offspring on the beach to rest while they fish. But this was winter and I'd never seen a harbor seal on our beach that wasn't wounded or dying.

I dreaded going down to the beach to attempt another seal rescue—the last time had been so heartbreaking. Last summer, several of us beach watchers had guarded a harbor seal pup as it lay thrashing and terrified on the rocks, its silken sides streaked with blood. Unlike most of the seals who end up on this beach—victims of fishermen's bullets—this pup's sides had been gashed by animal teeth, either orcas' or another seal's. So tiny and defenseless, the pup had lain looking up at us as if we were more threatening than any sea monsters. We had kept our distance, waiting the three hours for the wildlife rescue shelter to send their volunteer in the hope of saving the seal before he died of internal injuries.

"He's just a baby," one of the children standing guard said. "Where's his mother?" We explained about the fishermen, who regard seals as competitors for the dwindling salmon runs.

"There's nowhere safe for them—not in the sea, not on land," a schoolteacher told her students in a soft voice. "Did you know the seal is called a 'pinniped,' which means 'wing-footed?'"

As we sat in a circle on the rocks watching over the seal pup, I started humming a long-ago lullaby my father had first sung to me in our forest. The little seal snuffled, lifted his bewhiskered snout, and let out a sigh not unlike that of any small creature being sung to sleep. For the first time he lay down and stopped his jerking, frightened, and futile acrobatics. He lay bleeding into the beach as several others joined in humming the sea chantey:

Sail, baby, sail out across the sea.
Only don't forget to sail
Back again to me.

It must have given the seal pup some solace, because his deep-set black eyes gazed up at us in the tranquil trance-stare of all infants, no matter the species. His breathing steadied, and by the time the wildlife volunteer arrived to hoist him into a cage and carry him back to the refuge, the seal pup was calm. Our neighborhood gang of seal savers got daily reports on the pup's progress—he was warm, well fed, and there was some hope of survival. But on the third day, the pup succumbed to a secondary infection and died.

"At least he was comfortable," the wildlife worker told us. "Spending his last days cold, hungry, and terrified on the beach would have been his fate if you hadn't found him. Maybe next time the little seal will survive."

So here it was—the next time. Another young seal lay in trouble on our beach. It never occurred to me that this seal might be different. As I speed-dialed my marine biologist friend Toni, who is active in pinniped conservation, I grabbed my binoculars to better study this juvenile seal. Blending in with the black-and-white rock-strewn beach, the seal's camouflage was perfect. His small body was a gray globe with mottled splotches like countries on a map made of sealskin.

This little seal looked right up at my third-story window and then did something wonderful. He yawned, a great gap-mouthed show of pink gums, neat rows of teeth, and a tongue on which still lay a silver fish. Then he arched up, black flippers flapping in the winter wind. I was already half in love with this half-grown seal, whose dark eyes now closed, front flippers wrapped around its belly, which rose and fell with reassuring regularity. Could this actually be a healthy animal needing nothing more from me but a nod at its leopard-skin beauty?

"You're lucky to even see a harbor seal alive on shore," Toni advised me. "The way marine biologists tell a healthy harbor seal is by the fact that we catch sight of it only for a second before it's gone. They're so shy and reclusive. Do you see any injuries?"

"No," I answered, intently studying the seal from flipper to whiskers. "Could he be . . . just . . . well, sleeping?"

Toni laughed. "I've seen seals haul up on the beach after a big feed or rendezvous and just crash for half a day—there are so few places left in the world for them to rest. Plus last night's storm might have worn him out. He's young still. Watch over him. You know the biggest cause of death for seals ashore is dogs."

"I'll stand guard," I said, "and keep you posted. Maybe everything's perfectly fine and this is just a day in the life of a healthy seal."

I moved my worktable to the window, and as the afternoon waned into winter dusk I watched the small seal as it slept. On the street above the beach, joggers ran obliviously by, school buses disgorged their screaming students, a recycling truck clanked bottles into its metal innards. All the while the little seal napped, only occasionally glancing up at the everyday noises. Once a huge black dog off its leash bounded toward the seal, and I ran down three flights of stairs and shooed the dog away.

"Oh, I'm so sorry," the dog's companion whispered when she saw the supine seal. Then she smiled and said in a Scottish accent, "Silkie, do y'a think?"

I shrugged and ran back upstairs to better watch over the seal. I took notes like a field scientist right in my own living room. Burps and sneezes, belly plump and furry. Silver whiskers and wide, expressive black eyes. It occurred to me as I stood sentry over this seal that the leisure to study and happily witness this seal's sleep was a rare privilege in these days of species so endangered. I remembered last summer's seal pup and how we had fretted and ached over its long agony on the beach. And I wondered if this calm and happy spirit on the beach below wasn't a gift to balance my memory of all the other seals who had died. It was like seeing life without alarm, without worry. Smiling, I remembered my favorite Lao-tzu quote: "In stillness, all under heaven rests."

Resting with the seal as he napped, I felt a companionable peace, a well-being from this well being below. After about four hours, the seal suddenly roused himself and stretched in a deep back bend. Yawning, he flopped and hopped down the beach to the edge of the surf. Back flippers tucked like tail feathers, he looked like a large bird. Resting with a rock under his chin, he sniffed the sea air, then yawned again, scanning the water. Gulls circled above as at last he heaved into a shallow wave, waiting to be lifted and carried away. Poised there between the worlds of land and sea, the seal did not look back at its beach refuge or me, standing sentry. In a perfect world the seal should have no concern for the dangers of humans or the shores we share with them. And I like to believe that winter afternoon nap was perfect, if only for a few hours.

A YEAR AFTER this napping seal incident, on a balmy June afternoon, I got a call from my neighborhood St. Francis, and the finder of my Siamese Manx cat Isabel.

"Quick, come down to the beach," Joyce pleaded. "There's a stranded sea lion and we think he's in trouble, breathing heavily, very lethargic, and a woman who can't stop crying thinks she sees blood on his fore flippers. I've called everyone from National Marine Fisheries to the local newspapers. No one has shown up except the cops and they don't know what to do since he's not a criminal."

I sighed and gazed out at the sand flats revealed by low tide. Just two days earlier, on June 14, we'd had the lowest tide of 1999, which laid bare not only geoducks and living black sand dollars, but human history as well—an old amusement park's pilings from the early 1950s.

Treasure hunters with headphones and metal detectors like long, trembling antennae scanned the rarely exposed wet sand looking for old coins, relics, momentos of a playful time past. Scampering along tide-pools were entire busloads of schoolchildren, tiny beachcombers in their green fluorescent life preservers and sunflower-yellow slickers. Low tide was their favorite summer field trip. How sad if they came upon a sea lion in such distress.

I grabbed a slicker of my own; even though it was bright sun outside, there was a cool wind off the water. When I walked down the beach, my binoculars swaying like a heavy necklace, I was surprised to see a crowd of people, not just the usual neighborhood beach watchers. There were even two security officers in their official black uniforms stationed on the cement steps leading down to the beach.

"Injured?" I asked the officer with a certain wariness that comes from having witnessed too many sea creatures dead or slowly dying on our beach. Just two weeks earlier a juvenile female gray whale, only one and a half years old, had washed up on our neighborhood beach. It was one of more than a hundred grays to die off the West Coast during the 1999 spring migration, signaling all was not well with our Pacific Ocean.

"You know, we really don't think this sea lion's in any trouble," the officer said with a wide smile. "Some of the Seattle Aquarium guys just came by to examine him and said he was molting and that's why he seems so tired. I guess molting your fur is a big job when you weigh five hundred pounds!" The guard tilted back his hat and revealed himself to be quite delighted to find himself assigned this sunny detail.

"So you . . . you're guarding the sea lion?" I asked, incredulous.

"Here for the duration," the officer nodded, reassuming his professional demeanor. "As long as it takes, we're here to protect him."

I grinned and surveyed their makeshift guardianship: pine sawhorses in a five-hundred-foot semicircle cordoned off the sea lion. Between these wooden horses was strung bright yellow tape—the kind used at crime scenes to keep intruders away. The center of all this protection, the California bull sea lion, was so huge that I hardly needed my binoculars, except to see his expression, which was lazy with the sun-lulled contentment of any other beachcomber.

As I joined the crowd behind the crime-scene tape, I felt a warmth that was deeper than sunlight, radiating out from the core of my body to include all these strangers. I realized then that this radiant warmth was simple happiness. Pleasure in being part of a species that found wonder in another creature's mysterious ways, gladness to find myself among people who watched this sea lion, willing him health, wishing him well.

"I've been standing guard since eight P.M. last night," an elderly woman said. "Actually thought the sea lion was giving birth with all that panting. But the Aquarium man says he's so healthy, fat from all the herring he's gulped. Panting because it's hard to lay on land so long without the buoyancy of the sea."

"I love this big guy," a bicyclist nodded. "What a hero he is. I've been diving with California sea lions. Man, they aren't afraid of any-thing. No wonder. Look how much bigger than us he is!"

Leo Shaw, the education director at the Seattle Aquarium whom I'd last seen on this beach with the dead gray whale, welcomed me back with a story. "Big is right," he said, "and much to be respected. One of the guys at the aquarium, C.J., made the mistake of turning his back on a fur seal and the seal reached out so fast and chomped C.J.'s bottom. Fortunately all he got was a mouth full of leather wallet!"

"That sea lion looks just like my uncle after a bender," a man from Parks and Recreation said good-naturedly, then grinned.

We all laughed out loud, at which sound the sea lion suddenly roused himself, rolled over and lifted his massive head. Through the binoculars we marveled at his luxurious fur sloughing off his back in quilt-like patches, glinting silver. Where his skin had shed, his muscu-lar, blubbery body looked newly minted. Lifted up like this to listen and catch some scent on the wind, the sea lion was majestic, stately in his animal poise.

At that moment a young man broke through the crowd, carrying a white plastic bucket as he made straight for the sea lion.

"You there!" yelled the Parks and Recreation man. "See the signs posted? This is a federally protected marine mammal. Go back!"

We were all amazed at this fellow's wrong-headedness. Everywhere there were signs showing drawings of a human figure approaching a seal inside a circle with a prohibitive red slash across this interaction.

"I'm just giving him water!" the young man shouted back and kept making progress over the rocky beach toward the resting sea lion.

"That creature's got an entire ocean next to him," the Parks official called back. "He knows exactly where *he* is!" Then the Parks man said in a low voice, "I reckon between the two, sea lion and kid, the sea lion is the smarter."

We all tried not to laugh too loud as one of the officers protecting the seal reminded us, "I've heard in California that yelling at a resting sea lion is a $10,000 fine."

"Bit of an exaggeration," Leo said. "But you can get fined for harassment of marine mammals."

"I'll bet that's the same sea lion we saw several nights ago on our beach," a young mother said, adjusting a child on each hip. "But my kids chased him away. I'm so glad he found a refuge here."

Refuge, I thought, and open hearts. Even the security officers guarding him seemed to bask in his presence, as well as in the glowing sun. "This is my favorite detail of the whole job," the other security officer, a woman named Gabrielle, said. "Usually we just guard banks and parking lots. This is the best!"

We all fell silent watching our huge companion rouse himself as the late afternoon tide lapped closer and closer to him. Raising up on his fore flippers, the sea lion opened his mouth to sniff the sea, so close now to him. "This will be the true test," Leo whispered. "If he moves away from the tide to stay on the beach, he may be in trouble. But if he swims away strongly, we'll know for sure he's healthy."

As the rising tide eased toward the sea lion, he held his dignified pose, his head uplifted like a king of this beach. He nodded to the passing great blue herons, the osprey diving for delicious herring right under the sea lion's nose, the river otter who flopped on all four flippers onto the beach with a flat, white flounder flapping in his mouth. In a comic double-take, the otter suddenly noted the sea lion and stood absolutely still, his small, almost catlike face registering dismay, then reassurance, as the sea lion ignored him. The lion feigned boredom as the otter carefully crept past him as if his claws were tiptoes.

Soon the sea lion was poised in waves rising up to his massive shoulders. "That'll cool him off," someone said of our 42°F. Puget Sound.

As the sea rose around him, the sea lion shook his entire body and then with one powerful thrust of his tail flippers, he slipped into the waves. We could hear his sigh and hoped it was gratitude or relief from his twenty-hour sojourn on our beach.

"Let's hope it was just R and R, or shore leave that kept him here so long," one of the officers said as we all communally held our breath, hoping for the best for the sea lion who had become another neighbor to us.

The surf rose as the sea lion gracefully dove and then surfaced immediately. "He may decide to haul up on this beach again later tonight," Leo said, "or make it a permanent refuge. He may well be back."

"We'll be here," said the security officers.

"So will we," all the neighbors echoed, "whenever he needs to nap near us."

I bowed my head to hide my blurred eyes, though my sunglasses were ample protection. And I was not the only one moved as we watched our neighbor sea lion swim in strong strokes farther out to sea, where he promptly raised a front flipper like a black sail.

"He was sleeping," Leo laughed. "He's one healthy sea lion."

We couldn't help ourselves: we shouted out and clapped our

applause, even though sound carries quite far over Puget Sound. Perhaps we wanted the sea lion to hear our rejoicing for his return. Perhaps we wanted him to know he was always welcome back—to our home beach and his.

———

IT IS THE day after the sea lion chose our neighborhood beach to nap. One neighbor called at the crack of dawn to say the sea lion returned briefly for a midnight snooze. Another neighbor called happily to report a sighting of the same sea lion who shared a day and night with us.

"I know he's the same one," she said with authority, then added with some awe and pride, "I . . . I, well, I recognize him."

And this morning, as I gaze out to sea, searching this beautiful, blue ark we have made of our beach, our daily world, I also catch sight of our sea lion. He is sleeping now mid-waves outside my studio, his massive body like living flotsam floating on lazy swells. Marine mists of blue-violet and mystical gray drift along with him as the sea lion rests on the surface of this inland sea, one flipper sculling. He lolls and rolls, lifting his snout to yawn and arch his long spine before a slip-under dive below, where herring are dense and so easy this summer in Puget Sound—multitudinous schools of them in a huge, flashing silver ball.

I imagine this sea lion gliding through a great circle of flickering herring like a dream of abundance, a flood of food and sustenance. He will have enough, he will find another beach, the land given back to us all after God's long-ago deluge. I pray the sea lion will also find on this rocky, often dangerous land other people who will recognize him as another mammal, as kin, a neighbor belonging in this shared ark.

The sea lion sculls along, using his strong flippers like a rudder to steer. At last he disappears into the early morning mists. And I find that all I can do is sing, softly and gratefully, the lullaby of this world, this animal *mundi*:

> Sail, baby, sail, out across the sea.
> Only don't forget to sail
> Back again to me

The sea lion surfaces far off, with fish spilling from both sides of his bewhiskered snout. I smile as in his wake seagulls skitter, dip, and steal some of his catch. Today there is enough for all of us on this beach, on this spinning, sea-encircled planet.

HELP TO BUILD A NEW ARK
FOR THE ANIMALS

Whale Stewardship Project
Box 88558, Southport Street
Toronto, ON M6S 4Z8
rtw@idirect.com

TerraMar Research (Dolphins)
321 High School Road, NE
PMB 374
Bainbridge Island, WA 98110
www.TerramarResearch.com

Wild Dolphin Project
P.O. Box 8436
Jupiter, FL 33468
www.wwwa.com/dolph

Orca Conservancy
2403 S. North Bluff Road
Greenbank, WA 98253
www.tokitae@pugetsound.net

Wolf Action
Defenders of Wildlife
1101 Fourteenth Street, NW
Suite 1400
Washington, DC 20005
www.defenders.org

IFAW (International Fund for Animal Welfare)
411 Main Street
P.O. Box 193
Yarmouth Port, MA 02675
www.ifaw.org

Mission: Wolf
P.O. Box 211
Silver Cliff, CO 81249
www.indra.com/fallline/mw

National Resources Defense Council
40 West 20th Street
New York, NY 10011
www.nrdc.org

Wolf Haven International
3111 Offut Lake Road
Tenino, WA 98589
www.wolfhaven.org

Ocean Mammal Institute
(800) 226-8216
www.oceanmammalinst.com

World Wildlife Fund
Washington, DC 20037
www.worldwildlife.org

Ark Trust
www.arktrust.org

Alaska Wildlife Alliance
P.O. Box 202022
Anchorage, AK 99520-2022
awa@alaska.net
www.akwildlife.org

PAWS (Progressive Animal Welfare Society)
15305 44th Avenue, W.
Lynnwood, WA 98037

Jane Goodall Institute
P.O. Box 14890
Silver Spring, MD 20911-4890
www.janegoodall.org